Enacting History

Enacting History is a practical guide for educators that provides methodologies and resources for teaching the Holocaust through a variety of theatrical means, including scripted texts, verbatim testimony, devised theater techniques and process-oriented creative exercises.

A close collaboration with the USC Shoah Foundation *I Witness* program and the National Jewish Theater Foundation *Holocaust Theater International Initiative* at the University of Miami Miller Center for Contemporary Judaic Studies resulted in the ground-breaking work within this volume. The material facilitates teaching the Holocaust in a way that directly connects students to individual people and historical events through the art of theater. Each section is designed to help middle and high school educators meet curricular goals, objectives and standards and to integrate other educational disciplines based upon best practices. Students will gain both intellectual and emotional understanding by speaking the words of survivors, as well as young characters in scripted scenes, and developing their own performances based on historical primary sources.

This book, with foreword by Michael Berenbaum, is an innovative and invaluable resource for teachers and students of the Holocaust; it is an exemplary account of how the power of theater can be harnessed within the classroom setting to encourage a deeper understanding of this defining event in history.

Mira Hirsch is Director of Education at Theatrical Outfit (Atlanta), a freelance professional theater director and an educational consultant for the National Jewish Theater Foundation.

Janet E. Rubin is a faculty member at Eastern Florida State College where she teaches Speech and Theatre and directs theater productions. She is Past President of the American Alliance for Theatre and Education.

Arnold Mittelman is President of the National Jewish Theater Foundation (NJTF) and Founding Director of NJTF Holocaust Theater International Initiative at the University of Miami Miller Center for Contemporary Judaic Studies overseeing its research, production and education programs.

Enacting History

A Practical Guide to Teaching the Holocaust through Theater

Mira Hirsch, Janet E. Rubin
and Arnold Mittelman

Foreword by Michael Berenbaum

Routledge
Taylor & Francis Group

LONDON AND NEW YORK

First published 2020
by Routledge
2 Park Square, Milton Park, Abingdon, Oxon OX14 4RN

and by Routledge
52 Vanderbilt Avenue, New York, NY 10017

Routledge is an imprint of the Taylor & Francis Group, an informa business

© 2020 Mira Hirsch, Janet E. Rubin and Arnold Mittelman

British Library Cataloguing-in-Publication Data
A catalogue record for this book is available from the British Library

Library of Congress Cataloging-in-Publication Data
A catalog record has been requested for this book

ISBN: 978-1-138-60873-3 (hbk)
ISBN: 978-1-138-60874-0 (pbk)
ISBN: 978-0-429-46646-5 (ebk)

Typeset in Bembo
by Newgen Publishing UK

Mira Hirsch: For Sophie and Nate

Janet E. Rubin: Dedicated with love to my sister, Shirley Friedland, and my brother, Harvey Rubin

Arnold Mittelman: Dedicated to Susann Green (wife), Tyler Mittelman (son), Justine Shayman (daughter), Ashton and Cameron Shayman (grandsons)

Contents

Images

All of the following are available from the United States Holocaust Memorial Museum.

Foreword

I have been enthusiastically involved with the NJTF Holocaust Theater International Initiative since its inception not only because of my deep respect for its founder, Arnold Mittelman, a man of the theater, but because of the power and the impact of theater to present the Holocaust.

The case for the impact of theater is overwhelming.

The play, *The Diary of Anne Frank* has had a massive impact first on Broadway in the 1950s and again in the 1990s, but more importantly in schools and colleges where it has been performed for more than 60 years. I am familiar with all the critiques of the *Diary* – it is not really about the Holocaust for it ends just as the Holocaust begins for Anne and her family; the version we have is sanitized, dejudaized, universalized and cleansed of all the tensions between mother and daughter that were essential to the original version of the *Diary*. I share these critiques, yet, valid as they may be, no one can deny the impact of the play that brought the events of the Holocaust to the consciousness of adults and students alike.

Permit me an anecdote: I had the rare privilege of accompanying Miep Gies, the Frank family's protector, their lifeline to the outside world, on a trip to several locales in the United States and witnessed what happened. Women of all ages approached her and embraced her. Women she did not know felt they knew her because they had played her, they were her and had difficulty believing that she did not know them. I came to understand that playing a role in theater is to become intimate with the character, to come out of the self and at the same time to put all of one's self into the character and thus to live the part, to become the role.

The Deputy, a powerful and controversial consideration of Pope Pius XII, the Vicar of Christ, raised many of the issues of the role of the Pope during the Holocaust and actions and inactions of the Church that was judiciously silent at best, if not complicit. The play first performed in Berlin in 1963 and translated for London in the same year challenged Christians to confront the role that Christianity played in perpetrating the

Holocaust. It led to front-page controversy in newspapers, magazines and journals and blistering publications by scholars pro and con. It also attracted readers for more scholarly work and even penetrated the walls of Vatican City. After *The Deputy* the debate was public and both defenders of the Church and their accusers understood that the issue was joined. It had to be engaged.

Judgment at Nuremberg, the play first broadcast and performed in 1959 on the CBS television series Playhouse 90, offered a post-war generation insight into the guilt and innocence and perhaps more importantly the self-justifications offered by the perpetrators, not only the story they told to their judges in order to avoid incarceration, but also the story they told to themselves in order to shave in the morning or to embrace their spouse and children.

In addition to teaching and writing, I help shape Museums and thus engage in public history. Thinking about the offerings of this book, I was reminded of what two colleagues taught me. Carolynne Harris, with whom I worked on the Dallas Holocaust and Human Rights Museum, was fond of saying that there are three types of Museum visitors: *skimmers, swimmers and deep divers*. And the content of a Museum must not only address, but satisfy all three.

Rabbi Eli Mayerfeld, CEO of the Holocaust Memorial Center Zekelman Family Campus in Michigan, always challenges me to remember that there are many different ways of learning. Some learn by reading, others by seeing, some by hearing, still others by touching, and many learn most effectively by doing.

Using these exercises, students are given the opportunity to learn by doing. They must creatively engage the material, seeking a way not only of understanding what they are reading and hearing, but facing a second, formidable challenge of presenting this material to their fellow students, their primary audience, and perhaps only incidentally to their teachers. They must work in teams, in a manner that requires teamwork because no single individual can do it all alone. Working in tandem is an important educational antidote to the radical isolation that characterizes much of youth culture and, not incidentally, much of what we teachers demand of our students. To grapple with survivor testimony requires that one engage, and ultimately empathize, with the survivor. One must listen attentively in order to grasp what is being said and what remains unsaid. And then one must absorb and internalize what has been heard and seen in order to present it to the class.

Peer learning is educationally effective. Students learn from one another all the time and peer pressure, especially if the teaching is effective and empowering of the students, does not permit the student merely to skim the material. One cannot stick to the surface and expect to be effective.

Students who engage with the characters they play soon become what Carolynn Harris calls deep divers, looking for additional material to read, for films to see, for survivors to visit in order to better know their character. More than 40 years ago we did a study for four Holocaust curricula and gauged students' interest. Teachers reported that they were doing nothing different in the classroom, yet Librarians – as we called them in those days – reported that they were flooded with requests for more information, that students whom they had seldom or never seen were walking in and asking for help and students were actually talking to their parents about what they were learning in school. These findings have been consistent for generations of students, when skimmers become swimmers.

As we imagined new ways of using the resources of the United States Holocaust Memorial Museum, we created a cart of artifact facsimiles to engage students in learning by touching. The ironclad rule of most museums is "look but do not touch." And yet, visitors, young and old alike, want to touch. Danny Spungen has created a significant personal collection of Holocaust artifacts. Not being bound by the rule of Museum creators, he allows students to hold the artifacts in their hand and to learn by touching, often holding the artifact close to themselves. You will read in these exercises how to use facsimiles of artifacts for learning by touching. It will teach students how to see the story behind the artifact and what is worth preserving in our all too disposable world.

Effective teaching means that we must turn skimmers into deep divers. It means that we must engage all the modalities of learning so that our students became active, engaged with the material, with the subject and also with one another.

One final word: Why the Holocaust?

This material also allows students to engage with Holocaust survivors, now in the twilight of their life. They were a small minority of the victims – many more were murdered than survived – the question they faced was what to do with the accident of their survival. They too had to rebuild their lives in its aftermath. Over time they came to answer the question "Why did I survive?" not by a statement about the past but by what they did with their lives in the aftermath.

Because they have faced death, many will have learned what is most important in life: life itself, love, family and community, and what Holocaust survivor and Academy Award Winner Gerda Klein called "a boring evening at home." The small things, the simple things we have all taken for granted, cannot be taken for granted but must be treasured and appreciated anew.

For Jewish survivors, the survival of the Jewish people became paramount. The final statement of Jewish history and Jewish memory must be about life and not death, no matter how pervasive that death.

For many survivors, bearing witness conferred a sense of meaning in the aftermath of atrocity. They have told the story of the past, to keep a promise they made to those they left behind. More importantly, in the hope – however slim – that it can transform the future.

What of the role of Holocaust memory in the contemporary world?

In a world of relativism, it has taken its place as the Absolute. We don't know what is good. We don't know what is bad. But we do know that the Holocaust is evil, absolute evil. It is for that reason why people use the word in the plural as they attempt to call attention to their suffering – the Black Holocaust, the Holocaust of the American Indians, the Holocaust in Kosovo, Rwanda, Bosnia. The Holocaust is the nuclear bomb of moral epithets. It is an event of such magnitude that the more we sense the relativism of values, the more we require the Holocaust as the foundation for a negative absolute – absolute evil. This may well be the reason why the leaders of European nations have rediscovered the importance of the Holocaust for contemporary moral education. This may also be the reason why it becomes the focal point for Papal visits to Israel, for German society and for American society. It may also be why Holocaust deniers deny an event that all reasons, all standards of rationality demonstrate cannot be denied. It is in this function as negative absolute that the Holocaust may loom largest in the coming years.

Consciousness of the Holocaust has moved way beyond the Jewish community. In the past half a century the bereaved memories of a parochial community have been transformed into an act of conscience. Survivors *have responded in the most deeply Jewish way of all: remembering suffering and transmitting that memory in order to fortify conscience, to plead for decency, to strengthen values and thus to intensify a commitment to human dignity.* That is how the Biblical Jews taught us to remember that we were slaves in Egypt and that is why the Biblical experience has framed the struggle for freedom ever since.

One cannot undo what has happened. Historians can answer the question *how* only in the most technical sense, detailing event after event; as you shall read, theologians, writers, poets and philosophers, psychologists and artists have not answered the question *why*.

Yet we can answer the question of what to do with this history. Embrace it, study it, wrestle with it and ultimately transform it into a weapon for the human spirit to enlarge our sense of responsibility, to alleviate human suffering and strengthen our moral resolve.

Before you is a wonderful tool. Go read it! Go use it!

Michael Berenbaum
American Jewish University
Los Angeles, CA

Michael Berenbaum was Project Director overseeing the creation of the United States Holocaust Memorial Museum and was the first director of its Research Institute before serving as President and CEO of the Survivors of the Shoah Visual History Foundation, which took the testimony of more than 52,000 survivors.

Acknowledgments

National Jewish Theater Foundation–Holocaust Theater International Initiative (NJTF HTII) at University of Miami Miller Center for Contemporary Judaic Studies, its Advisory Board Members and Donors. Initial *Enacting History* book research funded by Marvin Leibowitz and Anne E. Leibowitz Foundation.

USC Shoah Foundation The Institute for Visual History and Education IWitness Program.

United States Holocaust Memorial Museum (USHMM) Photo Archives.

Individuals:
(NJTF HTII) Michael Berenbaum, Alvin Goldfarb, Haim Shaked;
(USC Shoah Foundation) Kim Simon, Kori Street, Jenna Leventhal;
(USHMM) Bret Werb;
(Routledge Press) Ben Piggott, Mary Rose MacLachlan.

All playwrights whose talents and insights created the plays, scenes and monologues selected.

All survivors whose courageous testimony we utilized to inspire and educate for hope not hate.

All educators who when using this book will provide an artistic moral compass for their students.

How to use this book

Enacting History consists of ten chapters which follow a chronology from the onset of the Holocaust through the aftermath of the Holocaust. Each chapter begins with historical context pages that serve as essential background information that should be read and studied prior to working on the theatrical activities in that chapter. Whether you are using the theater scenes and activities as a way for students in core curriculum classes to better understand the historical context from which they are drawn, or using the context pages as a way for students in theater classes to better understand the characters/individuals they will be portraying, the contextual information provided with each chapter will be an integral component of your process.

This book may be used as a supplement to your Holocaust teaching, or as a primary source, depending on the planned depth and breadth of your curriculum. In either case, these theater activities will allow students to submerse themselves in the stories and plights of individuals who endured some of the darkest hours in modern times, enabling them to view history through a personal lens. Through acting and performance, student learning will evolve from a passive experience to an active one, and students will be able to gain greater empathy for the individuals they are portraying and greater understanding of the times in which those people lived. Additionally, as audience members watching the theatrical work of their peers, students will be exposed to multiple historical narratives, giving them an even broader learning experience.

Each chapter features three different types of theater activities: 1. Scripted scenes and monologues; 2. Verbatim testimony historical narratives with tableaus; and 3. Devised theater activities. The scripted scenes, historical narratives and devised theater texts have all been selected for their relevance to the subject matter in each chapter and for their ability to further elucidate the historical information provided in each chapter's context section.

Each form of theater is described in detail within this chapter, with "How to" instructions, definitions of the theater terminology used in the activity, best practices, and a suggested lesson plan. You may choose to utilize one type of theater exclusively, or assign scene work across the spectrum of all three activities. Depending on your Holocaust learning goals, you may focus on activities from only one chapter of the book, or multiple chapters.

The activities you choose to use will depend on your comfort level with guiding your students in the creative process of that particular theatrical form. All three types of activities have been designed to be successfully fulfilled by students who may have no theatrical training, as well as by those who have extensive theatrical experience. The same can also be said for the teachers who are leading the activities. Exploring history by creating theater should not be restricted only to those who call themselves "actors," or acting teachers, but should be an accessible method of education within reach of all willing educators and their students.

An important component of each of these theater activities is that they culminate in performance. The art form of "theater" does not actually take place until there is a shared experience between performer and audience. Whether your presentations are readings, fully staged scripted scenes, historical narratives with tableaus or devised theater, the act of performing for an audience elevates the activity for the performers by empowering them to affect others with profound and powerful stories. Through the act of performing for their peers, the students, in a sense, will become teachers, and the result is one in which the experience and the material will stay with those students for an extended period of time and with greater significance. The "audience" can consist of the other members of the class, students from other classes, the entire school or invited guests – it doesn't matter (nor does the type of space you are performing in) – as long as there is some sort of audience to listen, watch, learn, engage and respond.

How to: scripted scenes and monologues

The scripted scenes in this book have been selected both for their relationship to each chapter's content and for age-level appropriateness for middle school, high school and college students. With only a few exceptions, the scenes feature characters who are close in age to the students who will be performing them. In portraying characters who are children, teens and young adults, student actors will be able to better relate to the historical circumstances which form the backdrops for each scene. While most of the scenes and monologues are technically fictional, in that they do not utilize verbatim testimonies or historical transcripts as text, they have all been selected from carefully researched plays, most of which are based on true stories, real people, and actual historical events. Acting in scripted scenes based on history, written by professional, published playwrights, gives students the opportunity to immerse themselves in bringing to life characters who may be very different from themselves, and who are, undoubtedly, going through experiences very different than any that they, themselves, have gone through. By portraying these characters, students will have the closest experience possible to "walking in the shoes" of another person, and will gain greater knowledge and understanding of the way the historical events of the Holocaust impacted individuals and communities.

The scripted scenes may be presented as readings or as fully staged pieces of theater. You may choose to assign scenes from only one chapter, or you may have students perform scenes from multiple chapters, or even all ten chapters, in order to represent each of the chronological periods of the Holocaust as laid out in this book.

Within the scripted scene sections in each chapter, one supplemental – or "spotlight" – activity has been provided to help your students delve deeper into a specific scene or monologue. This activity may be assigned to the particular group of students working on that scene, or may be explored by the entire class.

While it is not a requirement, students may be interested in reading the full scripts from which their scenes and monologues have been taken. This is helpful from an acting standpoint, as well as from an educational standpoint. Information regarding each script can be found on pages 179–183. (Note: performing scenes from these plays in an educational, classroom setting requires no additional permission; however, more formal performances of scenes or full plays outside of a classroom setting will require additional permissions from publishers and/or authors. See individual play information for publisher websites to request performance rights.)

As with all of the activities in this book, this activity should culminate with a performance in front of an audience.

Terminology and best practices for readings

Readings – a performance is considered a reading when actors are using scripts and there is no blocking (staging) involved in the performance.

Beats – these are brief or moderate pauses in which something shifts. Perhaps it is a new thought or a new idea. Perhaps the emotion of the character changes. Just as in music, where the rests are as important as the notes, the beats in a scene are just as important as the words. By allowing for beats and breaths, the actors allow their characters to become more real and more alive, and the audience will be able to believe that the characters are thinking and processing rather than simply *speaking*.

Best practices for performing scene and monologue readings

1   Both in rehearsal and performance, actors should stand at music stands with their scripts on their stands. Raise or lower the stands to a height of approximately chin level. This will help the actors to be able to look at their scripts without obscuring their faces and without having to lower their heads.
2   If the scenes or monologues are more than two pages in length, secure them in three-ring binders to ensure that the pages do not get out of order.

3   When actors are reading from scripts, it is very helpful if they highlight their parts. They should not highlight their character's name or any of the stage directions, just the lines that they are reading. This will help them stay on track and not inadvertently read something that is not a line of dialogue.

4   Assign a student to read any stage directions that are necessary for the audience to have a clear understanding of the action that is taking place. The group should decide which of the stage directions are vital to the audience's understanding of the scene; which ones will help the audience visualize what is happening. The student reading the stage directions should rehearse with the other actors to ensure the fluidity of the scene.

5   While they will technically be "reading" from scripts, the actors should be familiar enough with their lines to look up from the page and make eye contact with their scene partners from time to time. This will help the audience see the connection between the characters, making the script come more alive. For actors performing monologues, it is also important for them to lift their eyes off the page and look out toward the audience. This will allow the audience to see the actors' facial expressions and to better connect with their characters. (Actors should not look *directly* at individual audience members unless they are reading a speech which has been written as an address to the audience.)

6   The actors should project their voices so that everyone in the audience can hear every word they are saying, and articulate so that all of their speech can be clearly understood. Additionally, it is important that they do not rush their speech. Projection, articulation and pacing should all be part of the rehearsal process. Ultimately, it cannot be emphasized enough that the words of the playwright are of paramount importance, and it is the actor's job to make sure they are all spoken with adequate volume, clarity and precision. Actors should not change any of the playwright's words.

7   Students actors often wonder if they should use accents when they are performing scenes set in other countries. The general rule is this: if the characters are actually speaking in another language, even though the play is written in English, the lines should be spoken in un-accented English; if the characters are supposed to be speaking in English, and English is not their native language, then their English speech would be accented, and the actor can speak using the accent of that character's native country. In several scenes, the use of accents/dialects could be helpful to the audience's understanding that a particular character is not speaking his or her native language; however, if the actor is not adept at performing the accent, it could end up being a distraction rather than an asset, and it would be better to perform the role without an accent.

8   Actors should find the "beats" in their scenes and monologues. Some actors find it helpful to mark the beats in their script with lines, slashes or other notations that designate divisions or pauses.

9   **Prior to performing their scene or monologue, each group should introduce their piece using the description that accompanies each of the scripted scenes and monologues, as well as the play's short synopsis, found on pages 179–183.**

Scripted scenes (readings) – suggested lesson plan

Duration of activity: two class periods of 50–60 minutes each.

Day #1

Preparation: 1. Select scenes and monologues from the chapters that are best suited for your Holocaust learning and which you feel are most appropriate for your students. 2. Make the necessary number of copies of each scene and monologue. It is important the students have hard copies of their scripts. 3. Make enough copies of the *Scripted scenes and monologues* worksheet (p. xxvi) for each of your students.

Physical requirements: No requirements.

STEPS:

1 *Assign* scenes and/or monologues and roles to students.
2 Allow students approximately 10–15 minutes to *read through* their scripts and *highlight* their parts.
3 Have students sit with their scene partners to *read their scenes aloud* together. If some students are performing monologues, have them pair up and take turns reading their monologues aloud to each other.
4 Instruct students to *fill out the scripted scenes and monologues* worksheet. Some of the questions will need to be answered in partnership with the other member(s) of the scene group; others are specific to the character that each student is playing.
5 If there is time, have students *read their scenes aloud again* in their scene groups, using their responses on the worksheet to help inform their acting choices.

Day #2

Preparation: If possible, secure enough music stands for the total number of actors in the largest scene group.

Physical requirements: 1. Music stands. 2. An open space to serve as the "stage."

STEPS:

1 Students will assemble in their groups and *rehearse* their scenes. Instruct them to keep all of the *Best practices for readings* (pp. xviii–xix) in mind as they work.
2 Allow each group the opportunity to *rehearse with music stands* if possible.
3 In the second half of class, have each group/individual *perform a reading of their scene or monologue*. Make sure to have each group introduce their performance using the background information provided with each scene and monologue.

You may also choose to have students share some contextual information from the context section of the chapter from which their scene was taken.

4   At the conclusion of all of the presentations, *facilitate a discussion session* in which you ask the students the following:

a   Did you learn anything new from any of the scenes? What did you learn?

b   What moments stood out to you in each scene? Overall?

c   As actors, did participating in this activity give you a better understanding of the Holocaust? In what ways?

d   As actors and/or audience members, how was this experience different than learning about the Holocaust through reading a book? Listening to a lecture? Watching a movie?

Terminology and best practices for staged scenes

Blocking (noun or verb) – sometimes referred to as the "staging," blocking is the action of the actors; the movements that are taking place in the scene. As choreography is to dance, blocking is to plays. Blocking refers to both the larger movements of the actors in relation to the space – such as entering, exiting and crossing the stage (moving from one area to another) – as well as to smaller movements which relate to other actors or objects, such as picking up a plate, or placing an arm around another character's shoulder. Sometimes blocking choices are indicated in a script; other times, they are not. The blocking of a scene can serve to tell the story as much or more than the lines of dialogue. It is important that the blocking of a scene accurately matches the playwright's intentions to the best of the actors' and director's abilities.

Blocking (verb) – a second definition of "blocking" is obscuring something or someone from the audience's view. Actors must be careful when blocking their scenes, that they are not blocking other actors from the audience!

Staying in character – this phrase refers to one of the most important jobs of the actor. Actors are tasked with creating characters and not "breaking" from this by doing any of the following: laughing, when the character should not be laughing; making facial expressions or gestures that are not in keeping with what the character would actually be doing; looking at the audience (unless the playwright has intended for the character to "break the fourth wall" and address the audience); or improvising speech by changing or adding to the lines that the playwright has written. All of these behaviors take the audience out of the play, focus attention on the actor playing the role, rather than the character they are supposed to be embodying, and ultimately destroy the illusion of the world that the actors are striving to create.

Breaking the fourth wall – this is theater terminology which refers to actors looking directly at the audience and addressing them as if they are another character in the play. The expression comes from the naturalistic theater convention of constructing sets with designs that incorporate three walls to designate a room. In naturalistic plays, the actors must pretend that the room's fourth wall is actually there, and that the audience is not sitting where that wall would technically be. In "breaking the fourth wall," actors remove the illusion of the imagined wall and invite the audience into the action.

Off-book – when actors are off-book they have memorized their lines and no longer require a script or "book."

Best practices for performing staged scenes

1   When actors receive their scenes, they should highlight their parts, marking only the actual words they will be reading. They should not highlight their characters' names or any stage directions.

2   When blocking their scenes, actors should decide where the audience is sitting and stage the scene so that the audience can see all of the action. Scenes should always be rehearsed with the placement of the audience in mind.

3   In staging their scenes, actors should be mindful of not blocking other actors from the audience's view.

4   Actors should keep their faces open to the audience, particularly when they have lines.

5   These scenes may be performed with scripts or off-book. This choice will undoubtedly be influenced by the amount of time that has been allotted for this activity. However, if actors are performing *with* scripts, they should be familiar enough with the material to be able to look up at their scene partners to make honest connections with them. Eye contact between actors is critical in making the leap from a simple reading to a *performance*. Relationships are at the heart of most plays, and these can only be portrayed honestly by actors making connections with each other through eye contact.

6   Actors must stay in character, and keep their portrayals as real and honest as they possibly can.

7   Actors should "stay in their scenes," by keeping the focus of their eyes on the characters to whom they are speaking and on objects that are important to their character. Actors should not look at the audience unless the playwright has intended for the character to break the fourth wall and address the audience with his/her speech.

8   The actors should project their voices so that everyone in the audience can hear every word they are saying, and articulate so that all of their speech can be clearly understood. Additionally, it is important that they do not rush their speech. Projection, articulation and pacing should all be part of the rehearsal process. Ultimately, it cannot be emphasized enough that the words of the playwright are of paramount importance, and it is the actor's job to make sure they are all spoken with adequate volume, clarity and precision. Actors should not change any of the playwright's words.

9   Student actors often wonder if they should use accents when they are performing scenes set in other countries. The general rule is this: if the characters are actually

speaking in another language, even though the play is written in English, the lines should be spoken in un-accented English; if the characters are supposed to be speaking in English, and English is not their native language, then their English speech would be accented, and the actor can speak using the accent of that character's native country. In several scenes, the use of accents/dialects could be helpful to the audience's understanding that a particular character is not speaking his or her native language; however, if the actor is not adept at performing the accent, it could end up being a distraction rather than an asset, and it would be better to perform the role without an accent.

10   Actors should find the "beats" in their scenes or monologues. Some actors find it helpful to mark the beats in their script with lines, slashes or other notations that designate divisions or pauses.

11   **Prior to performing their scene or monologue, each group should introduce their piece using the description that accompanies each of the scripted scenes and monologues, and, optionally, with the play's overall description, found on pages 179-183.**

Scripted scenes (staged) – suggested lesson plan

Duration of activity: four class periods of 50–60 minutes each.

(NOTE: If you only have three days for the activity, Day #3 may be skipped.)

Day #1

Preparation: 1. Select scenes and monologues from the chapters that are best suited for your Holocaust learning and which you feel are most appropriate for your students. 2. Make the necessary number of copies of each scene and monologue. It is important that the students have hard copies of their scripts. 3. Make enough copies of the *Scripted scenes and monologues* worksheet (p. xxvi) for each of your students.

Physical requirements: No requirements.

STEPS:

1   *Assign* scenes and/or monologues and roles to your students.
2   Allow students approximately 10–15 minutes to *read through* their scripts and *highlight* their parts.
3   Have students sit with their scene partners to *read their scenes aloud* together. If some students are performing monologues, have them pair up and take turns reading their monologues aloud to each other.

4   Instruct students to *fill out the Scripted scenes and monologues worksheet*. Some of the questions should be answered in partnership with the other member(s) of the scene group; others are specific to the character that each student is playing.

5   If there is time, have students *read their scenes aloud again* in their scene groups, using their worksheet responses to help inform their acting choices.

Day #2

Preparation: 1. Locate small props, furniture and costumes pieces that can enhance the staging of the scenes you have selected. 2.Create open spaces in which multiple scene groups can work simultaneously.

Physical requirements: Spaces in which all scene groups can work on their feet.

STEPS:

1   Have students assemble in their scene groups and begin blocking their scenes and monologues. Instruct them to follow the *Best practices for performing staged scenes* (pp. xxii–xxiiii).

2   Survey the room as your students rehearse, assisting them with their blocking and character choices, using their responses on their worksheets to help guide them.

3   Work with each group to help them select appropriate props, furniture and, possibly, costume pieces.

Day #3

Preparation: Consider inviting other classes to watch your scene presentations on Day #4. Alternately, consider filming the scenes and sharing them with other classes at another time.

Physical requirements: 1. Spaces in which all scene groups can continue to work on their feet. 2. The props and costumes selected by the students on Day #2 should be readily available.

STEPS:

1   Have students continue rehearsing their scenes with their selected props.

2   Reserve the second half of class for scene sharing, allowing each group to present their scene or monologue to the class for critical feedback.

3   Allow student response, in addition to your own response, to each scene or monologue. Responses should be framed as follows:

a   Some things that are currently working successfully in this scene presentation are …

b   Things that your group can work on to improve your scene are …

c   This scene made me feel …

Day #4

Preparation: 1. If you have invited additional classes to see your performance, set up the room to accommodate these additional audience members. 2. Consider making a printed program with a scene list which includes the names of the plays from which the scenes are taken, as well as the names of the playwrights.

Physical requirements: (see Day #3)

STEPS:

1   Groups will continue to *rehearse* their scenes.
2   Groups will *present* their scenes to the rest of the class and any invited guests.
3   Make sure to have each group *introduce their performance* using the background information provided with each scene and monologue. You may also choose to have students share some historical information from the context section of the chapters from which their scenes were taken.
4   At the conclusion of all of the scene presentations, *facilitate a discussion session* in which you ask the students the following:
    a   Did you learn anything new from any of the scenes? What did you learn?
    b   What moments stood out to you in each scene? Overall?
    c   Were any of the scenes more effective than others? Why? What made those scenes so effective or impactful?
    d   As actors, did participating in this activity give you a better understanding of the Holocaust? In what ways?
    e   As actors and/or audience members, how was this experience different than learning about the Holocaust through reading a book? Listening to a lecture? Watching a movie?

Scripted scenes and monologues actor worksheet

Name of play: _____

Name of playwright: _____

This scene is associated with the chapter about _____

Answer the questions below to get a better understanding of the character you are playing. These questions, which have been loosely adapted from "Respect for Acting" by Uta Hagen, will assist you in making choices about your character and will help you infuse your scene with specificity and honesty.

Who is my character? (name, approximate age, personality characteristics, etc.)

Where and when does this scene take place? (year, season, city, country, etc.)

What are the given circumstances? (Refer to the historical context section of the chapter in which this scene appears, as well as any background information provided about the play.)

What is my character's relationship to the other character(s) in the scene? Or, if this is a monologue, whom is my character addressing, and what is my character's relationship to that person, or to others mentioned in the monologue?

What does my character want?

What is my character doing in this scene to get what s/he wants?

How to: verbatim testimony historical narratives

This activity incorporates the theater tools of monologue and tableau, asking its participants to create, rehearse and perform short scenes which combine verbatim speeches transcribed from the USC Shoah Foundation's collection of IWitness testimonies of Holocaust survivors, witnesses, and liberators with tableaus of their creation (https://iwitness.usc.edu/SFI/). As one student performs a historical narrative monologue using a verbatim text, the others in the group dramatically enhance the presentation of that monologue by staging accompanying tableaus, which give the monologue visual interest, helping to illuminate the story.

Of the three types of theatrical activities in this book, this is probably the most accessible to "non-actors," as most of the participants in the scenes are not required to speak as part of their performances. There is no dialogue between characters, and no memorization of lines. This makes the activity less threatening to those students who may not be comfortable with performing, and enables all students to have the experience of creating a piece of theater which will leave an indelible impact on an audience without having to step too far out of their comfort zones.

With each passing day, the number of living Holocaust survivors decreases. Soon, there will be no survivors left to give firsthand accounts of what they saw and what they lived through. This makes the existence of the Shoah Foundation's video testimonies all the more important. A large number of the individuals in these videos have already passed away, as the vast majority of the interviews were conducted in the mid-1990s with subjects who were well into their 60s and 70s. The verbatim testimony historical narratives activity gives students the opportunity to tell the stories of those who can no longer tell them, safeguarding their memories, as well as the memories of the millions who did not survive. Significantly, most of the survivors in these recordings were children or teenagers during the Holocaust, making their stories particularly relatable to young people. By keeping alive the words of these witnesses and survivors, students participating in this activity will be helping to ensure that the phrase "never again" is more than just an axiom.

The activity should be introduced by showing the class the "This is what I've scene" demonstration video that is on the IWitness website. "This is what I've scene" is the name of the verbatim testimony historical narrative activity that was created by the authors of this book specifically for the Shoah Foundation's IWitness site: http://iwitness.usc.edu/SFI/Activity/DoActivity.aspx?stp=a67ea83e-9884-4b96-b8a4-4458da314613. In order to access the "This is what I've scene" activity and this accompanying demonstration video, the teacher must create an account with IWitness: https://iwitness.usc.edu/SFI/Account/Register.aspx.

Terminology of scene components and best practices

Historical narrative monologue – This is a story told by a single character that is factual/historic in nature. The historical narrative monologue activities in this book are verbatim transcriptions of filmed interviews with people who survived the Holocaust, witnessed the events of the Holocaust or provided aid, refuge or liberation to those suffering in the Holocaust. The following *best practices* will assist your students in delivering strong narrative monologues:

1   The student in each scene group who is selected to read the monologue should be comfortable with speaking in front of an audience and should be able to project loudly enough and articulate strongly enough to be heard clearly by all audience members.

2   The narrator should watch the video of the person s/he is playing multiple times and make observations regarding the following: a. When does this person become emotional? Are there lines, words or sections which are difficult for this person to say? b. Where does this person take pauses? How do the pauses impact the telling of the story? c. Is this person very animated? Does s/he use her/his hands a lot? Or is s/he very still?

3   The narrator does not need to memorize the text, but should be familiar enough with the language that it feels like the s/he is *sharing* the story, not *reading* it. The narrator should frequently lift his/her eyes off the page to look up at the audience. Additionally, narrators should feel free to "connect" with the scene by focusing on the tableaus – either as the actors are shifting into position, or once they have assumed their freezes. This will encourage the audience to see the tableaus as images that are coming from inside the mind of the narrator.

4   If a music stand is available, allow the narrator to place the monologue script on the stand and adjust it to just the right height, so that the actor is not looking too far down, and the stand is not obscuring his/her face.

5   The narrators should first rehearse alone, and then with the entire scene group. Once they are working with their full ensembles, narrators should incorporate a sound or gesture that will be used to signal a change of tableau, such as stomping their feet, snapping or ringing a bell. One device that works well for this is a small "pet training" clicker. (These can be purchased at pet stores or online.) The sound of the click and the small gesture of pointing the clicker toward the tableau ensemble gives the impression that the narrator is changing the picture, as in a slide show or PowerPoint presentation, making the narrator an active participant in bringing his/her memory back to life.

6   Narrators should not attempt to portray their subjects as the age they were at the time their testimony was recorded. They should keep in mind that while their subjects were senior citizens in the video interviews, most were children, teens or young adults during the Holocaust when the events that they are describing took place. Additionally, the narrators should not try to emulate or imitate the accents of their subjects, unless they are extremely adept at doing so. It is far better to speak in their natural voices than to use accents that sound silly or that will distract the audience from the content of the stories.

7   Narrators should consider when to take pauses, even if the person they are playing did not necessarily pause in those spots. Placing small beats, or pauses, on either or both sides of certain words or phrases can give those words additional punch and purpose. Encourage them to mark their scripts with notes and symbols that will remind them of where to breathe, where to slow down and where to express more heightened emotion or emphasis. Additionally, they should time their delivery to correspond with the ensemble's movements from stage picture to stage picture,

and if using musical underscoring, should rehearse with this to see how it affects the rhythm and tempo of their speech.

8   **Narrators should utilize the brief introductions provided with each verbatim testimony as part of the scene performance to give the audience context for the scene**.

Tableaus – As in the visual arts, tableaus in the performing arts are frozen pictures which tell stories. Theatrical tableaus are created by actors positioning themselves in formations which convey information to the audience both about the action that is taking place and the emotions that the characters are experiencing. In creating tableaus, it is important that the actors fully commit to three things: 1. *The physical action* – by engaging their muscles with the necessary energy that would be required to complete an activity, actors clearly express to an audience what their character is "doing" without any need for spoken dialogue. This is a basic principle of pantomime, but in "frozen" form. For example, if an actor is portraying the lifting of a heavy piece of furniture, s/he must flex the muscles that would actually be engaged in such an activity in order to properly convey the weight of the object. 2. *The character's emotion* – actors must also fully commit to the emotion of the scene and allow that emotion to be reflected in their facial expressions. It is crucial that the actors "stay in character," meaning, maintain the emotional truth of the moment, and not slip back into being themselves, or smiling or laughing when that would be an inappropriate choice for the character. 3. *The character's focus* – last, the focus of the actor's eyes is a critical component to creating an effective tableau. The actor must focus his/her eyes on the person, object, or action that is most important to the character at that moment. This seemingly simple directive is the one that is most often overlooked by young actors, and is the one "fix" that can most radically improve the look of a stage tableau and of the audience's understanding of that tableau.

All of the actors in each scene group will collaborate to construct a series of theatrical tableaus which will depict various moments described in the historical narrative monologue. The goal is to stage between five and eight clear, powerful and visually interesting stage pictures which will accompany and help dramatize the narrator's reading of the monologue. It is helpful if the actors think of the tableaus like illustrations in a book. If this were a printed story, where would they choose to insert an illustration? Which moments of the story have the strongest potential to be compelling visual images? Which moments are the most significant and worthy of being highlighted by a physical manifestation?

Notes on prop and costume usage – Props and costumes give a sense of place and time to a scene and create visual interest. A simple hat, armband or vest can help delineate one character from another, and can fill in important information for your audience. Each chapter's *verbatim testimony historical narrative* section offers suggested props and costume pieces. Many of these items can be found at used-clothing stores, fabric, hobby or crafts stores, or better yet, in the homes of the theater-makers. School costume rooms and prop closets are excellent resources. What's most important is that any props or costumes that are used should *add* to the clarity and storytelling of the scene, not diminish it. So, for example, if the scene is set in 1940, and a telephone would be a helpful prop for the scene, it is actually better to mime that prop than to use a cell phone. Using a prop that is completely anachronistic will take the audience *out* of the action rather than bringing them *into* the action. While these pieces do not need to be 100 percent authentic, they should bear enough resemblance to the intended object or garment that their usage contributes positively to the storytelling.

Notes on musical underscoring — If chosen wisely, musical underscoring can greatly enhance these presentations by adding emotional weight to the scenes. Selecting the right music is crucial, as is the volume at which the music is played. Only instrumental music should be used as underscoring. Search for music that reflects the emotional qualities of the scene, and which augments those qualities without overpowering the narrative. Some composers whose work fits this description are: Ludovico Einaudi, Helen Jane Long, Dustin O'Halloran, Yiruma, Max Richter, Phillip Glass and Peter Jennison. Works for solo instrumental performance such as piano, violin, clarinet, flute, etc, can also be very appropriate and impactful.

STEPS:

1   Ensemble members should begin crafting their tableaus by using the *tableau story-board* (p. xxxv). Have students draw, to the best of their ability, what is taking place in each tableau. Underneath each picture, they should write the line in the narration that will accompany that physical image.
2   Ensemble members then decide which role or roles each actor will play in each tableau. (If an actor is playing more than one role in the scene, it is important that s/he wear small costume pieces that will delineate one character from another.)
3   Actors will then select several props and costume pieces that will help enhance their storytelling. These should be items that are easy to find. Objects like bowls and blankets can go a long way in fleshing out the details of the moment being depicted in a tableau.
4   Next, the actors will stage their tableaus. In doing so, they should always keep the audience in mind. Can the audience clearly see all of the actions? The facial expressions? Encourage the actors to make big physical choices and to commit to them. Without the extra component of dialogue, their physicality will be the only means by which they can communicate. Emotions, physical exertion, energy and exhaustion should all come through in their facial expressions and body positions. They should make definite choices and commit to them, holding their freezes and not breaking character.
5   After setting specific staging for each tableau, the group will combine the images with the narration. The narrator should be very clear about when it is time to move to the next tableau by using the agreed-upon signal. The actors should rehearse how they will move to the next tableau, and how they will add or discard props and costume pieces between pictures. The movement between tableaus is

almost as important as the frozen images themselves. This movement should be smooth and purposeful. Narrators may need to adjust their timing and/or add pauses in order for the actors to get into position for each new stage picture.

6   If the actors are using musical underscoring, they should rehearse with that as well. The music can have a big impact on the narrator's delivery and the overall rhythm of the piece.

7   It is now time to perform the scenes. Allow each group a few moments to set up. It is probably best if you have a designated spot for your narrators with a chair and a music stand that can remain in place throughout all of the scenes. If you are utilizing a large space for your performances and have access to a microphone, it is a great asset to have a microphone on a stand for the narrators. If you are incorporating musical underscoring in any of the scenes, set up your speakers so that it can be heard by the whole audience, but make sure that the volume is adjusted so that it serves to *underscore* the narration and does not obscure the narrator's words in any way.

Verbatim testimony historical narratives – suggested lesson plan

Duration of activity: three to four class periods of 50–60 minutes each.

Day #1

Preparation: 1. Create a login for the USC Shoah Foundation IWitness website: https://iwitness.usc.edu/SFI/. 2. Pre-screen the "This is what I've scene" demonstration video: http://iwitness.usc.edu/SFI/Activity/DoActivity.aspx?stp=a67ea83e-9884-4b96-b8a4-4458da314613.

Physical requirements: 1. An open area to conduct the theater activities. There should be enough open space to create a small "stage" on which five or six students can move around comfortably without bumping into each other or into furniture. 2. A computer with wi-fi access.

STEPS:

1   *Introduce* the technique of creating *theatrical tableaus* with the following theater activity:
- Divide students into groups of six to eight.
- Give each group of students one of the following words: love; disappointment; surprise; fear; jealousy; joy; sorrow. These words should be shared "secretly" so that students outside of each group won't hear the other groups' words. Instruct each group to create a single stage picture, or "tableau" which will so clearly illustrate their given word that the audience will be able to

guess it. You might offer this instruction: "Imagine that, collectively, all of the members of your group make up a single statue in the park. The statue has a plaque on it with one word – which is the word I have given you." These tableaus should be depictions of *stories*, with the given words describing the overall emotion of the story, *not* literal representations of the words themselves – such as actors making heart shapes with their hands for the word "love," or students all wiping tears from their eyes for "sorrow." Each actor in the tableau should have a specific "role" and there should be a clear storyline that the audience can glean from the picture.

- Allow each group to include one or two props in their tableau. These can be any items that are on hand in the classroom.
- Give the groups up to ten minutes to stage and rehearse their tableaus. Encourage them to keep the audience in mind when staging, making sure that all of the actors and their facial expressions will be visible to the viewers. Remind them to focus their eyes on what is important to their character in the scene. They should not look at the audience. Encourage them to create pictures that are visually interesting by having actors on different levels (sitting, standing, lying on the ground, kneeling, etc.) and by positioning themselves at different angles.
- Present the tableaus. Invite the groups up one at a time. Before the actors get into place, ask the audience to close their eyes. Once the actors are in their frozen position, ask the audience to open their eyes. This creates a bit of "theater magic" usually achieved through lighting or the opening of a curtain and will make each tableau that much more impactful. Have the actors maintain their freeze as the audience takes in the picture and begins guessing the given word.
- Discuss the students' work. Which tableaus were most effective? Most memorable? Why?

2 *Introduce* the "This is what I've scene" concept of creating scenes using tableaus paired with historical narrative monologues.

3 As a class, *watch* the demonstration video on the IWitness website: http://iwitness.usc.edu/SFI/Activity/DoActivity.aspx?stp=a67ea83e-9884-4b96-b8a4-4458da314613.

4 *Discuss*: What was effective about the scene that the students presented in the video? How did their tableaus enhance the telling of the narrative?

Day #2

Preparation: 1. Pre-select the narrative testimonies that you are assigning to your students. If you and your students are not utilizing the e-book, photocopy one testimony per group. 2. Make one copy of the storyboard template for each group. 3. Set up a table with props and costume pieces that students can select for inclusion in their scenes. (Note: prop suggestions are provided at the end of each chapter's *verbatim testimony historical narratives* section.)

Physical requirements: 1. Each group will need access to a computer and wi-fi. If your students have their own laptops, make sure they bring them to class for this activity. If you will need to use your school's computer lab, make sure you have made arrangements for that and that each scene group has access to a computer or, if they will be listening individually with headphones, that each student has access to a computer and headphones. 2. A table or tables large enough to display the props and costume pieces that you have assembled.

STEPS:

1   *Divide* students into scene groups of approximately five to six per group.
2   *Assign* testimonies to each group. Choose testimonies from the chapters that are most relevant to your Holocaust learning.
3   Have each group *watch* the video testimony of their assigned survivor/witness/liberator by using the website address that accompanies that particular testimony. This is a crucial step. *Seeing and hearing the actual person give his or her testimony is a critical part of the process.* (Optional: give each group two selections from which to choose after watching both testimonies.)
4   Have each group *determine* which moments in their narrative they want to illustrate in tableaus. Six is the suggested number of tableaus per scene, but some narratives may require more or less to tell the story effectively.
5   Have each group *choose* a narrator and *cast* all of the roles in their scene.
6   Narrators should *rehearse* their narratives while the ensembles *develop* a "story board" for the scene (use the *tableau storyboard* on p. xxxv).
7   Allow one or two students from each group to select between three and five props/costumes from the prop table. Make a list of which items each group is using so there will be no confusion going forward.

Day #3

Preparation: 1. Consider inviting other classes to watch your scene presentations on Day #4. Alternately, consider filming the scenes and sharing them with other classes at another time. 2. If your students will be using musical underscoring for their scenes, make sure you have speakers available and have tested them with whatever playback system (computer, smartphone) you will be using. 3. If you will be pre-selecting the musical underscoring tracks, have those ready to share with the students.

Physical requirements: 1. Make sure that the room is set up so there is an open "stage" area at the front of the room. 2. The props and costumes selected by the students on Day #2 should be readily available. 3. If you have access to a music stand, this will be helpful for use by your narrators. 4. A few furniture pieces – such as chairs and small tables – will be very useful to the actors in staging their scenes.

STEPS:

1   Actors will get up on their feet to *create* their tableaus. The narrators may serve as "directors," giving feedback as to how to make each stage picture clearer and more effective.
2   Each group will *select* the word or words in the narrative on which the actors will move to the next tableau. The narrator should mark these in his/her script. The narrators will be indicating – by either a sound or gesture – when it is time to "change the picture."
3   Optional: Each group will *select a musical track* to underscore their scene. (Alternately, you may pre-select these for each group, or not include music at all.)
4   Each group will *rehearse* the full scene, putting together the narrative with the tableaus, rehearsing both the tableaus themselves and the movement from picture to picture. (If you only have three days to complete this exercise, leave enough time for the performances of the scenes and jump to Step 2 in Day #4.)

Day #4

Preparation: 1. If you have invited additional classes to see the performance, set up the room to accommodate these additional audience members. 2. Consider making a printed program with a scene list which includes the names of the people whose testimonies you are sharing, as well as their basic biographical information.

Physical requirements: see Day #3.

STEPS:

1   Each group will continue to *rehearse* their scene.
2   Each group will *present* their scene to the rest of the class.
3   At the conclusion of all of the scene presentations, *facilitate a discussion session* in which you ask the students the following:
    a   Did you learn anything new from any of the scenes? What did you learn?
    b   What moments stood out to you in each scene? Overall?
    c   Did you respond more to the words of the story or the images? Or to the combination of both? Discuss.
    d   Were any of the scenes more effective than others? Why? What made those scenes so effective or impactful?
    e   As actors, did participating in this activity give you a better understanding of the Holocaust? In what ways?
    f   As actors and/or audience members, how was this experience different than learning about the Holocaust through reading a book? Listening to a lecture? Watching a movie?

Historical narrative scenes

Tableau storyboard

Create a storyboard of your tableaus. Underneath each drawing, write the line that is being read as this tableau is being formed. (If your scene requires additional tableaus, use a second sheet.)

1	2

3	4

5	6

How to: devised theater activities

This form of theater can be difficult to pin down because theater-makers describe it in so many different ways. For the purposes of this book, devised theater will be defined as *a method of creating a performance piece using source material that was not originally created or intended for theatrical performance.* Unlike traditional theater, devised theater typically does not have a linear structure based on plot. These performance pieces are more likely to be abstract in nature, using theme as a central guidepost rather than storyline, making devised theater more akin to poetry than to prose.

Devised theater projects are not unlike the visual art form of collage. Like the collage artist, the theater devisor selects materials with different textures, colors and shapes, and carefully arranges them in a format designed to elicit particular emotions or ideas from the viewer. Where a collage artist might incorporate swatches of fabric, pieces of magazines, paints, adhesives and natural or found objects, the theater devisor incorporates an assortment of written, visual and auditory source materials in the creation of his/her work.

In this book's devised theater exercises, these source materials have been preselected as the "scene components" for each activity; however, the theater devisors are asked to make many choices regarding the use of these given source materials. (Due to the sensitive nature of the subject matter of this book, the crafting of fictionalized stories is discouraged, and it is recommended that only the given, unfabricated texts that are provided are used in these activities.)

Types of source materials that are included in this book's devised theater activities include:

- Documentary photography
- Historical documents – laws, proclamations, declarations
- Newspaper articles
- Letters
- Poetry
- Song lyrics
- Music
- Children's games
- Interview testimonies.

One suggested devised theater activity has been created for each of this book's ten chapters. Each includes: 1. Scene components; 2. Texts; 3. Staging considerations, choices and tips.

Terminology of scene components and best practices

Tableaus – see page xxix in the *How to: verbatim testimony historical narratives* for a definition of and best practices for creating tableaus.

Choral speech – choral speech refers to the variety of ways in which text can be spoken by multiple members of an acting ensemble. Utilizing these techniques can lend a poetic quality to the text, and allow the actors to emphasize particular words and ideas without changing any of the words of, say, a historical document. These techniques include: 1. *Unison speech* – all ensemble members speaking the same words at the same time; 2. *Echoed or repeated speech* – ensemble members repeating words or phrases that have already been spoken by other actors, or repeating their own lines for effect; 3. *Alternating speech* – segments of sentences or paragraphs divided up among ensemble members so that varying voices are taking part in communicating one idea; 4. *Overlapping speech* – ensemble members speaking lines with a layered effect, overlapping the lines of those speaking before them. This can be used in conjunction with repeated text so that the lines are heard in their entirety in the beginning, and then in fragments later on.

Choral movement – choral movement is a form of choreography that is not necessarily "dance." Choral movement can add visual interest to a scene, helping to highlight words, phrases and ideas by punctuating them with intentional gestures that are performed by the acting ensemble in a variety of ways. These may include: 1. *Unison movements* – such as gestures, rising, sitting, jumping, etc., that are done together as an ensemble; 2. *Repeated movements* – movements that are done again and again, repeated either by a single actor or a group of actors; 3. *Contagion movements* – physical actions that are performed sequentially by the ensemble creating a ripple effect (think "The Wave" traveling around a stadium); 4. *Movement motif* – a piece of movement that is repeated a number of times in the course of one scene, often emphasizing a certain theme.

Group breaths – breathing is often the most overlooked aspect of acting. Just as in music, where the rests are as important as the notes themselves, the moments where actors pause and breathe can be as significant as the dialogue. Group breaths are deliberate actions where multiple ensemble members take full breaths – deep inhalations followed by deep exhalations – simultaneously. This creates a feeling of unity, and can convey a shared understanding or agreement, or may simply portray a shared moment among the characters/performers. These breaths should be purposeful and unhurried. There should be a stillness onstage when they occur, enabling a processing by the audience of what has *just* occurred and making room for whatever is *about* to occur.

Split stage – a blocking technique in which actions are taking place in two or more areas of the stage, depicting different scenes which are being performed concurrently. These could be two scenes that are both set in the same timeframe, or may depict things that are happening in two different time periods. A split stage is useful when you want to compare and contrast different scenarios by showing things "side by side" that in reality, would not literally be taking place in proximity to each other. When utilizing this technique, it is often powerful to alternate back and forth between the different actions. To do this effectively, have one scene group freeze in tableau while the other is active, and vice-versa.

Notes on object/prop and costume usage – small props and costume pieces can greatly enhance your devised theater scenes. Props and costumes give a sense of place and time to a scene and create visual interest. A simple hat, armband or vest can help delineate one character from another, and can fill in important information for your audience. Props and costume pieces should be kept very simple! Some of the devised theater activities include suggested props and costume pieces; others leave this to the discretion of the theater-makers. Many prop and costume pieces can be found at used-clothing stores, fabric, hobby or crafts stores or, better yet, in the homes of the theater-makers. School costume rooms and prop closets are excellent resources. What's most important, is that any props or costumes that are used should *add* to the clarity and storytelling of the scene, not diminish it. So, for example, if the scene is set in 1940, and a telephone would be a helpful prop for the scene, it is actually better to mime that prop than to use a cell phone. Using a prop that is completely anachronistic will take the audience *out* of the action rather than bringing them *into* the action. While these pieces do not need to be 100 percent authentic, they should bear enough resemblance to the intended object or garment that their usage contributes positively to the storytelling.

Notes on music and musical underscoring – musical underscoring can greatly enhance a scene presentation by adding emotional weight to the scene and/or providing a historical framework, if the music is from the era in which the scene takes place. Selecting the right music is crucial, as is the volume at which the music is played. Music with sung lyrics should only be used when there is no spoken dialogue; otherwise, the dialogue will become obscured. When the music is serving as underscoring, it is extremely important that the volume does not overpower the spoken word. Music such as anthems, marches and nationalistic or religious hymns can offer interesting texture and context in a scene, whether accompanied by physical staging (tableaus or movement), or alternating with moments of dialogue/text. Likewise, instrumental musical choices can provide another layer of expression to a scene, with a unifying soundscape bolstering the action. When choosing underscoring, search for music that reflects the emotional qualities of the scene, and which augments those qualities without overwhelming the dialogue and action. Some composers whose work fits this description are: Ludovico Einaudi, Helen Jane Long, Dustin O'Halloran, Yiruma, Max Richter, Phillip Glass and Peter Jennison. Works for solo instrumental performance such as piano, violin, clarinet, flute, etc, can also be very appropriate and impactful. Have fun searching for the music that will best enhance the scene.

How to get started on your devised theater scene – notes for directors and students

1   As a scene group, read aloud any text materials supplied for the activity. Discuss how these words make you feel. What do you want your audience to get out of hearing these words?

2   As a group, discuss any images supplied for the activity. How do these photos, pictures make you feel? What is happening in these images? How can you convey those feelings and ideas to your audience in a visual way?

3   If the teacher is not serving as the director, appoint a director. This should be someone who will not appear in the scene, but who will be able to stand on the outside during your rehearsal process, taking the point of view of the audience in order to make sure that you are conveying the ideas, images and sentiments that you want the audience to grasp.

4   Discuss how to interweave the given components in order to make your performance captivating and clearly understood. Try reading/performing/physicalizing these components in different ways. Get on your feet and experiment! Some ideas will work better than others, but you won't know until you try them. Don't say "no" before giving something a try.

5   Keep it simple. Trust that a single gesture or a single line of poetry can have great power when delivered with purpose and conviction. Have faith in the concept of using "a part for the whole," meaning that you don't have to show or tell "everything." Finding the movement, word, image, object, or phrase with the most significance can speak volumes. This is a fundamental poetic principle, and it will take you far in the creation and presentation of your devised theater scene.

6   Commit. Commit. Commit. If you believe in what you're doing and are able to stay "in the moment," and invest all of your energy into your performance, the audience will come along every time.

Sample devised theater scene

The following is a scene which was created by a company of teenage actor/devisors who were members of the Atlanta theater group Project Impact Theatre back in the late 1990s. Using only the text from the Reverend Martin Niemöller's poem "And Then They Came for Me," the scene was devised using the format of a game of musical chairs. It has proven so effective, that it has been used continuously for over 20 years in the social-issue theater performances given by Project Impact Theatre, and its subsequent incarnation, Project Tolerance. In response to the scene, student audience members frequently remark that although they had heard this poem before, they never fully understood its meaning until they saw it performed in this format. This response gives credence to the idea that devised theater can be a powerful and effective tool for teaching the Holocaust. By adding a physical manifestation to what was previously "just words," devised theater can contextualize those words, giving them greater meaning, greater resonance and greater longevity in the viewers' minds. Making associations through the use of juxtaposition, paradox, comparison, metaphor and analogy allows for a deeper level of thought and interpretation on the part of both the artists and their audiences. Devised theater both allows and encourages these associations.

Feel free to have your students perform this scene. And when doing so, be sure to credit Reverend Niemöller, as well as the Project Impact Theatre ensemble.

"And Then They Came for Me"

Text by Reverend Martin Niemöller;
Scene by the Project Impact Theatre ensemble under the facilitation and direction of Mira Hirsch

Seven actors:
- Guard
- Child (with jack–in–the–box)
- Players 1–5

Props/set pieces
- Five armless chairs
- One red armband (note: do not use Nazi insignia)
- Blank white mask
- Jack–in–the–box toy (The character in the box should be an old–fashioned clown character. Do not use a toy with a recognizable commercial cartoon figure.)

Guard stands USL. He wears a red arm band and an expressionless white mask.
Five actors enter and sit in one of five chairs – three facing the audience, two behind them facing upstage.
Child sits on floor or on a small box DSR operating the jack-in-the-box.
Bell rings.
Everyone rises from their chairs.
Guard removes one chair.
Child begins turning the jack-in-the-box. When the music stops, everyone scrambles for a chair. (NOTE: Actor #5 must get a chair in each round of the game.)
One person is left chair-less. Guard drags this person USR as Player #5 rises and says …

Actor #5
In Germany, first they came for the Communists,
And I didn't speak up, because I wasn't a Communist.

Other Players rise. Guard removes another chair.
Child turns the jack-in-the-box. When the music stops …
Another Player is left chair-less.
Guard drags this person USR as #5 rises and says …

Actor #5
Then they came for the trade unionists, and I didn't speak up, because I wasn't a trade unionist.

Other Players rise. Guard removes another chair.
Child turns the jack-in-the-box. When the music stops …
Another Player is left chairless.
Guard drags this person USR as #5 rises and says …

Actor #5

Then they came for the Jews, and I didn't speak up, because I wasn't a Jew.

Other Players rise. Guard removes another chair.
Child turns the jack-in-the-box. When the music stops …
Another Player is left chairless.
Guard drags this person USR, as #5 rises and says …

Actor #5

Then they came for the Catholics, and I didn't speak up, because I was a Protestant.

Other Players rise. Guard removes another chair.
Child turns the jack-in-the-box. When the music stops …
Another Player is left chair-less.
Guard drags this person USR
Player #5 sits in last remaining chair, and sighs, believing s/he is out of danger.
Guard walks up behind #5, who is the last person left and pulls the chair out from under him/her.*

Actor #5

(From the floor.) And then they came for me …

Guard lifts #5 from the floor and holds his/her arms behind his/her back …

Actor #5

And by that time, there was no one left to speak up.

Guard drags Actor #5 off USR with others.

*Rehearse this carefully so that the person in the chair is controlling the falling, and is not actually being surprised by the chair being removed. Decide on a physical or vocal cue that will indicate the exact moment that the chair should be pulled away. This requires a great deal of trust, cooperation and rehearsal between the actors so that no one gets hurt!

Devised theater activity – suggested lesson plan

Duration of activity: three to four class periods of 50–60 minutes each.

Day #1

Preparation: 1. If you/your students do not have access to the e-book version of this book, make copies of the above sample devised theater scene "And Then They Came for Me." 2. Pre-select the devised theater activities that you are assigning to your students. If you and your students are not utilizing the e-book, make at least one copy of the assigned activity for each scene group, and/or provide an electronic copy to the group's members.

Physical requirements: If you are staging the sample scene: 1. Create an open area in which to comfortably stage the "And Then They Came for Me" scene. 2. Assemble the props and furniture necessary for staging the scene: five armless chairs, a jack-in-the-box; a red armband; a white mask (optional). (If you are *reading* the scene without staging – no physical requirements are necessary.)

STEPS:

1   *Introduce* the technique of devised theater by sharing with your students the definition and description found on page xxxvi. Discuss the appeal and benefits of creating theater in this manner. Discuss the possible challenges and how they might be overcome.

2   *Select seven students to perform* the sample devised theater scene "And Then They Came for Me." Allow them some rehearsal time before performing. *Alternately, have two students read the scene aloud*, with one reading the stage directions and the other reading the lines of Actor #5. Discuss the scene, asking the following: Is it an effective piece of theater? Why or why not? After seeing the scene performed (or hearing it read) do you have a different impression of devised theater? Of its ability to impact an audience? To impact its devisors?

3   *Divide* students into scene groups of approximately six to ten per group.

4   *Assign* a devised theater activity to each group. Choose activities from the chapters that are most relevant to your Holocaust learning.

5   Have each group *read* the activities' instructions and texts together as an ensemble.

6   Instruct the groups to *begin discussing* their assigned activity.

Day #2

Preparation: 1. Set up a table with props and costumes pieces that the students can select for inclusion in their scenes. 2. Secure/create enough open areas for each group to work on their scenes "up on their feet." This may require finding additional space(s).

Physical requirements: 1. A table or tables large enough to display the prop and costume pieces that you have assembled. 2. Furniture pieces such as small tables, chairs, blocks, etc.

STEPS:

1   Students will meet in their scene groups for approximately 15 minutes to *discuss ideas for staging their scenes*. They may choose to appoint a director, or may choose to direct collaboratively.

2   *Students should get on their feet and begin exploring* the choices they have made. In this stage of the scene's development, it is important that multiple voices are heard

and that multiple ideas are tried. *Visit with each group*, observing the students' processes, giving critical feedback when necessary. *Encourage* experimentation and collaboration.

3   Each group should appointment one student to *"write" the group's script*. This will be best accomplished if that student begins with the electronic copy of the devised theater activity so that s/he can easily rearrange the lines of text into the agreed upon order and format, inserting stage directions, etc. as necessary.

4   At the end of the class period, *have your students submit three things*: 1. Their working script; 2. A list of any additional props that they would like to use for their scene and who will be responsible for finding/bringing in these items; 3. A list of music and/or sound cues that they will be incorporating in their scene, and who is responsible for locating these.

Day #3

Preparation: 1. Consider inviting other classes to watch your scene presentations on Day #4. Alternately, consider filming the scenes and sharing them with other classes at another time. 2. If your students will be using music and/or or sound effects for their scenes, make sure you have speakers available and have tested them with whatever playback system (computer, smartphone) you will be using.

Physical requirements: 1. Set up the room so there is an open "stage" area at the front. 2. The props and costumes set out on Day #2 should be readily available, as should any furniture pieces the students have chosen to use.

STEPS:

1   Each group will *rehearse* their full scene, incorporating any props, costumes, sound or lighting cues. (NOTE: If you only have three days to complete this exercise, leave enough time for the performances of the scenes and jump to Day #4, Step 2.)

2   Observe each scene group, giving critical feedback.

Day #4

Preparation: 1. If you have invited additional classes to see your performance, set up the room to accommodate these additional audience members. 2. Consider making a printed program which includes any relevant background information for each scene, as well as the names of the student devisor/actors in each scene.

Physical requirements: (see Day #3)

STEPS:

1   Each group will continue to *rehearse* their scene.
2   Each group will *present* their scene.
3   At the conclusion of all of the scene presentations, *facilitate a discussion session* in which you ask the students the following:
    a   Did you learn anything new from any of the scenes? What did you learn?
    b   What moments stood out to you in each scene? Overall?
    c   Were any of the scenes more effective than others? Why? What made those scenes so effective or impactful?
    d   As actors, did participating in this activity give you a better understanding of the Holocaust? In what ways?
    e   As actors and/or audience members, how was this experience different than learning about the Holocaust through reading a book? Listening to a lecture? Watching a movie? Watching a traditional scripted scene or play?

1

Propaganda, the growth of Nazism, the Nuremberg Laws and Kristallnacht

Context

Germany had been a democracy, so how were Adolf Hitler and the Nazis able to take over and control the state? Some context is helpful to understanding what allowed this to transpire.

Germany had suffered a humiliating loss in World War I. The Treaty of Versailles was perceived by Germans to be unfair. Germany was required to pay reparations and it depended upon the United States for loans. The Great Depression, however, crippled the US economy and created a ripple effect felt in Germany. The Nazis promised prosperity and blamed Jews for the country's economic woes. Further, their avowed antisemitism appealed to certain segments of the population. Antisemitism had a long history in Europe, albeit stronger at certain times than others, and was a useful tool for assigning blame to Jews for Germany's problems.

The German Workers Party originated in 1919 as a small, far right group, one of many fringe Bavarian political groups which shared the belief that Jews were manipulators who had contributed to Germany's loss in World War I. They associated Jews with Communist revolution and they decried the Weimar democratic government. On September 19, 1919, Adolf Hitler attended a German Workers Party meeting in Munich. As a German intelligence agent, he had been sent to observe; instead, he became involved. Anton Drexler, the group's leader, was impressed by Hitler and invited him into the Party.

Hitler became active not only in party propaganda, but also in drafting the 25 Points. This document, published on February 24, 1920, outlined Nazi ideology. Core values included antisemitism, racial stereotyping, a hatred for the Treaty of Versailles, a desire for more living space (land for Germans), a classless Germany, and a physically fit population. The doctrine embraced the notions of absolute power, press restrictions, and censorship. Democracy was shunned and state-sponsored terror against perceived criminals and enemies was suggested. On the same day that the 25 Points doctrine was published, the German Workers Party changed its name to the National Socialist German Workers Party (NSDAP), better known as the Nazi Party.

Hitler quickly was seen as the Party's leader and his Third Reich ultimately would adopt the antisemitic, anti-Marxist, anti-capitalist, and anti-democratic principles of the NSDAP. Hitler was charismatic, and his fiery rhetoric made him a popular speaker at rallies. His speeches and writings attracted men in the early 1920s who later would become prominent figures in the Reich: Julius Streicher created and ran the hate-filled publication *Der Stürmer*; Herman Goering shaped the Nazi police state; Hans Frank became President of the Reichstag and Minister of Justice; Ernst Rohm organized the Storm Troopers; and Rudolf Hess became Hitler's deputy party leader. More people joined the Nazis when France and Belgium crossed into German territory, an action taken when the country could not make reparations payments.

The Nazis first tried to take control of Germany by force. This failed, and Hitler was convicted of high treason. In prison, he wrote *Mein Kampf* (*My Struggle*) in which he explained his hatred of Jews and other central beliefs.

> Everything was here: the enormity of the threat posed by the Jews; the centrality of the issue of race; the importance of policing who was allowed to breed; the need for Germany to gain territory in the east ...
>
> (Rees 34)

These were fundamental beliefs for Hitler, and they would be at the forefront when he came to power. Hitler was paroled from prison on December 21, 1924.

The Nazis next tried to gain power through the electoral process and then by political maneuvering. Using this strategy, the Nazis went from getting 26 percent of the vote in May 1928 to becoming the second largest political party in the Reichstag in 1930. By 1932, they were the largest party in the Reichstag, holding 230 seats.

Working-class people were central to the party's growth. Nazis targeted rural areas with propaganda. They attracted more Protestants to the party than any other religious group. Support came from the lower middle classes, small businessmen, artisans and agricultural workers. By targeting certain demographics and regions of the country, the NSDAP became identified as a party of the masses.

Hitler became Chancellor of Germany on January 30, 1933. On February 23, 1933, the Reichstag burned. Although the fire was arson, the "Reichstag Fire Decree" was issued the next day. It suspended the people's right of assembly, negated the right to free speech and free press, allowed the state access to telephone conversations and mail, as well as the right to search houses, seize property and jail people without a trial. It enhanced Hitler's power.

The Enabling Act passed on March 24, 1933 permitted Hitler to bypass the Reichstag and allowed the Reich Cabinet to govern. It laid a legal foundation for dictatorship. To further strengthen their hold on the government, the Nazis took over policing and local government.

All too frequently, the SA would terrorize a neighborhood, prompting the central government to declare that local authorities were unable to cope. A new, Nazi leader would then be appointed to take control. On March 31, 1933, the state governments were dissolved and reconstituted in a manner that favoured the NSDAP representatives. In this way, the NSDAP expanded its reach across Germany.

(Sharples 50)

Further, by eliminating political competition, the Nazi Party was, less than half a year after taking power, the only lawfully recognized political party in the country.

The Nazi government wasted no time in tightening the noose. On March 28, 1933, Hitler called for Jewish businesses to be boycotted. That occurred on April 1, 1933. Storm Troopers stood in front of Jewish shops. They painted slogans on shops such as "The Jews are our misery" that told patrons not to shop at Jewish enterprises. This action, however, was not as successful as the Nazis had hoped.

Laws were passed in 1933 that limited the number of Jewish doctors and lawyers who could practice their professions. A law also limited the number of Jewish students allowed into the state schools and universities. Another banned Jews from civil service jobs. Dachau, the first concentration camp, was established in March 1933 to incarcerate political prisoners.

Significant events also occurred in 1934. "The Night of Long Knives" took place on June 30. Hitler had Ernst Rohm, head of the SA, and 20 of his followers killed. Because of their role in this, the SS (Schutzstaffel or Protection Squad) was elevated to a top paramilitary force and Heinrich Himmler became head of the Nazis' security forces. Even more momentous, on August 2, German President Paul von Hindenburg died. Hitler used the Enabling Act to merge the presidency and the chancellorship into one office. With that, he became Germany's dictator.

The Nuremberg Laws were passed in 1935. These separated Jews from the rest of the population. Jews were defined not by their religion but by their grandparents' religious affiliations. With these laws, Jews lost the right to marry, their political rights, as well as the right to employ non-Jews. They could not display the national flag. Young people defined as Jews, even if they did not practice the religion or had converted to Christianity, could not take pre-college exams or pursue professions that required a state exit exam. They could not participate in Hitler Youth groups or the Reich Labor Service. The law for The Protection of German Blood and Honor outlawed sexual relations between Jews and non-Jews. The Flag Law made the swastika flag the official flag of the nation. The Reich Citizenship Law revoked the German citizenship of Jews. Roma and Sinti (Gypsies) also were subject to these laws.

More laws designed to alienate Jews from the rest of the population were passed between 1937 and 1939. With these laws, Jews could not attend public schools. They lost their businesses and property. They could not attend cinemas or theaters, could not live or walk in certain parts of cities, and were not allowed into vacation resorts.

A defining event of 1938 was Kristallnacht, or "The Night of Broken Glass." On November 9 and 10, synagogues, Jewish cemeteries, Jewish businesses and homes were vandalized. The name comes from all the shattered glass that resulted from the assault. During Kristallnacht, Jews were humiliated, arrested, murdered, raped and taken to concentration camps. Although SA, State Police and Hitler Youth out of uniform, as well as some neighbors and supposed family "friends" of those targeted were responsible for instigating the riots, the government placed the blame for the violence solely on angry Germans.

The precipitating event for Kristallnacht was the murder of Ernst vom Rath in Paris by Herschel Grynszpan, a young Jew. Angered by the expulsion of his parents from Germany, the teenager shot the diplomat. Hitler used this killing as the basis for Kristallnacht, saying that the vandalism and looting were undertaken by enraged Germans. Ultimately, however, the Reich said that the Jews were to blame and seized any insurance payments that they might have received for their losses.

The international community condemned Kristallnacht but did little to help the Jews. America allowed 12,000 Austrian and German Jews who were in the country to extend their stay but rejected measures to bring Jewish children to safety within its borders. Britain was more generous, allowing additional refugees into the country and rescuing 9,000 children via the Kindertransport program.

From its earliest days, the Nazi Party used propaganda as an effective tool. Youth were targeted as early as the 1920s and the party was promoted to them as a dynamic and vigorous movement. Similarly, farmers were portrayed as rugged individuals made healthy through outdoor toil, symbols of hard work and self-sufficiency. In addition, by having a large family, the farmer was seen to reflect the rebirth of Germany. Jews, on the other hand, were said to be dirty and to spread disease. Nazi propaganda dehumanized Jews and showed them as grotesque and demonic caricatures or criminals. They were portrayed as inferiors and enemies of the state.

Nazi propaganda could be cloaked in military rhetoric. It depicted Hitler as a messiah. The swastika often was used to symbolize a rising sun. These images were meant to communicate a new dawn or rebirth for Germany. And it was Hitler, the strong leader, who would shepherd this resurrection.

In 1933, Hitler created the Reich Ministry of Public Enlightenment and Propaganda and put Joseph Goebbels in charge. He was tasked with spreading the Nazis' message through all available means, including media, the arts and educational materials. Goebbels had long been involved with propaganda and antisemitism. At the end of 1926, for example, he targeted Berlin Jews and, in particular, Dr. Bernhard Weiss. In *Der Angriff*, his magazine, Goebbels routinely called the deputy police commissioner "Isidor," using the common Jewish name rather than Weiss' given name. Goebbels made frequent derogatory references to Weiss, even depicting him as a donkey. When Weiss took legal action and won, Goebbels spun the decision to say that it confirmed that Weiss was a donkey.

Nazi propaganda in the early 1930s focused upon economic interests linked to Jews. Goebbels used guilt by association as a propaganda apparatus. Department stores, for example, were treated as Jewish enterprises that destroyed small businesses. As Minister, Goebbels favored visual materials such as colorful posters, artwork, newspapers and films to promote hateful messages. Jews felt powerless against the state and Goebbels was a master at making Germans feel like they had come to their own antisemitic conclusions.

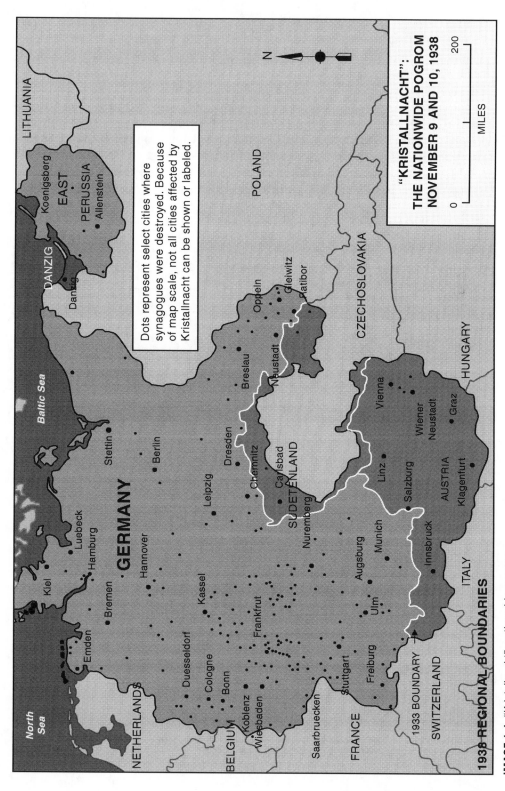

Dots represent select cities where synagogues were destroyed. Because of map scale, not all cities affected by Kristallnacht can be shown or labeled.

"KRISTALLNACHT":
THE NATIONWIDE POGROM
NOVEMBER 9 AND 10, 1938

0   200

MILES

IMAGE 1.1 "Kristallnacht": nationwide pogrom

The Nazis used technology as well as more basic devices to their advantage. Photographs, films, newsreels, loudspeakers, torchlit parades, rallies and radio promoted their ideology. Communal listening and shared experiences drew ordinary citizens to a belief that Germany could not be a united country if Jews were in it. Hitler's speeches were regularly broadcast. Jewish stereotypes were exploited, and Jews were depicted as an alien race that sucked the life from the nation. The Berlin Olympics were particularly successful for propaganda purposes. Germans won the most medals, an Aryan-looking athlete carried the Olympic torch into the stadium, and the Leni Riefenstahl film, *Olympia*, showed images of the games. The 1940 propaganda film, *Der Ewige Jude* (*The Eternal Jew*) compared Jews with rats. It also attacked Jewish bankers. Hitler was thought to have been involved in assuring that the film was extremely hateful.

IMAGE 1.2 Poster for the antisemitic museum exhibition Der Ewige Jude

Indoctrination began early. Teachers told Aryan students that they were better than Jewish students. The children's book, *Der Giftpilz* (*The Poisonous Mushroom*), was published in 1938 and its title story carried the message that although all mushrooms might look the same, they were not. The analogy was that Jews might look kind and nice, but they were deceitful and, like the poisonous mushroom, harmful. Another strategy promoted by Fritz Fink, a school inspector, was to teach a science that advocated people stay with their own kind, just as animals do. The idea was, therefore, that Aryan Germans should not mix with Jews. This was published in a pamphlet, *The Jewish Question in Education*, and reprinted in the antisemitic *Der Stürmer*. Teachers could use this natural order theory to justify the Nuremberg Laws.

Print media, newsreels and films were effectively used for propaganda purposes. When the Nazis took power in 1933, they virtually eliminated newspapers unfavorable to them and seized printing equipment. A decree issued on September 1, 1939 said Germans could not listen to foreign radio broadcasts. That meant that the only information about the war that they would get would be what the government told them, and the Nazis could spin that information to their advantage. When Germany started losing the war and the population began to see the Reich's weekly newsreels as propaganda, movie theater owners were told to lock the doors so that the patrons had to watch. Joseph Goebbels tried to manipulate the foreign press to shape the news in Germany's favor, and he eventually banned some foreign papers. He also restricted films from other countries, especially those from America.

In reflecting upon the Nazis' rise to power, it becomes clear that a number of events were required for this takeover of German democracy to occur. Unfortunately, these elements did come together. It is a stark reminder of what is possible when democratic values are not protected and preserved.

Scripted scenes and monologues

1. Monologue – *The Diary of Anne Frank* by Francis Goodrich and Albert Hackett, newly adapted by Wendy Kesselman

In this monologue, which opens the play, ANNE reads from her diary, recounting her family's journey into hiding which began that morning.

ANNE

July sixth, 1942. A few days ago, Father began to talk about going into hiding. He said it would be very hard for us to live cut off from the rest of the world. He sounded so serious I felt scared. "Don't worry, Anneke. Just enjoy your carefree life while you can." Carefree? I was born in Frankfort on June twelfth, 1929. Because we're Jewish, my father emigrated to Holland in 1933. But Hitler invaded Holland on May tenth, 1940. Five days later the Dutch surrendered, the Germans arrived – and the trouble started for the Jews. (*Pause.*)

Father was forced to give up his business – manufacturing products to make jam. We couldn't use streetcars, couldn't go to the theater or movies anymore, couldn't be out on the street after 8 P.M., couldn't even sit in our own gardens! We had to turn in our bicycles. No beaches, no swimming pools, no libraries – we couldn't even walk on the sunny side of the streets! Our identity cards were stamped with a big black "J." And … we had to wear the yellow star. But somehow life went on. Until yesterday. A call-up notice from the SS! My sister Margot was ordered to report for work in Germany, to the Westerbork transit camp. A call-up – everyone knows what that means! (*Pause.*)

At five-thirty this morning, we closed the door of our apartment behind us. My cat was the only living creature I said good-bye to. The unmade beds, the breakfast things on the table all created the impression we'd left in a hurry. (*Pause.*)

And our destination? We walked two and a half miles in the pouring rain all the way to … 263 Prinsengracht – father's office building! Our hiding place, the "Secret Annex," is right behind it upstairs.

2. Monologue – *The Survivor* by Susan Nanus, based on the memoirs of Jack Eisner

> *JACEK* is 15 years old. He is The Survivor of the play's title. This monologue opens the play.*
> *A spotlight comes up on JACEK wearing a Jewish armband. He addresses the audience.*

JACEK

I know what you want. I know why you came here. I've been waiting for you for a long time. You heard something. A story, maybe. Or you met someone with a number on his arm. Someone who said a few words that made you curious. Frightening words. Ugly words. Words like ghetto. Gas chambers. Crematoria. Words about death. Words about corpses. Words that wipe out the idea of living human beings.

Once there was a big city like Paris or New York. Where a lot of different people lived like everywhere else. It was a cultured place with a symphony and an opera and lots of elegant restaurants and cafes. I even sang in a choir there, and the audience was dressed in tuxedos and gowns. And then one day, the city turned into a jungle and disappeared.

Once there was a large group of people who lived in that city. They had their own schools and newspapers. Their own theaters, political parties, hospitals, even a language that was only theirs. And then one day, those people turned into ghosts and they disappeared.

Don't ask me *why* it happened. I don't know. Don't ask me *how* it happened. When you're fighting for your life, you don't have time to look around. Better to ask me *what* happened. Because that I can tell you.

This is a story, but no one made it up. It's unbelievable, but every word is true. It happened to so many people who never lived to tell about it. It happened to me and I did. I was fifteen then. I am fifteen now. For the rest of my life, I will be fifteen. There is nothing before, and nothing after. Only that same year, day after day, when I was fifteen.

This is a story about a group of kids. They were my friends and the last time we were together, we made a vow. If one of us lived, he would tell what happened. If one of us made it, he'd see to it that people would know.

* *YAH-tzek*

3. Scene for three actors – *T-Money & Wolf* by Kevin Willmott and Ric Averill

> *WOLF, 13 years old, is the younger brother of STEFAN, who is 16. The following scene takes place in the brothers' shared bedroom in Munich, Germany, in the 1930s.*
> *WOLF is half asleep in one of the beds. There is the sound of breaking glass and a flash of light. STEFAN is seen running through the light. One more crash and then silence. A window creaks as STEFAN sneaks into the bedroom.*

WOLF. Stefan? Stefan, is that you?

STEFAN. Shhhhh! Go back to sleep, Wolf.

WOLF. What's going on out there? Are you all right?

STEFAN. Everyone was there – burning and smashing. We threw rocks – it was like a carnival or a crazy cinema scene. You've never seen so much shattered glass.

WOLF. Did you get anything? The last riots, people were bringing stuff home!

STEFAN. You think I'm going to steal from a bunch of damn Jews?

WOLF. You're crazy, Stefan. What if the police had come by?

STEFAN. They watched us. They probably figured we were making their job easier. Cleaning up the neighborhood.

(*STEFAN's and WOLF's MOTHER enters the room.*)

MOTHER. Are you boys alright? I thought I heard something up here!

WOLF. (*Looks at STEFAN who motions him to silence.*) Stefan just opened the window, so we could hear. They're smashing glass all over the place.

MOTHER. (*As she closes the window.*) The police just stand around and watch. No one stops this insanity any longer.

STEFAN. Why should they? It's just Jew shops. Maybe they'll catch on and move to Poland, where they belong.

MOTHER. Stefan, you have friends in that neighborhood. Sarah, and …

STEFAN. *Wolf* has friends in that neighborhood.

WOLF. *(To Stefan.)* You didn't see if they …

STEFAN. From the window?

(MOTHER notices exchange, looks at STEFAN and realizes he is still partly dressed.)

MOTHER. What are you doing, Stefan? Sleeping in your shoes? You're not to be going out at night!

STEFAN. I'll go where I want, when I want …

MOTHER. I don't want any son of mine running with a gang of thugs, looting and burning! That's ugly …

STEFAN. What's so ugly about a fire?

MOTHER. Stefan, you're out of control. Go to sleep. We'll talk more in the morning. *(She exits.)*

STEFAN. It was beautiful, Wolf. At one store, Carl and I ran up to the glass and made faces, like the carnival. And the glass was kind of warped, so our faces leered and the fire from the shop across the street looked like it was coming from our heads. Then I stood back and smashed his reflection and he smashed mine.

WOLF. Did Sarah's place get hit?

STEFAN. How should I know? Don't worry, she'll probably move anyway. A lot of them are. That's what Tim told me.

WOLF. When? Was he with you?

STEFAN. Hell no, of course not. He's a rabbit. I talked to him after school. He said he saw Sarah's father talking to old man Mosher the night before last – about where they might go to set up shop. Look, kid, I know you like Sarah, but it's just not the right time to be seen with a Jew girl – Makes *me* look bad.

WOLF. Ahh, you've got Heidi.

STEFAN. Maybe. You never know with Heidi. Sometimes she fails to see the wisdom of being who I want her to be! But come with me tomorrow. We're having a meeting. There'll be some girls your age there, and Carl and some of my friends. You're a little young, but if you want to join, I'll get you in.

WOLF. They wouldn't want me.

STEFAN. They won't care if you're with me. But listen, Wolf, it isn't just a club – once you're in, you're in. You don't just change your mind. Are you ready to be a part of something bigger than you can even imagine?

WOLF. *(Hesitant.)* Yes – I mean, I want to be with you.

STEFAN. Smartest thing you've said all night.

SPOTLIGHT ACTIVITY

T-Money & Wolf

"Secret"

Create a scene which explores the choices people make when they are engaging in secretive, suspicious or dangerous behavior.

1   Divide the class into groups of two or more.
2   Each actor selects a character from the list below.
3   The group collectively selects one secret and one resolution from the list.
4   The group creates a scene from the elements chosen, making sure that the scene has an inherent conflict.
5   The actors perform the scene for the rest of the class.
6   Discuss the choices that the characters made. How do these characters and the scene relate to *T-Money & Wolf*? To the other scenes in this chapter?

Characters	Secret	Resolution
A friend	One character possesses stolen property	A relationship ends
Another friend	One character is hiding from someone	There is an arrest
A sibling	One character is involved in criminal activity	Someone lies
A parent	One character wants to impress a sibling	Someone is betrayed
An authority figure	One character is hiding something from a parent	Someone keeps a promise
A criminal	One character is sworn to secrecy	Someone is punished
An innocent person	One character knows that someone will get hurt	Actions bring suffering
A bully	One character has disobeyed a parent	Consequences result
An honest person	One character is disloyal	Someone is protected

Verbatim testimony historical narratives

1. From the testimony of Eva Bergmann – "Kristallnacht"

(https://iwitness.usc.edu/sfi/BrowseTopics.aspx?TopicID=39&ClipID=1225)

Born: November 16, 1916, Berlin, Germany
In this interview from May, 1995, Eva describes what happened when she was 21 years old and living in her birthplace of Berlin, Germany, the evening that Kristallnacht took place.

EVA

Kristallnacht. We were … it was at night when it began. Way at night. After eleven or twelve. We were already in bed. And we heard, all of a sudden, loud clattering in the street. We heard that it was glass, shattering of glass. And voices that were screaming. People were screaming. But we didn't dare to look out of the window. We were afraid. Only the next morning, we looked down and we saw on the street … we had a lot of Jewish groceries and tailors and carpenters. They were all Jewish around us. And we saw that the glass was lying on the street. People tried to sweep the glass away. And we were horrified.

And we went later on, much later around five o'clock, we went out and we saw the nearby synagogue. I could not tell you the name of the synagogue which was on the Russian Platz.* The glass was all taken out, and in the yard were the prayer books torn up and there were ashes all over. It was a horrible look. The temple, the synagogue, was hardly recognizable, and even though Mom and Dad, nor Hans, nor I, ever went to the synagogue … but what a horrible experience for the Jewish people. And we saw that some people were cleaning up the ashes in that courtyard. I do think they engaged Jewish people to do that clean up, not the Christians, because I read, later on, that some Jewish people had to be on their knees cleaning up the glass.

*Square or plaza

2. From the testimony of Esther Clifford – "Antisemitism"

(https://iwitness.usc.edu/sfi/BrowseTopics.aspx?TopicID=4&ClipID=1226)

Born: December 5, 1920, in Munich, Germany
In a 1996 interview, Esther recalls antisemitic propaganda published in the local Nazi newspaper in Frankfurt am Main, Germany, in 1934, when she was 14 years old.

ESTHER

As the years went by in 1934, there was a terrible paper being published. It was called Der Stürmer,* the Storm Trooper Newspaper. Everything seemed to be called Storm Troopers, or Troopers … And that was a horrible paper. That affected me terribly, because it was plastered on all these stores that sold newspapers. And in the morning, going to school, I would see Der Stürmer and people standing and reading them. And what did they list in Der Stürmer? They had people with long noses and saliva running from their mouth and looking typically – you know, they meant Jewish people because they always wrote about Jewish people with their long noses. And they were looking at little gentile children, greedily looking at the money that the children had in their hands, wanting to steal the money from these children. And they had terrible stories there that Jewish doctors were trying to inject gentiles with poisonous medication.

They had bankers that would swindle Jews out of their money. And here I was, walking to school and people were actually reading this. Young people, old people, people of all ages. And by the time I got to school, I couldn't learn. I wasn't thinking. I wasn't listening to the teacher. I was thinking about Der Stürmer ... So, going to school was getting harder and harder.

SHTER-mur

3. From the testimony of Margaret Lambert – "Antisemitism"

(https://iwitness.usc.edu/SFI/BrowseTopics.aspx?TopicID=4&ClipID=147)

Born: April 12, 1914, in Laupheim, Germany
In a 1995 interview, Margaret speaks about segregation and the exclusion of Jews, resulting from anti-Jewish laws, and explains how they affected her own life in Germany in 1933 when she was 19 years old.

MARGARET

It started in 1933, really. I had very good friends of whom I knew were members of the Nazi party since 1928. And she was one of my best friends. She didn't care that I was Jewish and I didn't care that she was a Nazi. She was one of my sports friends and we got along very well. But then, of course, in 1933, everything changed. Like, overnight, you could not go into a public place – no restaurants, no swimming pools, no movies ... nothing. You couldn't ... You were not allowed in any public place anymore. And people that you knew wouldn't talk to you anymore. Friends that you had, they would shun you. Most of them. Not because they hated us all of a sudden, but they were afraid. Because that was the way it was. You talk to a Jew and you'll be punished. It was very hard. I was 19 years old, and all of a sudden, I was shut off from everything. I got a letter from my sports club saying that I wasn't welcome there anymore because I was Jewish. And that was the thing I loved to do most, as I said before – sports. And all of a sudden that was finished. There was nothing I could do. We just were really vegetating, if you want to call it that.

4. From the testimony of Esther Clifford – "Fear"

(https://iwitness.usc.edu/sfi/BrowseTopics.aspx?TopicID=23&ClipID=1227)

Born: December 5, 1920, in Munich, Germany
In a 1996 interview, Esther discusses the events of Kristallnacht, which took place November 9–10, 1938, when she was 17 years old. She recalls the fear that drove her to flee her hometown of Frankfurt am Main, Germany.

ESTHER

I woke up one night, and there was a lot of noise, like the breaking of glass. And I looked out. I looked through the blinds and I saw that there were people throwing stones through the windows that I knew Jewish people lived there. And they were throwing stones through all the windows. Bricks and all kinds of things through those windows. And I realized – they're breaking all the windows of the Jews. And it's what became the infamous Kristallnacht – Crystal Night.

So I put on ... I dressed myself warm, and I ran out of the house. I was afraid ... I was always afraid to stay in the house since I was deported once before. And I run out of the house ... I run to the next block and someplace nearby was this synagogue – Breuer* Synagogue. And that synagogue was in flames and there were young people standing there throwing stones through these beautiful windows. It was a gorgeous synagogue. It was well known, and it was up in flames. And I was standing there at the corner in awe. The synagogue was something. We went to that synagogue, even that recent Friday, the recent Sabbath. And now, the synagogue was in flames. I couldn't get over that. But I realized very quickly that I can't push my luck, and I kept on running. I thought this was just taking place in our street. And I just kept on running and running ... any place. Just to get away from this chaos. And then I realized that they were still throwing bricks in many other windows. And I went to this main street where we had the store and all the windows were broken. They had Juda** written in big letters. *Juda.* And I ran back again. I didn't know where to run. I thought, there must be a place where they didn't throw these, but wherever I run, they were throwing bricks.

And then, I was so out of breath, I sat down on a bench thinking, "What should I do? Where am I going to go now?" I remember looking up at these nice houses and above the sky was red from all the fires from all the synagogues that were burning. And then I was looking down on the bench where I was sitting. In big letters it said "Juden Verboten." Jews are not permitted to sit here. I thought, "I have to get up. Somebody's going to find me on that bench." And I decided – I had a little money – I decided to run to the railway station because my second sister Mary was still in Munich. And I thought, "I'll go to Munich, because this way, I'll go away from here." And that's what I did. And while running, I saw so many men being pulled out of these houses, and children crying "Give me my father back!" and women crying at the windows.

And I got to the railway station and I got to a train. And the train took me to Munich. And I thought, "I'm glad I'm getting away from that chaos." But when I got to Munich, the same thing was happening there.

*BROY-er
**YOO-deh

Suggested props/costumes for Chapter 1 historical narrative scenes

- Men's and women's sweaters, jackets
- Men's and women's hats and scarves

- Old/torn books (plain covers)
- Dirty rags
- Metal or wood bucket(s)
- Newspapers (black and white only)
- Broom
- Composition notebook and pencil
- Book satchel
- Soccer or volleyball
- Sports trophy
- Envelope and "letter"
- Small suitcase
- A brick
- Bench

Devised theater activity

Combine two historical documents to create a scene which juxtaposes a law which infringes on human rights with a declaration which seeks to protect them.

Scene components

1   Word-for-word texts from both "*the Law for the Protection of German Blood and German Honor*" and *the Preamble to the UN's Universal Declaration of Human Rights*
2   No fewer than three *group breaths*
3   No fewer than four instances of *choral speech*
4   No fewer than four instances of *choral movement*
5   *Musical underscoring* or musical interludes

Texts

1   *The Nuremberg Laws* were antisemitic laws designed to separate Jews from the general population of Germany. Adopted by the Reichstag (German Parliament) on September 15, 1935, these "racial purity laws" set up the framework for what would become the Holocaust.

Law for the Protection of German Blood and German Honor of September 15, 1935 (Translated from Reichsgesetzblatt I, 1935, 1146–1147.)

Moved by the understanding that purity of German blood is the essential condition for the continued existence of the German people, and inspired by the inflexible determination to ensure the existence of the German nation for all time, the Reichstag has unanimously adopted the following law, which is promulgated herewith:

Article 1

1   Marriages between Jews and citizens of German or related blood are forbidden. Marriages nevertheless concluded are invalid, even if concluded abroad to circumvent this law.
2   Annulment proceedings can be initiated only by the state prosecutor.

Article 2

Extramarital relations between Jews and citizens of German or related blood are forbidden.

Article 3

Jews may not employ in their households female subjects of the state of German or related blood who are under 45 years old.

Article 4

1   Jews are forbidden to fly the Reich or national flag or display Reich colors.
2   They are, on the other hand, permitted to display the Jewish colors. The exercise of this right is protected by the state.

Article 5

1   Any person who violates the prohibition under Article 1 will be punished with a prison sentence with hard labor.
2   A male who violates the prohibition under Article 2 will be punished with a jail term or a prison sentence with hard labor.
3   Any person violating the provisions under Articles 3 or 4 will be punished with a jail term of up to one year and a fine, or with one or the other of these penalties.

Article 6

The Reich Minister of the Interior, in coordination with the Deputy of the Führer and the Reich Minister of Justice, will issue the legal and administrative regulations required to implement and complete this law.

Article 7

The law takes effect on the day following promulgation, except for Article 3, which goes into force on January 1, 1936.
Nuremberg, September 15, 1935
At the Reich Party Congress of Freedom
The Führer and Reich Chancellor
[signed] Adolf Hitler
The Reich Minister of the Interior
[signed] Frick
The Reich Minister of Justice
[signed] Dr. Gürtner
The Deputy of the Führer
[signed] R. Hess

2   *The Universal Declaration of Human Rights* was proclaimed by the United Nations General Assembly in Paris on December 10, 1948, as a common standard for all peoples and all nations. Crafted largely in response to the grotesque human rights abuses which took place in the Holocaust, the Declaration sets out a list of fundamental human rights that, ideally, would be universally acknowledged and protected throughout the world.

Preamble of the Universal Declaration of Human Rights:

- Whereas recognition of the inherent dignity and of the equal and inalienable rights of all members of the human family is the foundation of freedom, justice and peace in the world,
- Whereas disregard and contempt for human rights have resulted in barbarous acts which have outraged the conscience of mankind, and the advent of a world in which human beings shall enjoy freedom of speech and belief and freedom from fear and want has been proclaimed as the highest aspiration of the common people,
- Whereas it is essential, if man is not to be compelled to have recourse, as a last resort, to rebellion against tyranny and oppression, that human rights should be protected by the rule of law,
- Whereas it is essential to promote the development of friendly relations between nations,
- Whereas the peoples of the United Nations have in the Charter reaffirmed their faith in fundamental human rights, in the dignity and worth of the human person and in the equal rights of men and women and have determined to promote social progress and better standards of life in larger freedom,
- Whereas Member States have pledged themselves to achieve, in cooperation with the United Nations, the promotion of universal respect for and observance of human rights and fundamental freedoms,
- Whereas a common understanding of these rights and freedoms is of the greatest importance for the full realization of this pledge,

Now, therefore, The General Assembly proclaims this Universal Declaration of Human Rights as a common standard of achievement for all peoples and all nations, to the end that every individual and every organ of society, keeping this Declaration constantly in mind, shall strive by teaching and education to promote respect for these rights and freedoms and by progressive measures, national and international, to secure their universal and effective recognition and observance, both among the peoples of Member States themselves and among the peoples of territories under their jurisdiction.

Staging considerations, choices and tips

1   How do these texts relate to each other? Are there any similarities? What are the differences? You do not need to use *all* of each text, but you must incorporate elements of both documents. Do not alter the language in any way.

2   How can your theatrical piece best point out the contrasts – or juxtapositions – of these very different "laws?" Find ways to interweave the texts to highlight these juxtapositions.

3   What would you like your audience to come away with after watching this piece of theater? What do you want them to learn? What kind of conversation would you like your presentation to start?

4   What does your scene "look" like? How will you incorporate the movements and the breaths to highlight certain words and phrases? Will the actors reading the Nuremberg Laws interact with those reading the UN Declaration? Or will each group remain in their own areas of the stage?

2

Perpetrators, collaborators and bystanders

Context

There is no doubt that the master architect of the Final Solution was Adolph Hitler. He had, however, plenty of help in his effort to annihilate European Jewry. Hitler and his accomplices viewed the Jews as Germany's enemy. They drew into their murderous machine a variety of contributors from all walks of life.

The undertaking to exterminate the Jews was a de-centralized operation that functioned like a well-oiled machine. It included people from various callings, from those who committed the murders to those who undertook small but necessary roles in the eradication process. There were, of course, the infamous. They are noted in the following chart.

Name	Function
Adolf Eichmann	Eichmann ran the Office for Jewish Emigration and arranged transportation for deportations.
Dr. Josef Mengele	At Auschwitz, Mengele selected prisoners for labor or for death. He also conducted heinous medical experiments upon prisoners.
Heinrich Himmler	Himmler was the head of the Schutzstaffel (the SS), the elite guard that murdered countless Jews and turned Germany into a police state.

Name	Function
Reinhard Heydrich	Heydrich was Himmler's assistant and was the person who proposed the Final Solution as an end to the Jewish problem.
Herman Wilhelm Goering	Goering headed the secret police unit of the SS known as the Gestapo, or Special State Police.
Paul Joseph Goebbels	Goebbels oversaw the Nazi Ministry of Propaganda.
Rudolf Hess	Hess was a Nazi Party Deputy and a personal aide to Hitler.
Martin Bormann	Bormann was Rudolf Hess' Chief of Staff and rose to become Secretary to the Führer in 1943.
Albert Speer	Speer served as Minister of Armaments and Munitions.

Some of the government organizations involved in the slaughter of the Jews and other perceived enemies of the state not only include those mentioned above, but also the Reich Chancellery, the Interior Ministry, the Justice Ministry, the Party Chancellery, the Reich Chamber of Culture, the Education Ministry, the Economy Ministry, the Finance Ministry, the Transport Ministry and the Foreign Office. It is worth keeping in mind that this is only a partial list.

Far less well-known were the myriad civil servants, military and militia personnel, local mayors, indigenous police, industrialists and professionals who made necessary contributions to the Final Solution. Innumerable skills were required for the far-reaching destruction to occur. Members of the Einsatzgruppen, the mobile killing squads had, for example, a direct role as murderers. Lawyers were tasked with finding legal justifications for unjustifiable actions against the Jews. Doctors first drove Jewish colleagues out of the medical profession and later engaged in practices such as sterilization and medical experiments. The German State Railway supplied train cars that transported countless victims to the camps. The German Central Bank held stolen currency and gold that funded mass murder. When it came to industry, Volkswagen is an example of a German company that used forced labor, so much so that eventually the German plant encompassed an area that housed four concentration camps and eight forced labor camps. Another firm, Topf and Sons, manufactured the ovens used to cremate bodies at the camps. Despite it being illegal to burn more than one body at a time, this company has the dubious distinction of designing and installing ever more efficient ways to get rid of multiple bodies through the gassing and cremation processes used for killing. It is sobering to realize that by the end of the war, according to the article "Perpetrators, Collaborators and Bystanders" found in *The Holocaust – The Nazi Genocide against the Jewish People*, "there were 900,000 Germans in the SS and several million in the regular armed forces, police and government bureaucracies. There were 500,000 clerical and 900,000 manual workers in the railway network, which was key to

IMAGE 2.1 Adolf Hitler salutes ranks of German Youth from his car during a Reichsparteitag (Reich Party Day) Parade

transporting Jews to the camps" (1). The behavior of the perpetrators ranged from hesitant to sadistic. The former may have had qualms, particularly when it came to killing, but the latter relished their tasks.

That German citizens benefitted from the actions of perpetrators cannot be argued. Note these grim statistics:

> In one six week period, 222,269 sets of men's suits and underclothes, 192,652 sets of women's clothing, and 99,922 sets of children's clothes, all collected from gassed victims at Auschwitz, were distributed among civilians in Germany. A total of between 15 and 20 billion Reich Marks were deposited in German banks, representing the proceeds of the theft of the savings, property and possessions of murdered European Jews.
>
> ("Perpetrators, Collaborators and Bystanders" 1)

Perpetrators had help. Collaborators may not have been as directly involved in the effort to destroy the Jews, but they were not without responsibility in the process. Countries throughout Europe played a role by depleting their Jewish populations. Some were Germany's allies; some were occupied countries. Jews were expelled from both. Those who devised or applied anti-Jewish laws throughout Europe also could be considered collaborators. In some of these countries, collaborators included extremists who enjoyed helping the Germans. In some Axis countries, paramilitary organizations, military and police were responsible for terror, deportation, or murder. In certain areas, collaboration extended to auxiliary units that were used as perimeter guards or who served within the camp system.

Ordinary citizens within Germany became collaborators, in that they were expected to report suspicious behavior by Jews to German authorities. They also had few, if any, reservations about taking over Jewish apartments or possessions once the rightful owners began their journeys to their fates. Whether they were motivated by antisemitism, opportunities, nationalism, or ethnic or political hatred, these individuals and nations each played a hand in constructing unimaginable horror.

In addition to perpetrators and collaborators, there were bystanders. This term has two meanings when applied to the Holocaust. According to the United States Holocaust Memorial Museum, the first would include those who could be thus classified because of their distance from the events taking place. The second were those near to or present at the events as they unfolded. Into the first category could be placed Allied governments because they did not prioritize rescuing Jews, neutral countries, officials within the United States and Britain who did not act upon warnings about the carnage taking place, Jewish organizations, and religious institutions. Into the second could be placed those who neither willingly hurt nor helped victims and who therefore harbored the self-perception that they were not involved in what was happening around them.

Some bystanders became rescuers but more often they either enriched themselves due to the plight of others, said nothing, or taunted the condemned. Nevertheless, if bystanders were aware of what was happening, they stayed silent. There are several reasons for their inaction. Some felt that since it was not happening to them that it had no direct personal effect. Some were antisemitic. Some profited from the troubles of the Jews. Some feared harsh Nazi reprisal for helping those targeted. It is worth noting that, "Throughout the Holocaust, not a single government, social group, scholarly institution or professional association in Nazi-dominated Europe openly declared its solidarity with the Jews. That includes the Catholic and Protestant churches" ("Perpetrators, Collaborators and Bystanders" 3).

Regardless of the degree to which they were involved, perpetrators, collaborators, and bystanders shared accountability for the planned annihilation of a people. Each played a part in one of mankind's most heinous undertakings.

Scripted scenes and monologues

1. Monologue – *And Then They Came for Me: Remembering the World of Anne Frank* by James Still

YOUNG BOY/HITLER YOUTH is a 12-year-old boy who appears at the beginning, middle and near the end of the play. This monologue is a compilation of those three appearances. The ellipses represent the breaks in time between each of those scenes.
YOUNG BOY hurries on stage, out of breath, excited. He sees the audience and addresses them directly, as if he were talking to a friend. (In a full production, as he performs the first scene, he is putting on a uniform – one piece at a time, casually transforming himself as he talks.)

YOUNG BOY/HITLER YOUTH

This is the greatest country in the world! No more unemployment, no more inflation, no more violence in the streets. My father says big government is to blame for our problems. And the Jews. And the immigrants, the Blacks, the homosexuals, the mentally and physically handicapped … RATS are the lowest form of animals and the JEWS are the lowest form of mankind. If we can get rid of the Jews the world will be a better place. That is what the Führer says. *Heil, Hitler!*

I've been a member of the Hitler Youth since I was seven. *Heil, Hitler!* We say "*Heil, Hitler!*" if we meet a friend on the way to school. We say "*Heil, Hitler!*" at the beginning and end of every class. The Postman says "*Heil, Hitler!*" If our parents don't say "*Heil, Hitler!*" we are supposed to report them and they will be arrested.
…
When I am promoted in my unit to the Hitler Youth, our leaders give me a little puppy and they tell me to keep the puppy with me day and night, to feed it and care for it, to let it sleep with me – to make it my property and responsibility. As the Führer has said: "We will be one people, one nation." And the youth – we are going to be *that* people and *that* nation. *Heil Hitler!*
…
After I had the puppy for about six months, after I had kept it with me day and night, fed it and cared for it – loved it – we were told to report to a Unit meeting. And to bring our puppies. Our leaders welcomed us. They praised us. They told us we were the future of Germany. And then they ordered me to take my puppy – they ordered all of us to take our puppies – they ordered us to strangle our puppies. (*Pause.*) I … they told us if we didn't do it – we'd never be chosen, we'd never be SS, we'd never be real

Germans. (*Pause, struggling.*) "I promise at all times to do my duty for the Führer, so help me God." (*Beat.*) I did it. I did what I was told. I strangled my puppy. An order – is an order. Yes? (*Mixed emotion.*) I have been a member of the Nazi youth groups since I was 7. (*Finding new strength.*) I will fight in Germany's total war. It is win or die for Germany. (*Beat, then salutes, passionately.*) *Heil Hitler!*

SPOTLIGHT ACTIVITY

And Then They Came for Me

"Hitler Youth"

1 Have a student read aloud the monologue (above) from James Still's play, *And Then They Came for Me* (Dramatic Publishing, Woodstock, IL, 1999).* Instruct all of the students to pay attention to how the boy felt about his puppy. Did his feelings change and, if so, how?
2 Have the students write a character analysis of Young Boy that addresses the following:
   ■ How is the character like me?
   ■ How is the character unlike me?
   ■ What does the character say about himself?
   ■ What actions reveal his character?
   ■ How do his feelings about Germany impact his actions?

In analyzing this character, students may determine that the boy, like many children, really cares about his pet. This helps to humanize the character. Why then does the boy follow orders to kill the puppy? What motivates the change in him?

3 Next, have all students pair up and improvise a scene based upon the following scenario:
   Who: Two teenage friends
   What: One is involved with a group that the other perceives to be a bad influence. This friend tries to persuade the other person to leave the group.

Ask for volunteers to perform their scenes for the rest of the class. When these have concluded, discuss the arguments that were used for remaining in or leaving the group. Next, apply these to the boy in the play. Why was being in the Hitler Youth so important to him? What role did peer pressure play in the improvisation? In the monologue? Should orders be obeyed if they are perceived to be wrong or harmful? Why or why not?

*A part of this activity has been reprinted with permission from *Teaching About the Holocaust Through Drama*

2. Scene for two actors – *East of Berlin* by Hannah Moscovitch

In the flashback portion of this scene, RUDI is a 17-year-old high school student, attending a German language school in Asuncion, Paraguay, in 1963. HERMANN is RUDI's classmate, who knows a startling secret about RUDI's father. (The ellipses between two of RUDI's lines represent a speech of Hermann's that was cut for age appropriateness.)

RUDI. (*Speaking to the audience.*) We were in science class. We were cutting up beetles and looking at the insides of them, and Hermann said something like "That's what your father did to the Jews." It was a sort of … joke. I was surprised. I didn't get the joke. I asked him about it. Here's what Hermann said to me.
(*Transition. It's 1963. RUDI and HERMANN are in science class at the German-language school in Asuncion, Paraguay.*)
HERMANN. It's an analogy. (*Beat.*) An analogy, a parallel? I'm not saying it's an accurate analogy, but it's close enough that I thought you might react, for instance, with emotion –
RUDI. What are you talking about?
HERMANN. Your father. My father commanded in Poland, it's not as though he was some sort of war hero either, all right.
RUDI. What are you talking about?
HERMANN. Your father. Am I going too fast for you?
RUDI. What about my father?
…
I don't know what you're talking about.
HERMANN. Your father. During the war. Don't you … know about the war?
RUDI. Know what?
(*Beat.*)
HERMANN. Forget it. I don't know why I'm – Just, here, fill in the chart, I'll get rid of the tray –
RUDI. Hermann!
HERMANN. Or, fine, I'll fill in the chart, but we both know you're better at it.
RUDI. My father served in the army, during the war.
HERMANN. Yes. That's – yes. That's what he told you?
RUDI. Yes that's what he told me! (*Beat.*) What!? Hermann, what? What are you talking about? You're talking about my father. You're saying my father …? What are you saying?
(*Beat.*) Tell me what you're saying.
(*RUDI gets hold of him.*)
Tell me what you're saying!
HERMANN. Your father was an SS doctor!
(*RUDI lets him go.*)
Did you know that? You didn't know that?
RUDI. He – no! He was a troop physician, in Russia, then he was promoted to captain, went back east, served as an officer …?

HERMANN. Yes …

RUDI. What?!

HERMANN. No, he – yes he went back east, he was … transferred to the … camps.

RUDI. The camps.

HERMANN. The camps, yes, the trains, on the ramp, selections? To the left, to the right? You know what Auschwitz is, don't you?

(*A reaction that indicates RUDI sort of knows, but isn't sure.*)

The camp? With the Jews? Doctors, experimenting – it's why you're so good at science, you got his … (*Beat.*) He probably also served at some of the work camps. You don't get sent to Auschwitz right away. There were doctors who killed themselves there, SS doctors; you had to have the right temperament for it so they were careful who they sent –

RUDI. He wasn't in the SS. (*Off HERMANN's look.*) He wasn't in the SS! His jacket, his military jacket is Wehrmacht –

HERMANN. He probably exchanged his SS uniform for an army jacket when the Allies were close to Berlin. "The Russians are coming! The Russians are coming!" "Here, lend me your jacket."

RUDI. No. No, it's his jacket, it fits him, it's his –

HERMANN. Then he kept an old jacket. (*Beat.*) I don't know, from watching you, I get the sense you're not … stupid – don't you wonder why you're in Paraguay?

RUDI. We lost the war!

HERMANN. If – listen – if everyone who lost the war *left* Germany, there wouldn't be anyone *in* Germany, would there?

RUDI. This is stupid, there's no way my father …! Are you saying he – in the camp he – but if he was a doctor – I don't understand. (*Beat.*) There's no way my father …!

HERMANN. Then forget it.

3. Monologue – *East of Berlin* by Hannah Moscovitch

> In this monologue, RUDI tells the audience what happens after his schoolmate, HERMANN shows him a book called The Final Solution which includes a photo of RUDI's father and proof that he was a Nazi who conducted horrible experiments on Jews in Auschwitz.

RUDI. I went home. My father was on the front lawn, kneeling down, looking at the grass. It was dying a little around the edges, and he was telling one of the servants to water it again. He asked me how my school day was. I asked him how he liked it at Auschwitz.

I remember the sound of blood in my ears, and my father calling to me as I walked into the house. (*Beat.*)

He came after me. (*Beat.*)

I stood there in the front hallway and asked my father questions about the war. They were the first real questions I'd ever asked about it. (*Beat.*)

I told him I wanted to know about the mistakes he made at the camps. (*Beat.*)

He didn't answer. He just … stood there and looked at me, with his … pink eyelids, and his well-manicured nails, and the slight stoop in his shoulders. (*Beat.*)

I called him a murderer. (*Beat.*)

He told me not to raise my voice. (*Beat.*)

We had a … physical fight. I hit him a couple of times. I blacked his eye and I split his lip. He was mostly just trying to defend himself, he didn't hit me back, he just … turned towards the wall, and … let me hit him. (*Beat.*)

My mother was screaming in the background the whole time. (*Beat.*)

Afterwards, she kept saying, "What happened, what happened?" My father said, "It's over, it's fine, it's over." (*Beat.*)

He … needed an X-ray, he was breathing badly, he thought I might have fractured one of his ribs, so I … drove him to the hospital. I remember the hospital, dirty little hallways and no doctors, my mother and father sitting there, on the metal chairs, her arms around him, his nose all crusted with blood. (*Beat.*)

He looked very … beaten. (*RUDI laughs.*) He was already fifty-one years old then.

4. Scene for three actors – *T-Money & Wolf* by Kevin Willmott and Ric Averill

The bedroom of brothers WOLF (14) and STEFAN (17) in Munich, Germany, in the mid-1930s.

MOTHER. Wolf, Stefan? Are you up yet? Wake up. There were sirens in the night and Mrs. Schmidt told me Sarah's shop was half burned out. Where did you boys go last night?

STEFAN. Go away.

WOLF. Let us sleep.

MOTHER. Somebody threw a torch through Sarah's shop window.

WOLF. Is she all right? Are her folks all right?

MOTHER. No one knows for sure where she is. You boys don't know anything, do you?

STEFAN. No. We just went to the youth meeting. Look, we brought home some bread and sugar … (*Gets rations from under the bed, hands them to her.*)

MOTHER. Stefan, we don't need this! How much trouble are you in?

WOLF. You should have heard what they said at the meeting last night. Germany's changing and we're going to be a part of it.

MOTHER. You sound like your brother and he sounds like the …

STEFAN. Like what? Like I'm starting to think for myself?

MOTHER. Just the opposite! No son of mine comes up with the idea that Jewish shops should be destroyed.

STEFAN. (*Climbing half out of bed.*) There's not room for everybody in this country, Mother.

MOTHER. So let's get rid of … Sarah? She's a pretty bad person!

STEFAN. She's a Jew. Are you a Jew-lover? You want me to start telling people my mother's a Jew-lover?

MOTHER. Stefan! You forget who you're talking to!

STEFAN. I'm talking to you! (*Grabs her and turns her toward him.*) That's who I'm talking to!

MOTHER. (*Taken aback.*) My God, what would your father say?

STEFAN. My father? My father? My father was shot in a stupid war. A war we're going to finish! What would Father say? He'd say for his sons to follow a strong leader – to form a strong Germany – to achieve a greatness he was never allowed. Don't ask me what Father would say, cause you might not want to hear the answer. (*He storms out.*)

WOLF. Mother, I'll check on Sarah. But Stefan's right. You have to let us take care of things.

Verbatim testimony historical narratives

1. From the testimony of Edith Reiss – "Bystanders"

(https://iwitness.usc.edu/sfi/BrowseTopics.aspx?TopicID=6&ClipID=1123)

Born: June 23, 1916, in Lancashire, England
In this May, 1998 interview, Edith, a non-Jewish woman, describes how, when she was 23 years old, she returned to Germany, where her family had once lived, on a vacation. While there, she saw firsthand the increasing violence against the Jews in 1939.

EDITH

It must have been August 26th, 27th, something like that, of 1939. And I had taken pictures during my holiday in the Harz Mountains. And I had left them at a photographer's in the town of Göttingen. I went to pick up the pictures and there were several other people in the store. I had to wait. And as I was waiting, I heard a commotion outside the shop. And then I picked up my pictures and came out of the shop. And there I saw a man in the Brownshirt uniform* kicking an old man. And he was kicking him off the pavement into the gutter. And now there was a crowd of about maybe twelve people all standing around looking. As I came out of the shop, I was horrified to see what was happening. The Brownshirt walked away. The man was left in the gutter, and I immediately rushed to pick him up. And as I picked him up, I saw he had a patch on his coat that had the Jewish symbol "Juden"** – J-U-D-E-N – which meant "Jew." I picked him up, and as I did so, a person that was standing there touched my elbow and said "Don't get involved." So I said "Why not? Why can't you help this man?" And they used two words: "concentration camp." So, I helped the man along the street and then he turned to me – he said "I will be alright."

*Brownshirt: a member of the early Nazi militia founded by Hitler in 1921. They wore brown uniforms
**YOO-den

2. From the testimony of Rudolph Lahnstein – "Kristallnacht"

(https://iwitness.usc.edu/sfi/BrowseTopics.aspx?TopicID=39&ClipID=517)

Born: February 13, 1930, in Idstein, Germany
In a 1996 interview, Rudolph remembers hiding in a storage bin while his family's home in Idstein, Germany, was being ransacked during Kristallnacht, when young Rudolph was eight years old. He recalls that the men who did this were their neighbors, and one-time "friends" of his father.

RUDOLPH

He instructed all of us to go into the basement with the storage bin and lock the door. Lock the door! It's an eye and a hook and the door was wood with slats. You could see through it. And just go there and be silent, do nothing. No noise. And we did as we were told. And my father put himself on the inside of the front door and tried to barricade it, and within moments, the knocking on the door began. And it wasn't just a knocking. And my father wouldn't let them in. And it was locked and my father held his shoulders against it. But finally, the guys with the axes came through and knocked the door off, so obviously, he couldn't hold them back anymore. And here came this gang of people. And among them were some of the people he went to school with, some of his best friends, the guys from the card club. And I remember – my father, when we were playing cards in years past, he taught me how to play. And I learned pretty well and I knew all these people. I do remember that my father went to the one he knew the best, the one he thought was a friend of his. And he says, "I don't care what you do to me. But don't go into that storage bin." The man had been in our house many times. He knew where the storage bin was. And then they took my father and they just stood him up in the courtyard. In the middle of the courtyard. And it wasn't that big of a courtyard. It was just … a courtyard. And they instructed him, "Just stay there and don't move." (*Sighs.*) And that's when it began. I was so fearful. I could look through the slats of that wooden door and I could see my father up the stairs … I was looking up. And I wanted to go to him and scream. But I was instructed "no noise." And I didn't make any noise. And then it began. This terrible noise. All the windows were breaking in the house. Every window, every pane was gone. And that noise – it didn't stop. And the dishes that were broken … there wasn't a dish that remained unbroken. Everything was destroyed. And that noise – I still hear it. I guess the name "Kristallnacht" is apropos. Then the furniture came out from the top. Every piece of furniture that we owned,

I guess, came out the windows. And I remember my sister Vera whispering in my ear, "Let's pray. Let's pray." And I was like this (*Clasps hands tightly.*). And you could see the whites of my knuckles. I couldn't pray hard enough. And I just prayed for my father because I saw him and all the stuff coming down all around him and he's trying to duck it. Some hit him, some didn't. But he didn't move from his spot. And then, after what seemed like an eternity – it was over. It was over. I still didn't move. And when they were gone, my father came to life, as it were, went down to us in the storage bin and we just cried and hugged and hugged and cried and uh … excuse me (*Sniffs back tears.*). It's … uh … it's just something I will never forget.

3. From the testimony of Bronia Sonnenschein – "Ghetto Life"

(https://iwitness.usc.edu/sfi/BrowseTopics.aspx?TopicID=28&ClipID=942)

Born: July 12, 1915, in Złoczów, Poland
Interviewed in January, 1996, Bronia Sonnenschein recounts the Germans forcibly removing Jewish children from the Łódź ghetto and murdering them.
(NOTE: For the purposes of length and clarity, small edits have been made in this testimony.)

BRONIA

Rumkowski* stood in that marketplace. And he said, "This order has been given. In order to keep the ghetto alive, I have to ask you to give the best you have – your children." Now, anyone will understand, they can do whatever they want with you. But they cannot make you give up your child of your own free will. *Nobody* can do it. And what they said they'd do, they did. They said, "If you don't succeed, we will come in with our trucks and we will take the children." They ordered a curfew for the whole week. Nobody could go out and get their weekly rations. We got terribly, terribly hungry, and even more scared. And then they came in and everybody had to stand on the street with their children. And I see it like it would happen yesterday. It is something nobody will ever forget. It is carved in our hearts. When they came and just took one after the other of those poor, defenseless children – their mothers, jumping after them, or their fathers – and loaded them onto the truck. The truck came back empty in no time. Today, I know. After the war, we knew. There was gas in the truck. They didn't take the children far. They gassed them right in the truck. The curfew lasted for one week. They took 11,000 of our children and 8,000 men and women over 50.

And there was an incident. There was one man – I don't know his name. We were all poor, but he struck me that he was poor all his whole life before the war. His wife had died sometime before. He had a little boy. Shmuel** was the little boy's name. He had brown curly hair and large blue eyes. And he was so thin and he was so hungry and he was holding onto his father's hand. And they took little Shmuel. Put him in the truck. And this poor man. He stood there, and there was no little hand to hold on. I guess he had lost his mind. He didn't jump after little Shmuel. And so, little Shmuel was killed with the other children. Mercifully, his father died two days later. I can't forget little Shmuel. Together with *so* many children.

*Chaim Rumkowski was the head of the Jewish Council in the Łódź ghetto. He supplied the Germans with names of ghetto inhabitants to be deported to concentration camps, believing that his cooperation with the Nazis' requests would lessen the severity of the violence inflicted on his fellow Jews. His actions made him a very controversial figure. (Also see p. 37 in the context section of the chapter "Ghettos.")
**SHMOO-uhl

Suggested props/costumes for Chapter 2 historical narrative scenes

- Women's sweaters
- Men's sweaters, jackets
- Tattered clothing items
- A brown uniform shirt
- Men's and women's hats
- An old camera (as close to 1930s style as possible)
- An envelope with B&W photo prints
- A cane or walking stick
- Small suitcase
- Sticks and/or ax handles
- Deck of cards
- (Unbreakable) dishes
- Silverware
- Table and chairs
- Flat sheet of wood (ramp)

Devised theater activity

Devise a scene which demonstrates the danger of blind loyalty using the format of a game of "Simon Says."

Scene components

1 The children's game "Simon Says."

Background

Blind loyalty involves being loyal to a person or cause even when doing so asks the loyalist to act in ways that are immoral, unethical and potentially harmful to others. Many Nazi perpetrators, bystanders and collaborators were guilty of such behavior, which enabled the Holocaust to take place.

By juxtaposing the concept of blind loyalty with a childhood game, the banality of evil is exposed and we see how simple and childlike it is to follow orders and to not think for oneself.

Text

This devised theater activity does not have an exact text to incorporate; instead, the devisors are asked to use the format of the game "Simon Says" and to invent their own text which follows these instructions:

1   Begin with simple directives from your "Simon." These should be movements which are non-threatening – basic instructions such as "touch your toes," or "reach for the sky."

2   Simon's directives should become increasingly menacing, with commands which ask the players to inflict harm on each other, such as "pinch your neighbor," or "hit your fellow citizen."

3   Have one player become a "Protestor," refusing the commands and questioning where the game is going. The Protestor may question either Simon or those following Simon's commands.

4   Have Simon order the other players to stop the Protestor in some way.

5   Make Simon's final command to the players this: "Raise your right hand," accompanied by the gesture of making the Nazi salute. Do NOT give away this metaphorical association prior to the end of the scene by using costume pieces, props or language that indicate that the leader is a Nazi. Let this be a surprise to your audience.

Staging considerations, choices and tips

1   Consider having your Simon stand on a block or a (very stable) chair which makes him/her higher than the other actors. This will give your Simon the appearance of having power.

2   How will you arrange the players so that they can give all of their focus to Simon, yet still have their faces and reactions clearly visible to the audience?

3   While Simon Says is a children's game, the scene should become increasingly menacing and dangerous in its tone. Don't shy away from portraying the life and death aspect of what is at stake for the Protestor.

3

Ghettos

Context

Ghettos originated in Venice, Italy in 1516 when Jews were ordered to live in a designated area of the city. The 16th and 17th centuries saw this concept spread to other European cities, including Rome, Frankfurt and Prague. The Nazis did not invent the idea of ghettos; their purpose for establishing these areas of confinement is what made them unique. The Nazis saw ghettos as a means of isolating the Jewish population from the outside world and from each other. In addition, ghettos made it easier for the Germans to control their captives and to facilitate deportations to the camps.

Ghettos established by the Nazis varied in size from small to large. Some lasted days; others lasted years. Some were open while others were sealed by walls, fences or barbed wire. According to the United States Holocaust Memorial Museum, "The Germans established at least 1,000 ghettos in German-occupied and annexed Poland and the Soviet Union alone" ("Ghettos"). The first was established in Piotrikow Trybunalski, Poland in October 1939. As the Germans invaded and conquered territory, they forced thousands into confinement. Jews were ordered to live in communities of at least 500 people and between 1939 and 1943 there were thousands confined to at least 356 ghettos. Most of these were in Poland and Eastern Europe as that is where large Jewish districts already existed. In addition, the Germans did not wish to provoke Western Europeans by establishing ghettos there. Some living in the ghettos were locals; some came from other parts of the city or the countryside, and some came from other countries. This diversity made it less likely that they could organize for revolt.

In some cases, ghettos could be established quickly and Jews were given little warning that they were being forced to move into them. In Poland, for example, a knock on the door could mean that a Jewish family had only minutes to gather their possessions and leave their home. Everywhere, these forced relocations could mean that families might be transported to the ghetto in trucks or made to walk and carry

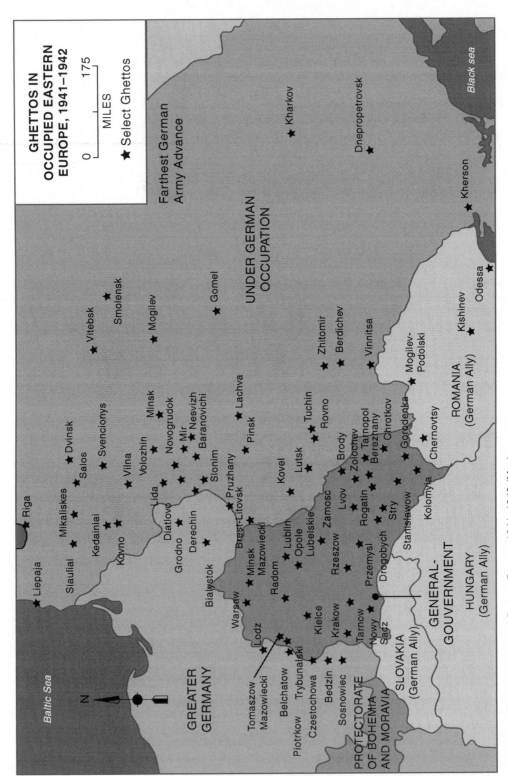

IMAGE 3.1 Ghettos in occupied Eastern Europe, 1941–1942 (Map)

their belongings with them. They could not use automobiles for transportation and there were limited horse-drawn carts available for this purpose. Not knowing how long they would be confined, detainees had to quickly decide what to take with them. Possessions left behind were seized by the Nazis as abandoned goods.

Conditions in the ghettos were deplorable. Jews had to wear armbands or badges for easy identification as Jews. Ghettos were often set up in derelict areas of a city. In larger cities, guards were placed at entrances to insure no one left these "Jewish residential districts" ("The Ghettos; 1939–1941"). To do so could mean death. Food was scarce and starvation claimed many lives.

> For teenagers whose bodies were growing and demanding nutrition, hunger was constant and overpowering. In the Warsaw Ghetto, food was rationed by the Germans according to calories. An average person needs about 2,000 calories a day. Teenagers require more … Even with the illegal smuggling of food into the ghetto, most people never got more than 1,100 calories per day.
>
> (Ayers 21–22)

In addition to starvation, there were many other causes of death in the ghettos. Cold winters and a lack of heat or adequate clothing resulted in people freezing to death. There might or might not be electricity. Overcrowded conditions, inadequate or no plumbing, and human waste and garbage in the streets meant that diseases could spread quickly. Typhus was spread by lice and if residents had no soap or hot water, they could not clean themselves to get rid of these vermin. Other diseases included tuberculosis, dysentery, malnutrition, intestinal issues and exhaustion. Heart failure resulted from stress. Orphaned children might have to resort to begging in the streets. Some froze to death in those streets during cold winters. According to Ayers, "In the Warsaw Ghetto alone, between November 1940 and April 1943, 100,000 Jews died from hunger or disease" (23).

Smuggling became necessary for survival in the ghettos. In addition to food, medicine, news, valuables, goods to trade and weapons were trafficked into the ghettos. The smugglers were frequently children and teens who were small enough or nimble enough to move into and out of tiny spaces, facilitating leaving and re-entering the ghetto undetected. Any residents with money or valuables could trade these for black-market goods. Some young people smuggled in order to feed their families. It was a risky business. Jews found outside of the ghetto faced immediate execution. Anyone caught smuggling faced brutal punishment from the Nazis, including private or public execution.

Some smugglers also were couriers. They carried arms, underground newspapers, false documents and money. Couriers also arranged escapes. Women were especially good in this role as it was harder to tell if they were Jewish. Unlike Jewish men, women were not circumcised.

Traditional roles were difficult to maintain. Ghetto residents competed for whatever forced labor jobs might be available in factories or workshops. These jobs could delay deportation. Because many fathers had either lost their jobs outside of the ghetto or been sent to camps or killed, the family unit in confinement was in disarray. Frequently, women had to provide for their families. In the Warsaw Ghetto, between six to seven people had to live in the same room, straining attempts at privacy. Ghetto teenagers might be involved in secret meetings or members of clandestine political groups. They were sometimes in communication with resistance groups and could get news to share with residents. Although schools, education, and religious services were forbidden by the Nazis, these were created and concealed from their captors by those imprisoned. Despite living in horrible circumstances, ghetto dwellers engaged as best they could in educational, cultural, political and humanitarian endeavors that helped themselves and others.

The ghettos were administered by Judenrat, or Jewish Councils. They were responsible for distributing food and water and making sure that there were services such as medicine, police, jobs, welfare, education, culture and heat. As resources were scarce and infrastructure lacking, they faced enormous challenges. Further, they had to do the Nazis' bidding. If they failed, they could be killed. Worst among their duties was compiling lists of ghetto residents to be deported. Some, like Adam Czerniakow, the chairman of the Warsaw Ghetto Judenrat, committed suicide rather than send fellow Jews to their deaths.

Although there were a number of ghettos, some are better known than others. In Poland, for example, there were five major ghettos: Warsaw, Łódź, Krakow, Lublin and Lvov. Examining Warsaw and Łódź can provide further insight into Nazi brutality and horror.

Outside of New York City, the largest Jewish community could be found in Poland, where 350,000 Jews were residing before Germany invaded. The ghetto was located on 2.4 percent of the city's land, although 30 percent of Warsaw's population was forced to live there. In 1939, as Ayers notes:

> More than 120,000 people were squeezed into each square kilometer. As the months passed, more Jews were transported to the ghetto from elsewhere in Eastern Europe, until more than a half million people lived there.
>
> (46)

Warsaw was sealed on November 16, 1940. It was a closed ghetto, with 11 miles of wall and barbed wire hemming in its 450,000 residents. More than 80,000 Jews died within its borders. Deportations to the death camps began in July of 1942. Attempts, however, to make the unbearable more tolerable were made. Artists and scholars engaged in creative and learned activities, including music, theater and books. These provided brief respites and were reminders of life before the ghetto.

The Warsaw Ghetto is perhaps best known for the uprising that occurred there as Jews, determined to resist the Nazis, put up a valiant fight. The Zydowska Organizacja Bojowa (the ZOB) also was known as the Jewish Fighting Organization and, in the fall of 1942, these teenagers and young adults decided to take a stand against their captors. By that time, only about 35,000 people were still in the ghetto and they recognized that the end was near for them. Although ZOB members were untrained and had few weapons, they decided to fight rather than die passively. Their leader was 23-year-old Mordecai Anielewicz and on April 19, 1943, he and the ZOB staged an uprising against the Nazis. The ZOB headquarters was surrounded on May 8 and the

Nazis, who had advantage over the rebels in terms of weapons and skill, pumped in gas. More than 100 were trapped inside and many, including their leader, chose suicide rather than capture. Approximately 75 ZOB survivors escaped into Warsaw's sewers two days later. The uprising was over.

The first permanent and second largest ghetto in Poland was established in Łódź in 1940. On February 8 of that year, the police president ordered the ghetto be created in a run-down area where 62,000 Jews already lived.

> The ghetto would cover an area of four square kilometers, including the Jewish cemetery, and would comprise 31,000 poorly built houses, almost none of which had running water or was connected to the sewage system. Here it was intended that 160,000 people live, hermetically sealed off from the world around them.
>
> (Benz 51–52)

The isolated ghetto was sealed on April 30, 1940. Leaving was punishable by death. Even talking to someone outside from over the barbed wire was not allowed. The ghetto had Jewish police, a prison, a court, a newspaper carrying information from the Jewish Council, its own money, an archive and a statistics department. None of these alleviated the constant hunger or the wretched conditions endured by those confined there.

Jews ordered to move into the ghetto had to leave possessions behind. With valuables and money gone, social class distinctions disappeared. Jews from Łódź, the district, and throughout the Reich were confined to quarters that lacked electricity and water. Furthermore, Sinti and Roma (Gypsies) also were housed in Łódź. They were treated harshly and confined to their own section of the ghetto. The Łódź ghetto population grew so large that schools had to be closed to make more room.

The Jewish Council Chairman was Chaim Rumkowski. A controversial figure, Rumkowski established a system whereby ghetto Jews, including children, were used as forced laborers in workshops and factories. Deportations to Chelmno began on January 16, 1942. Jewish Council members had to make lists of the people to be deported. In Chelmno, Jews were gassed in vans. Those who were not murdered there were sent to Auschwitz. The Łódź ghetto lasted until the summer of 1944 when it was liquidated.

The Łódź ghetto lasted 18 months longer than the Warsaw Ghetto. Approximately 12,000 survived Łódź. One in four ghetto residents died there. In the Warsaw Ghetto, one out of five or six died. Ghetto survivors were likely to meet their deaths in extermination camps.

Hungary presented a unique situation. Jews in Budapest were relocated to yellow star houses, also called Star of David houses. Just as Jews were forced to wear a yellow star, so too were these houses marked. There were approximately 2,000 of these apartments and they housed nearly 200,000 Jews awaiting deportation. Families were given one room, and often a dozen or so might live together in these cramped quarters. The dwelling entrance was guarded by an attendant and a curfew was imposed. Residents stayed in these houses for approximately six months until two large ghettos could be

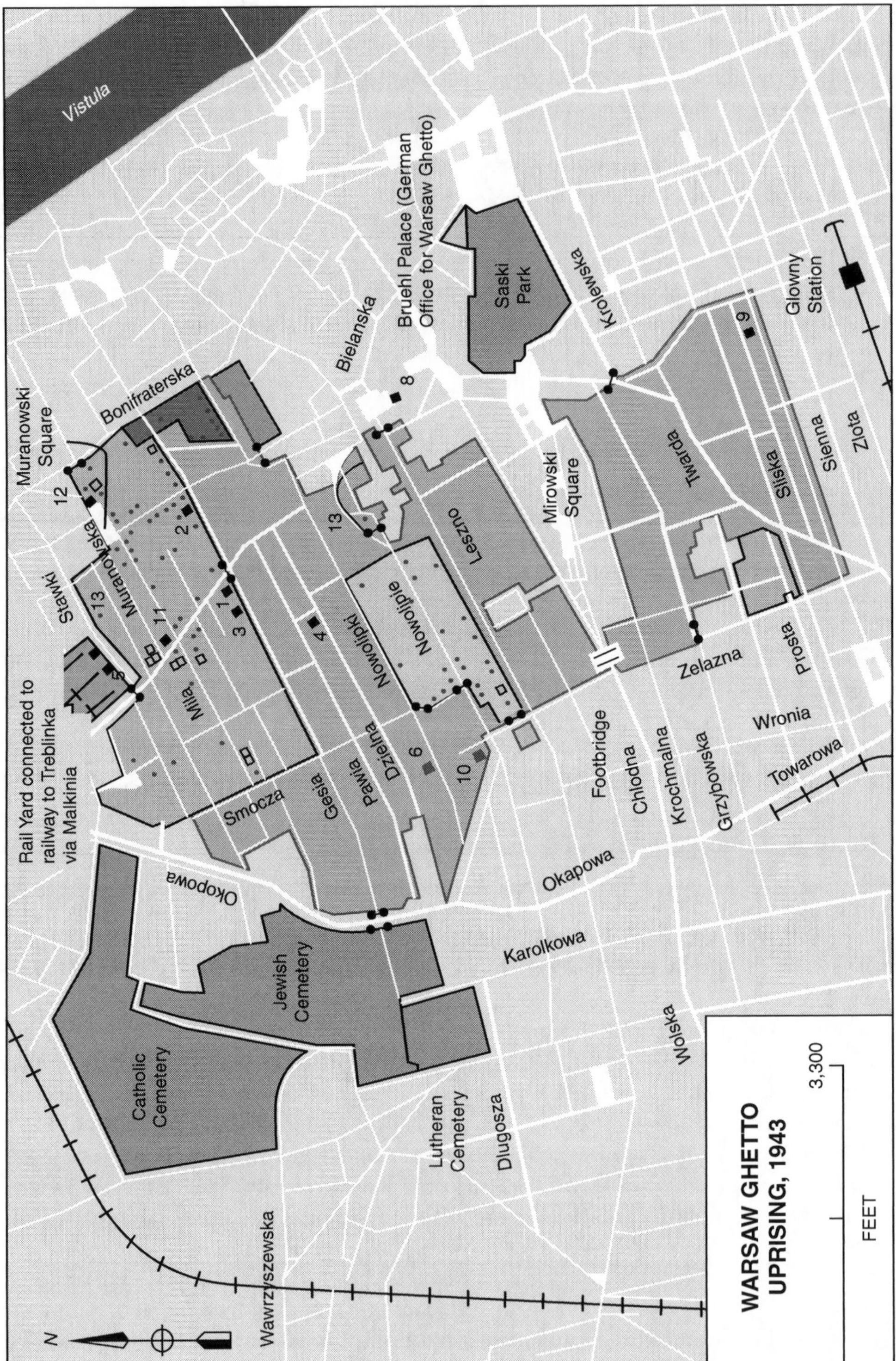

IMAGE 3.2 Warsaw Ghetto Uprising, 1943 (Map)

constructed. Yellow star houses were a way-station for Jews destined for deportation to death camps.

Overcrowding, starvation and disease killed an estimated 500,000 Jews in the ghettos created by the Nazis. Some deported from ghettos went to forced labor or concentration camps; most went to death camps. At war's end, apart from those in Budapest, no ghettos remained by the time Europe was liberated.

Scripted scenes and monologues

1. Scene for two actors – *The Survivor* by Susan Nanus, based on the memoirs of Jack Eisner

> *HELA is 13 years old and is the younger sister of JACEK* who is 15.*
> *HELA and JACEK are Jewish teenagers who are imprisoned in the Warsaw Ghetto in Poland. Along with a number of friends, they have been smuggling food and other goods into the ghetto.*

HELA. Stop treating me like a baby. I'm thirteen years old and perfectly capable of catching a silly little knapsack. Besides, ever since they closed the schools, there's nothing to do all day. I'm bored.

JACEK. (*To audience.*) My sister Hela wanted to help me. I never forced her. When she first asked, I said no. It was bad enough I was a smuggler without risking her life, too. But after Papa's business was confiscated, I decided to give Hela a chance. I needed her. (*He picks up a knapsack and calls out to her.*) Okay, ready? Catch! (*He tosses her the knapsack. She misses.*) Pick it up. Come on, quick!

HELA. That was impossible. No one could have caught that.

(*HELA brings JACEK the knapsack and moves back.*)

JACEK. This job requires the impossible. You have to catch it no matter what, Hela. I'll be on a moving streetcar. I can't guarantee perfect aim. Try again. Ready.

HELA. Ready. (*He throws it again. She misses.*) I'm sorry. I'm sorry. Do it again.

JACEK. You have to run faster. Keep your eye on the knapsack and run. Now!

(*JACEK tosses it. HELA catches it, but stumbles and almost falls.*)

HELA. Jacek, you did that on purpose! Do you have to throw it so hard?

JACEK. If you think that's too hard, how do you expect to catch it when it's full of potatoes? (*He tosses it again. She catches it.*) Good. Again.

HELA. (*Bringing him the knapsack.*) This'll really help, won't it? I mean if I catch the knapsack, then you can bring over more food.

JACEK. Yeah. Move back a little.

(*JACEK tosses the knapsack to HELA. She brings it back. They continue practicing as they speak.*)

HELA. Do they still have movies on the Aryan side?

JACEK. Sure.

HELA. And puppet shows in Krashinski Gardens?

JACEK. I don't know. I never get there. Now, I'm going to fill this with rocks. When you catch it, pull it close to your body so it doesn't fall.

HELA. I wish we had a park in the ghetto. I bet there are lots of flowers in Saxon Gardens right now. Tulips. I like tulips, don't you?

JACEK. (*Filling the knapsacks with rocks.*) They're all right.

HELA. After the war, I'd like to visit Holland. They have windmills there.

JACEK. Unless they've all been bombed out.

HELA. All of them?

JACEK. It's possible.

HELA. But the tulips, they'd still be there, wouldn't they?

JACEK. I don't know. Maybe.

HELA. But we learned in school that there are thousands of tulips all over Holland. How could the Germans kill every single flower? (*He doesn't answer.*) Jacek?

JACEK. What?

HELA. Next time you go, will you bring me back a flower? It doesn't have to be a tulip, it can be anything. (*No answer.*) Jacek?

JACEK. What?

HELA. Will you?

JACEK. Sure. You're my partner, aren't you? Catch! (*He throws the knapsack, full of rocks. She catches it, staggers, but doesn't drop it.*) Good girl, Hela! You made it!

*YAH-tzek

SPOTLIGHT ACTIVITY

The Survivor

There are several scenes from *The Survivor* in this chapter, a play that chronicles the risks undertaken by a group of young people struggling to survive under Nazi oppression. The following activities are designed to give students a deeper understanding of what life in the Warsaw Ghetto was like and how the bonds of friendship and courage became a solemn promise to tell the story of these brave youths.

"Ball toss activity"*

According to the United States Holocaust Memorial Museum, "Between 1940 and mid-1942, 83,000 Jews died of starvation and disease." In *The Survivor*, the young characters are engaged in smuggling food into the Warsaw Ghetto, both for sustenance and to sell. In the scene above, we learn that Jacek is smuggling food and tossing it into the ghetto from a moving streetcar. His sister, Hela, wants to help. If she is to assist him, he must teach her to catch a knapsack containing provisions that he will toss to her while the streetcar is in motion.

1   Have students form a circle and toss an inflated balloon to others in the circle, using a random pattern. Next, remove the balloon. The students must recreate tossing the balloon without using the actual object. They must try to replicate the size and shape of the balloon and accurately remember the pattern of who they tossed it to and who received it.
2   Repeat the activity with balls of various sizes, shapes and weights, using first the actual object and then recreating the ball toss without the object. Consider using ping pong balls, beach balls, and nerf balls before incorporating larger and heavier balls. (Stress safety when directing this activity.)
3   Select one of the balls and continue the ball toss using the real object. This time, however, include the following motivations for catching the ball:
   ■   If you catch the ball, you will win a prize.
   ■   If you catch the ball, the entire class will receive an A in this course.
   ■   If you catch the ball, you will escape punishment.
   ■   If you catch the ball, you will save a life.
At the end of the activity, discuss the effect that changing the motivation had upon the action.

*This activity has been adapted with permission from *Teaching About the Holocaust Through Drama*.

4   Have pairs of students work on the scripted scene, incorporating what they discovered in the ball toss activity into the performance of the scene.

(Statistics taken from the United States Holocaust Memorial Museum, "Warsaw." *United States Holocaust Memorial Museum Holocaust Encyclopedia*. United States Holocaust Memorial Museum, Washington, D.C., www.ushmm.org, May 29, 2017.)

2. Scene for two actors – *The Survivor* by Susan Nanus, based on the memoirs of Jack Eisner

HALINA* is 15 years old. She is pretty and blond, and is Jacek's girlfriend. MALA is also 15. She is HALINA's best friend.
The two friends have a plan to escape the Warsaw Ghetto by posing as Polish Catholics.

HALINA. Come on, Mala. Hurry up.
MALA. Maybe this is a bad idea.
HALINA. No. We decided to get out and we're going. Do you have your crucifix?
MALA. I'm wearing it.
HALINA. It feels funny, doesn't it? Like we're not really us anymore. How much money did you bring?

MALA. Thirty zlotys.**

HALINA. Thirty! But we need a hundred to pay that man.

MALA. Well, don't you have any?

HALINA. I have fifty and you're supposed to have fifty. What happened to the other twenty?

MALA. I gave it to my mother.

HALINA. What? Are you crazy?

MALA. We're leaving the ghetto and she's not. What did you expect me to do?

HALINA. Not without a hundred zlotys, we're not.

MALA. Halina, she's my mother.

HALINA. He told us not to show up without it. What if he gets angry? He could turn us over to the Gestapo.

MALA. She hasn't eaten in three days. She keeps giving all the food to my brothers. I couldn't leave her without any money. Be mad at me. I don't care. I'm not sorry. Go ahead by yourself if you want and I'll go home.

HALINA. It's too late for that. It's almost curfew.

MALA. So, I'll stay here. I don't care. Let them catch me.

HALINA. Will you keep moving? It took me two months to make this contact and we're not throwing it away.

MALA. I'm sick and tired of the whole thing! Just look at this disgusting dress. And these ratty old shoes. And my hair. I'm dirty and I stink! I don't care, anymore. I'm not going.

HALINA. Good, Mala. Why don't you just throw yourself off the wall while you're at it and save them the trouble?

MALA. It's not going to work. Pretending we're Polish is a stupid idea!

HALINA. It'll work if you stop complaining and listen.

MALA. We don't have enough money. That man isn't going to cross us over out of the goodness of his heart.

HALINA. I know. But I have this.

(*HALINA pulls out a chain with a small gold ring.*)

MALA. What is it?

HALINA. My mother's wedding ring. It's gold.

MALA. You're going to sell her wedding ring?

HALINA. He said to stand on that roof and signal. He has a rope ladder from his attic.

MALA. You've had that ring since I first met you in the ghetto.

HALINA. This way.

MALA. But Halina. That's all you have to remember your mother by.

HALINA. There he is.

(*HALINA signals and they move forward. Lights fade.*)

*Ha-LEE-na
**zLO-tehz — Polish currency

3. Scene for three actors – *The Survivor* by Susan Nanus, based on the memoirs of Jack Eisner

RUDY is 15 years old and comes from a Hasidic (very Orthodox Jewish) family.
LUTEK* is 15 years old from a rich Warsaw family.
HELA is 13 years old and is the younger sister of JACEK.**
RUDY, LUTEK, HELA and other teenagers have been smuggling food and goods into the Warsaw Ghetto to help their fellow Jews imprisoned there by the Nazis. Now they have begun smuggling weapons into the ghetto and are preparing to fight back in an uprising.
Lights up on RUDY, LUTEK, and HELA in the attic.

RUDY. Where are they? They should've been here by now.

LUTEK. Relax. Something probably came up. You know Jacek.

HELA. He had to stop and pay off Stash, remember?

RUDY. Well, they better hurry. It's almost curfew.

HELA. Let's see how we did this week. Where's my book?
(*HELA searches and takes out a schoolgirl's notebook.*)

RUDY. (*Pacing.*) I never liked Stash. Markowsky's a crook, but at least he's one of us. Stash could spill the whole operation to the Gestapo for a reward.

LUTEK. We pay him more. He's getting rich off of that drainpipe.

HELA. (*Consulting notebook.*) Last week, we fed two hundred and fifty-five people. Look. I have all their names. I'm saving them to show my children.

RUDY. This girl would save the wall if she could fit it into her scrapbook.

HELA. What's wrong with it? I want to remember.

LUTEK. You don't think you'll remember the Ghetto without souvenirs?

HELA. Not every detail. Anyway, how else will people in the future ever know what happened?

RUDY. What makes you think they'll want to? What makes you think you'll want to? I don't. As soon as this war is over, I'm going to do everything I can to forget it ever happened.

HELA. Like what?

RUDY. Like learning to fly. I'm going to be a pilot and live in the sky. Far away from the whole world.

HELA. You'd have to come down sometime.

RUDY. Only to visit you.

LUTEK. England is far enough for me. Buckingham Palace, the Tower of London, the British Museum. And every afternoon at four o'clock, they have tea. They sit quietly and they eat these things called crumpets and act like civilized human beings.

HELA. I want a camera. After the war, I'm going to get a job after school, no matter what Mama says, and I'm going to save up and get one. The Germans keep taking pictures and making movies and we don't have anything. I wish I had a picture of every one of us right now.

LUTEK. (*Looking out the window.*) I don't like it. They're late and the whole building is dark. Usually there's a candle or something.

HELA. Don't you see anyone?

LUTEK. Not Stash, not his wife, nothing. We need a signal. Some kind of sign if something goes wrong.

RUDY. A signal? A gun would be a lot more useful.

HELA. You know how to shoot a gun?

RUDY. What's to know? You point and pull the trigger.

LUTEK. There's a little more to it than that, Rudy.

RUDY. So. I'll figure it out. Too bad I didn't learn that instead of the Talmud.*** Yesterday, they beat up my father so bad, he could barely crawl. I told him, Tateh, shave your beard, it just provokes those bastards. But God forbid he should touch a razor to his face.

HELA. He has a right. It's what he believes in.

RUDY. Don't give me that. It's what he hides in.

HELA. That's not fair, Rudy. Lots of people still believe in God.

RUDY. And you, little sister? What do you believe?

HELA. Don't be sarcastic.

RUDY. I'm not. I want to know.

HELA. I guess I still believe, too. Every night, I say a prayer and ask God to watch over Mama and Papa and the rest of us, and so far, we've been pretty lucky. I got typhoid, and I got better, didn't I? And we're not starving and nobody's been arrested. Even though a lot of terrible things have happened. I still think God cares.

RUDY. What about Yankele?**** Did he care about him?

HELA. I don't know.

LUTEK. I'd like to believe. I always did before. It would make things easier if I thought all of this was happening for a reason. But every time I hear the Germans boasting how God is on their side …

RUDY. Whose side does it look like he's on?

LUTEK. Well, now that the Americans are in the war …

RUDY. I'm talking about us. The Yids. The swine. The dirty Kikes …

HELA. (*Losing control.*) How are we supposed to know? What do you want us to do? Give up? Say there's no hope? Let the Germans get away with everything?

*Loo-tek
**YAH-tzek
***TALL-mud, the source of Jewish law
****YAHN-keh-leh

Verbatim testimony historical narratives

1. From the testimony of Daniel Geslewitz – "Anti-Jewish Laws"

(https://iwitness.usc.edu/sfi/BrowseTopics.aspx?TopicID=3&ClipID=915)

Born: August 14, 1924, in Łódź, Poland
In an October, 1995 interview, Daniel Geslewitz describes how, after the occupation of Poland, the Germans created the Łódź* ghetto. Geslewitz was 15 in 1939, when he and his family were imprisoned there.
(Portions of this testimony have been omitted for brevity.)

DANIEL

In December, they issued an order that Łódź had to be made Judenrein** – free of Jews. They said that they would create a ghetto, and all the Jews would have to move into the ghetto. Live in the ghetto. And in the process of moving all the Jews from uptown – and they always did it in the night – they would surround a few blocks and everybody would have to leave the building. And you could only carry one valise. In the process, one night 400 were shot because they were too slow. [The Germans] did that, you know, for any reason. And the Jews started moving into the ghetto. They couldn't take their furniture with them. Only what they could carry. And you could see all the people carry on their back a mattress or whatever it was, and they moved into the ghetto. The ghetto was surrounded with barbed wire and you couldn't get in or out of the ghetto. They kept on moving in more and more from the other part of the city of Łódź. It was the poorest section of the city. There was no sewer. No running water. And they squeezed in, into the ghetto, if I'm not mistaken, 186,000 Jews in that small quarter. And in April, they closed the ghetto. Anybody who was in the ghetto couldn't get out. Anybody who was outside couldn't get in.

All of a sudden, food became a problem, because you couldn't get it. There was no food available. Before the war, we used to eat collectively (as a family). During the war, we couldn't eat collectively anymore. Everybody had to manage himself – his piece of bread should last him for a week, 'til you get the next piece of bread. So, the family was no more sitting around the table eating whatever mother would put on the table. It was everybody having to manage what he was getting by himself. You had to be very careful, because if you got bread that should last you ten days, you couldn't eat it in one day, because what are you going to eat the other nine days? You had to be very, very careful – self-controlled – to eat the bread and divide it for nine or ten days. And eating this was a whole ceremony. You didn't eat it fast. You had to eat it slowly, because you wanted to enjoy it for a longer period of time. Or you got potatoes or whatever. Anything that was edible we would eat. But not much was there. Not much edible was there.

My father died in 1942 in the ghetto. He died of hunger. Lots of people died from hunger. There was a terrible hunger in the ghetto.

*LUHDJ
**YOO-din-rine

2. From the testimony of Henry Greenblatt – "Ghetto Life"

(http://iwitness.usc.edu/SFI/BrowseTopics.aspx?TopicID=28&ClipID=110)

Born: November 1, 1930, in Warsaw, Poland
In a February, 1996 interview, Henry discusses living in the Warsaw Ghetto during the war and how, because he was small child, he was able to sneak in and out of the ghetto to get food.

HENRY

The most important thing was food. We, at that time, had some money saved up that my father saved for the purpose, probably, of opening up his dream business. And we started to go out of the ghetto. At that time, the ghetto wasn't closed tight. It was just a Polish policeman and a German staying by the gate. There was a gate that people could come in and come out by showing several documents. And I remember my father used to come to the Polish policeman and show him his identification as an invalid and the policeman would kind of feel sorry for him. Then, my father would pull out his eye, his glass eye and look pretty bad, and the policeman would let us out. The German didn't pay any attention at all. So we would go. I remember we went to the market. And we bought some food and we brought the food in and that continued for a few weeks.

Then, they closed up the ghetto and nobody was able to get out of the ghetto. I mean nobody – no adult – would take a chance to go out. The ghetto was designated to quite a few blocks and was cordoned off, and they built a high wall, probably about a ten-foot wall with glass on top of the wall, so that you could not scale that wall. It was impossible to scale that wall. On the other hand, they left a little bit of a hole at the gutter for the water to run through. So when it rained, the water was running through it. It was a small hole, but enough for me, as a little kid, to crawl through. So, I wasn't the only one that was crawling through. Other kids would crawl through, not knowing what happens on the other side. So you made your way through and would go out from the ghetto. I knew already the place that I went with my father to buy food and I'd buy some food. I couldn't carry too much. I would buy one bread, sometimes some potatoes, and a little bit of different things. It was pretty cheap, not to spend too much money, bring it into the ghetto, then my father would sell it. And we had a little bit always left over from that.

3. From the testimony of Eva Safferman – "Ghetto Life"

(http://iwitness.usc.edu/SFI/BrowseTopics.aspx?TopicID=28&ClipID=157)

Born: April 15, 1928, in Łódź, Poland
In this July, 1996, interview Eva speaks about her forced labor in the Łódź* ghetto, and how she managed to hide from the Germans during a roundup.

EVA

[In the ghetto] I went to school for a short while, and then they just closed all the schools and everybody had to go to work. So they sent me to a place that was making carpets. And then, after a short while, they disbanded it and sent all the young children to another factory – a factory that was making, I believe, uniforms for the Germans. And we worked there. And from there, the Germans asked the director of this factory occasionally to give them names of people they should evacuate.

And one day, there was a list and my name was on this list. And I knew that I had to hide if they would come and look for me. I had an uncle who was a policeman in the ghetto. So, when I saw my name, I went to him and I asked him, "Please, could you do something? You know the director of the place. They should take off my name from the list." And he did. He managed to take off my name. But unfortunately for me, my name was tagged twice, and the other name was still on this list.

And one day, they came to look for me. In this little place where we were, a couple of apartments were spread out. And we had a little bit of ground in the back. And all the tenants used to divide a little piece of ground and we used to grow some vegetables – radishes, beets, cucumbers. And we also had three fruit trees, which really helped us in the ghetto. So we used to divide whatever fruit would grow amongst the tenants. And everybody got a little bit. And one day, when I was in the back there, I heard somebody come in and yell "Eva Zissman!" And I had a bad feeling about it, because I knew my name was on the list. So I ran in the back and I lay down between the beets. The beets. And I covered myself with the beets. I put it all around. And they came to my mother and they asked her "Where is Eva?" and she said, "I don't know. I don't know where she is." So they said, "Well, we're gonna wait." And she says, "I don't know how long it's gonna be 'til she comes." But she says, "Here." She gave them a bag of apples. "Please write down that she's not here." So, ok. They took the apples. They went away. This was the first time that I was saved.

LUHDJ

4. From the testimony of Helen Fagin – "Ghetto Life"

(http://iwitness.usc.edu/SFI/BrowseTopics.aspx?TopicID=28&ClipID=166)

Born: February 1, 1922, in Radomsko, Poland
In a February, 1996 interview, Helen relays how she taught younger girls in the ghetto, and how the novel Gone With The Wind *helped her and the other young ghetto inhabitants cope.*

HELEN

We really had a very limited space. Not only the actual living space, but actually also the limited outside space. And that ghetto was keeping us very much together in a way that it *brought* us together as well. We would try to establish a semblance of a social life. A semblance of an intellectual life. For example, there were no schools. And my younger sister was very young, and I knew that she needed education. So, I established a clandestine school. And the girls would come to my room – I can't call it an apartment – and they would be in groups of five or six, and they would come every hour on the hour. And I would conduct classes with them. And I would spill out of my head whatever I remembered having learned in my school. The most incongruous subject matter. I would teach them Latin vocabulary. I would teach them geography. I would teach them anything I knew.

As a matter of fact, [later] I wrote an essay which I called "Gone With A Dream," because one of the things that I had read most recently, prior to establishing the school, was the Polish translation of *Gone With The Wind*. And, when the girls came, and they were so solemn and they were so sorrowful and they would say, "Please, please, tell us a story," I would say, "Okay. Today, I'm going to take you to an altogether different world." And I took them away to a Southern plantation in Georgia. And I was talking to them about Tara and about Melanie and about Scarlett and Rhett Butler. And their eyes would open and they would dream about it. And I remember one girl especially. A green-eyed girl who I thought would have looked just like Scarlett, and I said to her, "Goodbye Scarlett." And she would say, "No, I'd rather be Melanie." So – we were dreaming together.

Suggested props/costumes for Chapter 3 historical narrative scenes

- Women's sweaters
- Men's sweaters, jackets
- Tattered clothing items
- "Uniform" shirts
- Men's and women's hats
- Old (1930s/40s-looking) suitcases
- A small loaf of bread (real or fake)
- Pieces of bread (real or fake)
- Potatoes (real or fake)
- Burlap sack (with apples – real or fake)
- Burlap sack "filled"
- Clipboard with papers and pencil
- Branches/fronds ("Beet plants") – real or fake
- Loose papers

Devised theater activity

Create a scene using the poem "The Butterfly" *by Pavel Friedmann which explores the physical and emotional differences between Freedom and Captivity.*

Scene components

1   The poem "The Butterfly."
2   *Adjectives* describing the photo "Women Prisoners in Theresienstadt" (on the following page). Have each actor/devisor respond to the photo with two or three adjectives. Incorporate these words into your scene using different techniques of *choral speech*.
3   *Staging* which utilizes set pieces (chairs, tables, ropes, planks – anything!) which mark off, or restrict the playing area to a tight space.
4   *Staging* which contrasts with the above – representing open space and freedom of movement.

Text

1   "The Butterfly" was written by Pavel Friedmann on June 4, 1942. Pavel was imprisoned at Theresienstadt, which the USHMM's Holocaust Encyclopedia describes as a "ghetto-camp" (https://encyclopedia.ushmm.org/content/en/article/theresienstadt). On September 29, 1944, he was deported to Auschwitz where he died at the age of 23.

"The Butterfly"

The last, the very last,
So richly, brightly, dazzlingly yellow.
Perhaps if the sun's tears would sing
against a white stone …
Such, such a yellow
Is carried lightly way up high.
It went away I'm sure because it wished
to kiss the world goodbye.
For seven weeks I've lived in here,
Penned up inside this ghetto
But I have found my people here.
The dandelions call to me
And the white chestnut branches in the court.
Only I never saw another butterfly.
That butterfly was the last one.
Butterflies don't live in here,
In the ghetto.

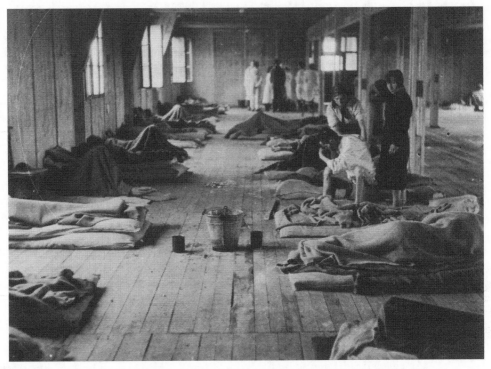

IMAGE 3.3 Image of "women prisoners in Theresienstadt" courtesy of YIVO Institute for Jewish Research

Staging considerations, choices and tips

1   How will you integrate the descriptive words associated with the photo with the text of the poem?

2   Will you use a prop to represent a butterfly? If so, what will you use and how will you use it? Will your butterfly be realistic or figurative? How will that impact your overall scene presentation?

3   What does freedom "look" like? What does captivity "look" like? How can you represent these concepts onstage with furniture, props and staging?

4

Concentration and extermination camps

Context

Concentration and extermination camps were a cornerstone of the Nazis' attempt to rid the Reich of perceived enemies and inferiors. A concentration camp is defined as "a camp in which people are detained or confined, usually under harsh conditions and without regard to legal norms of arrest and imprisonment that are acceptable in a constitutional democracy" ("Concentration Camps, 1933–39"). What many may not realize, however, is that the term does not define all the types of camps and internment locations established by the Nazis. The purposes of these facilities varied, as did the length of time that they were in existence. The number of camps and ghettos established from 1933 to 1945 exceeded 42,000. People were deported to the camps because of race, religion, nationality or politics. Imprisoned were intellectuals, political prisoners, criminals, Social Democrats, Communists, Roma (Gypsies), Jehovah's Witnesses, those the Nazis considered social misfits or inferiors, such as gays, beggars, tramps and alcoholics, and of course, Jews. The camps were run by the SS, led by Heinrich Himmler, and were differentiated by function. Similar to a prison, the Nazis saw camps as a way to separate certain groups seen as undesirable by the rest of society. Unlike a prison, those confined had not been convicted of crimes nor given a release date. For millions, the only way out was death.

Lagersystem was the term used for the system of camps created by the Nazis. These included camps for forced laborers and prisoners of war as well as transit camps, concentration camps and sub-camps, and death camps. Some had explicit reasons for being; others served multiple purposes. Labor camps, for example, were used as places where prisoners worked within the camp or in factories or stone quarries, on farms, or wherever else they might be needed. Smaller off-shoots of larger camps, sub-camps were often located near a venue that required enslaved workers. Labor camps were viewed as places where people could be worked to death. POW camps housed prisoners of war. Transit camps held deportees from occupied territories

IMAGE 4.1 Abraham Lewent's prisoner jacket

until they could be moved to forced labor, concentration or extermination camps. Concentration camps were detention or murder centers for perceived enemies of the state and forced laborers, and extermination camps were where millions were slain.

Dachau, established to the northwest of Munich in March of 1933, was the first concentration camp. Himmler put SS Lieutenant General Theodor Eicke in charge of organizing the concentration camp system and the structure that he implemented at Dachau became the model for how other camps were run. Upon arriving at a concentration camp, prisoners forfeited their possessions. Men and women were separated from each other. Children remained with their mothers. Personal clothing and shoes were replaced by a striped uniform and wooden clogs. Inmates would wear these clothes, day and night, for six weeks at a time. Each person was given a number and a colored triangle to sew onto his or her uniform. The following chart shows the color designation for each triangle.

Triangle color	Group identification
Green	Professional criminals
Red	Political prisoners
Purple	Jehovah's Witnesses
Pink	Homosexuals
Black	Social misfits

Triangle color	Group identification
Black or brown	Roma and Sinti (Gypsies)
One of the above as well as a yellow triangle or Star of David	Jews

One SS Death Head unit oversaw the areas inside of the camp while another group managed the outside areas. Each concentration camp had the same internal staff consisting of the:

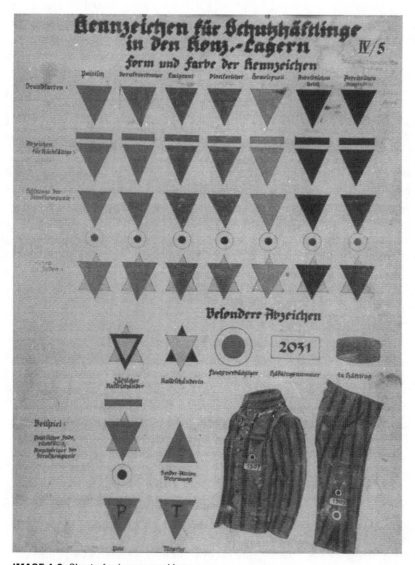

IMAGE 4.2 Chart of prisoner markings

1   Commandant's Headquarters (consisting of the commandant and his staff)
2   A protective detention office run by a Security Police officer who maintained prisoner records in terms of arrival, discharge, discipline and death and who received his instructions from the Reich Central Office for Security
3   Commander of the Protective Detention Camp
4   Administration and Supply
5   SS Physician

("Nazi Camps" 7)

In addition to the guards, most camps had barbed wire or electrified fences, ditches, watchtowers and vicious dogs. Camps had separate sections for women and men. Barracks designed to hold 250 to 400 prisoners might have as many as 1,200 occupants. There were three tiers of wooden bunks for sleeping, with three to five people in a space not designed for that many. SS guards appointed *kapos*. These were prisoners assigned to guard other prisoners and frequently they were selected for this task because of their propensity for violence. (It should be noted, however, that sometimes *kapos* helped prisoners, despite the danger in doing so.) Furthermore, prisoners were encouraged to spy on one another and report to their captors. A person could be rewarded for betraying others, but it was dangerous as either prisoners or the SS might murder the informant. Of all prisoner groups, Jews were singled out for obliteration.

Conditions were brutal. Prisoners were subjected to morning and evening roll calls (*appell*) where they might stand for hours in harsh temperatures. Not only did roll calls take place on the roll call square (*platz*); this square also could be the scene for punishments and executions that prisoners had to watch. Throughout the camps, those guarding the captives engaged in diabolical and sadistic behaviors. Inmates could be punished for real or imagined infractions. Any objects that could inflict pain might be used to deliver merciless beatings. Prisoners were attacked by dogs, hung, or murdered in the most gruesome ways. Blameless groups could be punished for the infractions of other prisoners. Some women were raped. Some of the camps had prisons or punishment units within them where solitary confinement might take place.

Death came in many forms. The most likely to perish were the youngest and the oldest, those deemed unsuitable for work. Either they were killed, or they succumbed to malnutrition, disease, exposure, stress or exhaustion. Prisoners who were able to work had the best prospect for survival. Teenagers ordinarily fared best.

Economic considerations came into play in notable ways. Camps were not expected to incur a cost for the Reich; they might even make a profit. Some ways of making money included companies paying the SS for prisoners that they could use as workers, selling or repurposing Jewish possessions taken from inmates and, after murdering Jews, using their hair, teeth and gold fillings for products or sale. As the war continued, more prisoners were needed as workers by businesses supporting the German effort and for replacement of workers who died from forced labor, adding to the coffers of the SS. Business considerations came to influence site selection for work camps, such as near quarries.

Being selected for forced labor was no guarantee of survival. The giant chemical company, I.G. Farben, was the first private company to use prisoners from Auschwitz.

Of the approximately 35,000 inmates who worked there, more than 25,000 died. Inmates also were used for construction projects, including those within the camps. The tasks could be grueling and for weak, underfed or exhausted workers, they could be fatal. The drudges were literally worked to death.

While not a forced labor camp, Theresienstadt is an example of an internment site that transformed from a ghetto into a concentration and a transit camp. Jews were moved from all parts of the Reich to this location in Czechoslovakia. Although not classified as a forced labor camp, work was expected of the inmates who were over 14 years old. Here is where artists, musicians, actors, writers, scholars and other important Jews from throughout the Reich were sent. The Nazis considered Theresienstadt to be a model camp and showed it off to visitors as proof that Jews were well treated. When the Red Cross came to inspect the site on June 23, 1944, they saw a place where artists performed, social activities were available to inmates, gardens were planted and barracks revamped. What they did not know was that deportations had increased prior to their visit, that artists used for propaganda purposes were killed after the dignitaries left and that inmates clandestinely created truthful records of the horrid conditions there. During its existence as a ghetto, 35,444 Jews died, and when it was a camp, 88,000 were deported. It was from Theresienstadt that, on October 30, 1944, 2,000 Jews were deported to Auschwitz on the last train to go to the extermination camp. Of the 15,000 children detained at Theresienstadt, it is estimated that only between 100 and 150 survived.

Theresienstadt was one of a number of major concentration camps. Other camps included Ravensbruck, Neuengamme, Bergen-Belsen, Sachsenhausen, Gross-Rosen, Buchenwald, Flossenburg, Dachau, Stutthof and Dora-Mittelbau in Germany, Mauthausen in Austria, and Natzweiler-Struthof in France. Theresienstadt, as mentioned, was in Czechoslovakia. Camps also existed in Ukraine, Latvia and The Netherlands. While death was ever-present at these camps, it was the extermination camps that were constructed to end millions of lives.

The extermination camps were Treblinka, Belzec, Sobibor, Chelmno, Majdanek-Lublin and Auschwitz-Birkenau. An estimated 3.5 million perished in these carnage centers. The Nazis' own figures from the end of 1942 give insight into the scale of murder.

24,733	Majdanek
101,370	Sobibor
434,508	Belzec
713,555	Treblinka

The death camps were located in Poland, a country that had been home to Eastern Europe's largest Jewish population. An estimated 91 percent of Polish Jews died during the Holocaust, with approximately 450,000 being murdered at Auschwitz. All six camps were located near railway lines to facilitate the daily and

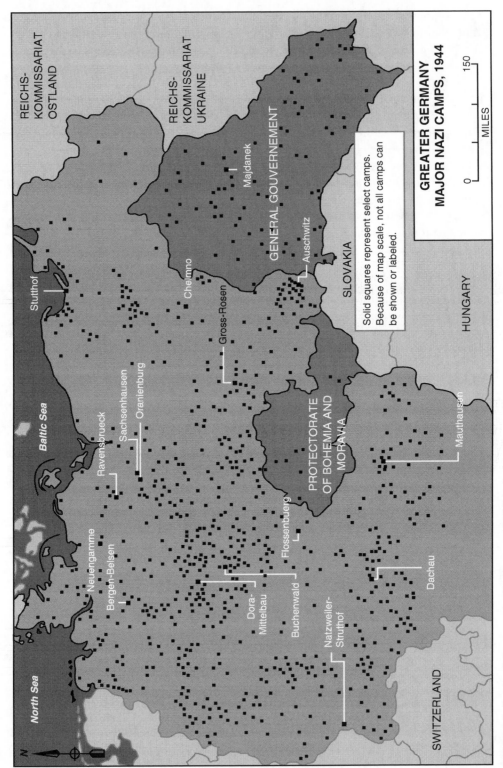

IMAGE 4.3 Greater Germany major Nazi camps, 1944 (Map)

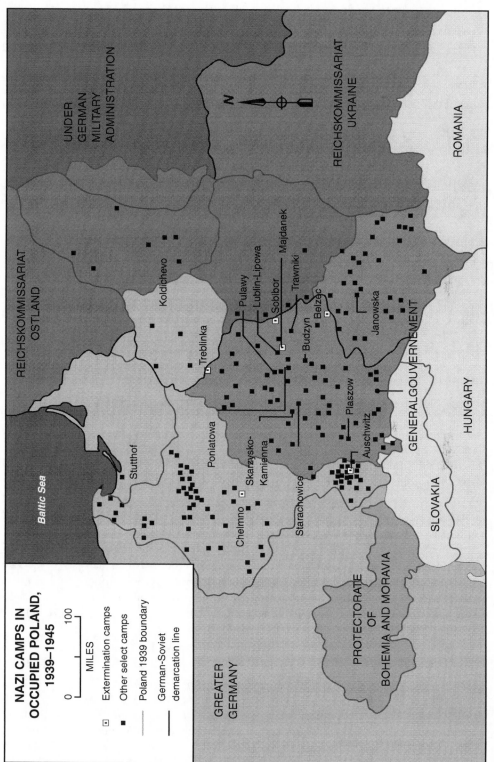

IMAGE 4.4 Nazi camps in occupied Poland, 1939–1945 (Map)

IMAGE 4.5 Two ovens inside the Dachau Crematorium

deadly transfer of Jews from ghettos and other camps. Within two hours of their arrival, passengers could be dead. There were both male and female guards at these facilities, although far fewer women than men did these jobs and their gender did not abate their brutality. The extermination camps had in common large crematoriums, ovens for burning corpses. They did not, however, have more than a few barracks; new arrivals were not expected to stay. Only about ten to twenty percent of an incoming transport might be spared.

Chelmno was the first camp to routinely use gas vans to kill Jews. The vans were disguised as Red Cross vehicles and they could contain as many as 70 people at a time and kill them using carbon monoxide gas. "By September 1942, 55,000 adult Jews, 20,000 Jewish children, and five thousand Gypsies from the Łódź ghetto had been sent to the gas vans in Chelmo" (Roleff). Estimates are that 170,000 to 360,000 died there.

Treblinka, the last of the death camps to be built, opened on July 23, 1942 and, with the exception of Auschwitz, more lives were ended there than at any other extermination camp. A railway spur led directly into the camp, making it easier to offload Jews from the trains and into the gas chambers. The camp was disguised as a transit camp and arriving Jews thought that they were going for showers and disinfecting upon arrival, not to their deaths. That deception failed when the number of Jews brought there increased and the Nazis could not rid the camp quickly enough of murder evidence. When that was the case, train cars had to be held, causing some of the waiting Jews to die in the cars. Most of the Jews from the Warsaw Ghetto died at Treblinka. In *The Holocaust: A New History*, Laurence Rees notes that:

> Around 850,000 people – some estimates say over 900,000 – were murdered here between summer 1942 and autumn 1943. And within that timeframe, the most murderous period was from the end of July until the end of August 1942 when an estimated 312,500 people were killed – around a quarter of a million of them from the Warsaw ghetto.
>
> (301–302)

Ironically, a medical doctor, Irmfried Eberl, ran the death camp. Rather than save lives, he was the only physician to be in charge of an extermination facility. Eberl was replaced by Franz Stangl, who had acquired killing experience through the T4 program, in which the infirmed were murdered.

While Treblinka was the site of a largely failed rebellion in August 1943, no such rebellion took place at Majdanek, which had been constructed as a POW camp in 1941. The camp was unique in that it was several types of camps – POW, concentration, extermination or combination concentration and death camp – rolled into one. The gas chambers were behind the shower blocks at the camp. The SS had to rev motors so that the screaming of those being killed could not be heard. Executioners could use either bottled carbon monoxide or Zyklon B gas to end life.

Sobibor, Treblinka and Belzec had a similar pathway to death for deportees. There was an arrival area, a narrow passageway from there to the gas chambers, and a separate pathway section for guards and *Sonderkommandos*, the term used to describe Jewish men who were forced to take prisoners to the gas chambers and then remove their dead bodies and take them to the crematoriums to burn. Any *Sonderkommando* who refused this task would find himself doomed. Belzec's gas chambers were built to kill more than 1,000 people at a time. At Sobibor, gas chamber capacity was increased from 600 to 1,200 people.

The most infamous of the extermination camps was Auschwitz. It was a complex mixture of camps and sub-camps. Auschwitz I was a concentration camp. Auschwitz II, also known as Auschwitz–Birkenau, was the extermination camp, with gas chambers and crematoriums at Birkenau, and Auschwitz III, also known as Buna–Monowice, was a labor camp. In addition, there was a POW camp and a number of sub-camps. The location was desirable as Auschwitz had railroad connections and it could be generally secluded from the areas around it. As an extermination camp, Auschwitz–Birkenau was a killing factory, with mass murders beginning systematically on July 4, 1942. In addition to Jews, Roma and Sinti (Gypsies) and non-Jewish Poles were murdered there. Over the main entrance gate stood the sign "Arbeit macht frei," meaning "Work will make you free." That was hardly the case and meant to deceive.

Rudolf Höss was the commandant of Auschwitz from May 1940 to December 1943. He oversaw the extermination camp. Höss "boasted that each of his four gas chambers could kill 2,000 people at a time. It is believed that about 1.5 million Jews were murdered there. Also killed at Auschwitz were approximately 19,000 Gypsies and 12,000 Soviet POWs. Another 50,000 died from other causes" (Roleff 18). In his autobiography, Höss notes that he would have never questioned or disobeyed orders to kill Jews and others brought to the extermination camp.

Between 6,000 and 7,000 people were needed to run the operation at Auschwitz, a small number compared to the staggering number of lives lost. Both SS and civilians worked there, including guards, messenger girls and medical personnel. Prisoners also were pressed into service. Inmates who worked in the storage buildings where the possessions of the deceased were stockpiled might pilfer items at great risk to themselves as these could be traded or bartered. *Kapos* were used in the selecting of prisoners for life or death; the SS made the choices but the *kapos* separated families, unloaded luggage, made sure prisoners lined up, took dead bodies from train cars, searched the transports for valuables and cleaned the railway cars and the platform. In addition to duties described earlier, *Sonderkommandos* helped those about to be gassed to undress, led out to be shot those who appeared troublesome, stoked the fires that burned the bodies, extracted gold from victims' teeth, cut their hair and awaited the same fate as the newly deceased. On average, those who did this work lived an additional four months, long enough to train their replacements before being executed themselves.

Auschwitz also was the scene of gruesome medical experiments. Prisoners were mutilated, dissected, infected and murdered in the name of science. The after-effects for those who survived the experiments often proved fatal. The notorious doctor, Josef Mengele, did research on twins and dwarfs that was horrifying. He fled to Berlin with the medical records when the Nazis tried to destroy evidence of their misdeeds.

When it became clear, in January 1945, that the Soviets soon would liberate Auschwitz, the Nazis made a concerted effort to destroy signs of the atrocities they had committed. They burned records, blew up the crematoriums and destroyed the warehouses filled with the possessions of their victims. Finally, they forced the remaining prisoners into death marches to German held territories. Many died or were executed along the way.

What was it like for someone who was transported to a death camp? The journey would be by train, with railroad cars crammed with people. There was a bucket in the car for a toilet. The only food and water would be what the passengers brought with them. The body of anyone who died during the journey was left in the car with the living until the train stopped, often days later. Some suffocated, as there was little ventilation in the cramped cars. Some froze to death in cold weather.

When the train stopped, the captives exited. Their luggage and possessions were left at the platform and their jewelry was given to the guards. Then, there was a selection, where SS men determined who would live and who would die. Those to be gassed went to the left; those spared to the right. The condemned were taken to changing rooms. Efforts to calm and deceive them might include signs telling them to remember where they hung their clothes so that they could retrieve them after being showered and deloused. Sometimes they were given soap and towels. They were then led to what they thought were shower rooms. In truth, they were gas chambers.

Those who went to the right were given prisoner uniforms. Their heads were shaved. At Auschwitz, their arms were tattooed. If they were given a cup or a bowl, it was a precious commodity as they needed it to receive food. After that came more humiliation, forced labor, roll calls and ongoing selections. Their lives could be taken at any moment.

Of the six million Jews murdered during the Holocaust, one and a half million were children and teens. Death, however, did not discriminate by age and for many who perished, their trip to the camps was their final stop on life's journey.

Scripted scenes and monologues

1. Monologue – *And Then They Came for Me: Remembering the World of Anne Frank* by James Still

> *YOUNG EVA is a 15-year-old Jewish teenager living in Nazi-occupied Amsterdam. In the following monologue, she narrates for the audience what happened the day her entire family was arrested by the Nazis and sent to concentration camps.*
> *(This monologue contains some lines which were originally written for other characters in the full script, as well as two lines (in bold) which have been added, based on stage directions, to clarify the action.)*

YOUNG EVA. My name is Eva Geringer. Today is my birthday. I am 15 years old. This morning I woke up. I went down to breakfast to open my presents. And then they came for me.

After we are arrested, my family is transported to Westerbork – a transit camp ... a kind of holding camp where there are thousands of other Jewish and Gypsy families. Waiting. A few days later they put us on another train. Two days, three days ... four days ... We don't know when it is day. We don't know when it is night. The train is like cattle cars ... A hundred people are pushed together in one car. Lying ... sitting ... Sometimes the train stops, the doors open, bread is thrown in, buckets of water for us to drink. Three days, four days ... It's hot. Boiling hot. And the doors are closed. And bolted shut from the outside. Where are they taking us?

The train stops. The doors of the train open. (*Sunlight floods the stage, blinding Young Eva and the others.*) At least we can stretch and breathe a bit of air. But then we saw on the platform the big sign "Auschwitz" and we knew this was the death camps. **My mother hands me a coat and hat and says "Put it on, Evi." It's hot but I put them on anyway.** The SS officer looks me up and down and finally indicates for me to go to the left. Soon Mutti* joins me. I'm the youngest person left in our group. As ridiculous as I look, this hat and coat make me look older and save my life.

*MOO-tee (Mother)

SPOTLIGHT ACTIVITY

And Then They Came for Me

"Poses"

Prior to engaging in this three-part activity, students should read Eva's monologue from *And Then They Came for Me*, on the previous page.

Part I

1   The teacher calls "Pose #1," and all students individually create a pose which reflects what Eva is doing and/or feeling at the beginning of the monologue.
2   The teacher calls "Pose #2," and the students strike a pose that reflects her feelings and/or actions during the middle of the monologue.
3   Finally, the teacher calls Pose #3, and the students create a pose that reflects Eva's feelings and/or actions at the end of the monologue.

Part II
Have the students divide into groups of three. One person in each group will play Eva, another student plays Mother, and the third student plays the SS Officer. Next, the above activity is repeated with the following variations:

1   When the teacher calls "Pose #1," the student playing Eva strikes a pose that communicates her feelings and/or actions at the beginning of the monologue.
2   When the teacher calls "Pose #2," the second actor joins Eva as her Mother. Together they demonstrate the feelings and/or actions that they are experiencing during the middle of the monologue.
3   When the teacher calls "Pose #3," the third person joins and all three create poses that reflect the feelings and/or actions of Eva, Mother, and the SS Officer at the end of the monologue.

Part III
For this phase, students may stay in their groups or form new groups of three.

1   Have the actors enact an original scene that involves Eva and two other characters. These can be Mother and the SS Officer or new characters based upon those mentioned in the monologue, such as family members, train passengers or camp personnel. The scenes can be created with or without dialogue.

After seeing all three phases, discuss how the activity provides insight into Eva's emotions in the monologue. Ask for volunteers to perform the monologue.

2. Monologue – *And A Child Shall Lead* by Michael Slade

MARTIN is 10 years old and is the "new kid" in the Terezin (Theresienstadt) concentration camp. He comes from a wealthy Prague family. He doesn't fit in on many levels. MARTIN has just arrived and has been placed in the boys' barracks. He doesn't understand what is happening, as he makes clear in this scene with the other boys. (The ellipses represent lines of dialogue from the other boys which have been omitted.)

MARTIN. Where's my room?
…
There must be some mistake.
…
You don't understand. I want to speak to someone in charge. I'm Martin Lowy. I didn't do anything wrong. They came to our house. They chased away the servants. They made us get in a line. I got separated from my parents. I tried to tell them, but no one would listen. I was pushed into a boxcar with all these people I didn't even know. They closed the doors. The train started moving, and when it stopped, we were here. It's a mistake. I'm Martin Lowy. My father is Vaclav Lowy. My mother is Etela. I have a little brother, Josef. I live at 317 Maisel Street in Prague.
…
I don't belong here! And I'm hungry. I haven't eaten since they took us from our house.
…
Where's the adult in charge?
…
I want to go home.

3. Monologue – *And A Child Shall Lead* by Michael Slade

MIROSLAV is a teenage boy who has been imprisoned in the Theresienstadt ghetto-camp. MIROSLAV has come up with the idea to create a secret newspaper chronicling actual events and conditions in Terezin. His friends agree to help him, even though the penalty if they are caught would be death. They name the newspaper "VEDEM," which means "we are leading" in Czech.
In this scene, lights come up on MIROSLAV in a hiding spot as he is writing.

MIROSLAV. (*With great urgency.*) Vedem Report. "Wandering Around Terezin." Today I visited the so-called hospital to report on it for this newspaper. Men and women of all ages, as well as children, were crowded into a long, dark, smelly corridor. There was barely enough room to stand. Crowds were pushing. Disease and suffering were everywhere.

I started to worry about the risks I was placing my own health in. The few doctors were overwhelmed with the number of patients and lack of supplies. Even so, they kept working, tirelessly, endlessly. Suddenly a man rushed in, "Dr. Herz!" he called, trying to catch his breath.

"You're on the list!" "What list?" Dr. Herz asked, still working, not even taking his eyes from his patient. "The Polish transport." The man answered. "You're leaving tonight." Dr. Herz stopped. He is one of only a handful of doctors in the camp. For a short time, the entire area was filled with a death–like silence. Finally, Dr. Herz spoke. "Then I will have to work fast. There is much to do here." He worked right up until the moment he had to leave for the transport.

4. Monologue – *The Survivor* by Susan Nanus, based on the memoirs of Jack Eisner

> *HALINA* is the 15-year-old girlfriend of Jacek (Ya-tzek). With her blond her and fair features, she survived for a time by posing as a Polish peasant girl.*
> *(We hear a sad mournful sound as the spotlight comes up on HALINA. She speaks as if speaking to Jacek.)*

HALINA. It seems like I spent my whole life waiting to be with you. On the Aryan side, in the concentration camp … You. You were the reason I got up and stood in roll call for hours. The reason I did slave labor in the munitions factory filling bullets with chemicals. The reason I didn't kill myself when they made me a prostitute for the SS.

When they separated us at Maidanek,** I tried to memorize your face. When they shaved my head, I worried what you'd think. When my period stopped I was afraid I could never have your child. But what scared me most was that you would die and I would be left alone. That I'd get through, but you wouldn't be there. And then one day, I realized that *I* was the one coughing blood, and *I* was the one getting sicker, and that *I* wasn't the one who was going to be left alone.

When we were liberated, they carried me out of Bergen–Belsen on a stretcher. They told me they were sending me to a hospital in Sweden and put me on a ship.

Only you could've found me there. When I heard your voice, it was like out of a dream. And I started calling your name and suddenly you were hugging me and kissing me and I could smell your smell and I couldn't stop crying. Because I wanted to live and be with you. I wanted to comfort you. I wanted to share whatever life was left. But it was too late.

(*Pause.*) I died in your arms. At least we shared that, didn't we?

*Ha-LEE-na
**my-DAH-nek

5. Monologue – *And A Child Shall Lead* by Michael Slade

> *MARTIN LOWY is 10 years old. He is imprisoned, along with thousands of other Jews, in the Terezin ghetto-camp in Czechoslovakia. He comes from a wealthy Prague family and he loves to draw.*

In this monologue, MARTIN writes a letter to his brother, even though he doesn't know where his brother or his parents are, and there is no way to send mail. He has decided to write letters anyway, and to save them until he sees his family again.

MARTIN. Dear Brother, Sometimes it's hard to believe I've only been here for six months. My memories of our life in Prague seem more and more like a dream. Like a story I was once told, but that never really happened. I don't remember ever not being hungry. I don't remember ever not being frightened. But the scariest part is that it's getting harder and harder to remember what you and Mommy and Daddy look like. I try to draw you all. I close my eyes and try so hard to picture your faces, but I can't. Would I recognize you if I saw you? Would you recognize me?

(*Pause.*)

They've started to do a lot of work around the camp. Old buildings are being painted. New structures seem to be being built. Gardens are being dug. They've put up a sign calling Terezin "The Jewish Settlement Area." No one is sure why. But the rumor is that the Germans have agreed to let the Red Cross visit. Hopes are high that conditions will change, and not a moment too soon. Despite the fresh paint, things have gotten so much worse. There is even less food. There is even more sickness. This morning, Alena and I saw a mother holding a small child … maybe one or two years old. It was so hungry it didn't even have enough strength to cry. A hawk was perched nearby on one of the fortress walls … watching. It knew the child was about to die.

(*Pause.*)

When I get out of here, when I grow up, I want to become a doctor … to take care of sick children.

Love, Martin.

P.S. I drew you a picture of the mother and the baby and the hawk.

6. Monologue – *The Survivor* by Susan Nanus, based on the memoirs of Jack Eisner

RUDY comes from a religious (Hasidic) Jewish family. He is telling Lutek the story of what happened when the Nazis came for him and his family.
Lights up on RUDY and Lutek in a hiding place. RUDY's face is dirty and his clothes are torn.

RUDY. (*To Lutek.*) They kicked in the door and started hitting us with clubs and pushing us down the stairs. We didn't even have time to get our coats. When we got outside, the street was full of people from every building on the block, and there were SS troops and Ukrainian guards with machine guns and dogs all over the place. It was impossible to escape. People were crying and begging, but my father didn't even look up. He'd put on his tallis* and was praying right in the middle of that hellhole.

I couldn't believe it. The Germans are whipping and pushing us toward the depot and he's praying Sh'ma Yisrael!** I kept looking for a way out. My mother was crying and holding onto me, and I didn't know what to do. And then I notice that the cattle cars are only guarded on one side and there's a chance to make a run for it. So, I tell him, "Tateh.*** Let's try to escape. I see a way out." And he says, "no, no, my son. This is God's will. Only the Messiah can change anything."

(*With tears of fury.*) Can you believe it? It's death, it's the end, and he's still waiting!****

*Prayer shawl
**Shɔ-MAH Yis-ro-ALE the most important prayer in Judaism, proclaiming that there is one God
***TA-teh Yiddish for "Father"
****waiting for the coming of the Messiah

7. Scene for two actors – *Anne Frank & Me* by Cherie Bennett

NICOLE BERNHARDT is a 16-year-old French Jew. She is also Nicole Burns, a non-Jewish American teenager in "another reality" set in contemporary times. Her high school class has been assigned to read "The Diary of Anne Frank," but Nicole has not completed the assignment.
ANNE FRANK is a 15-year-old girl who perished in the Holocaust after chronicling her life in hiding in a diary which became one of the most famous books of all time.
In this scene, NICOLE BERNHARDT is being transported on a train to a concentration camp, and has just met a girl named ANNE who is on the train with her. (The ellipses represent lines which have been cut for clarity and simplicity.)
(The girl turns around. It is ANNE FRANK, thin, huge eyes. Their eyes meet. Some memory is instantly triggered in NICOLE. She knows this girl, knows things about her. But how?)

ANNE. Spreekn U Nerderlander? (*Srpeck-in Ooo Ned-er-lahn-der?*) (*NICOLE just stares.*) So you speak French, then? Is this better?
…
Have you been in here a long time?
NICOLE. Seventeen days, starting just outside Paris.
ANNE. It smells like it.
NICOLE. Does it? I can't even tell anymore.
ANNE. It's all right. It's not important.
NICOLE. Look, I know this sounds crazy, but … I know you.
ANNE. Have you been to Amsterdam?
NICOLE. No, never.
ANNE. Well, I've never been to Paris. Although I will go someday, I can assure you of that.

NICOLE. I do know you. Your name is … Anne Frank.

ANNE. (*Shocked.*) That's right! Who are you?

NICOLE. Nicole Bernhardt. I know so much about you … you were in hiding for a long time, in a place you called … the Secret Annex …

ANNE. How could you know that?

NICOLE. (*Her memory is flooded.*) You were with your parents, and your older sister … Margot! And … some other people …

ANNE. Mr. Pfeffer and the Van Pels, they're all back there asleep –

NICOLE. Van Daans!

ANNE. (*Shocked.*) I only called them that in my diary. How could you know that?

NICOLE. And Peter! Your boyfriend's name was Peter!

ANNE. How could you know that???

NICOLE. You thought your parents would disapprove that you were kissing him –

ANNE. How is this possible?

NICOLE. You kept a diary. I read it.

ANNE. But … I left my diary in the Annex when the Gestapo came. You couldn't have read it.

NICOLE. But I did.

ANNE. How?

NICOLE. I don't know.

ANNE. (*Skeptical.*) This is a very, very strange conversation.

NICOLE. I feel like it was … I know this sounds crazy … but I feel like it was in the future.

ANNE. This is a joke, right? Peter put you up to this.

NICOLE. No –

ANNE. Daddy, then, to take my mind off –

NICOLE. No.

ANNE. (*Cynical.*) Maybe you're a mind reader! (*She closes her eyes.*) What number am I thinking of right now?

NICOLE. I have no idea. Do you believe in time travel?

ANNE. I'm to believe that you're from the future? Really, I'm much more intelligent than I look.

NICOLE. I don't know how I know all this. I just do.

ANNE. Maybe you're an angel.

NICOLE. That would certainly be news to me.

ANNE. Is the rest of your family here?

NICOLE. My mother. They killed my father.

ANNE. I'm sorry.

NICOLE. And my boyfriend. And my best friend. (*A beat.*) Do you think God is watching us, right now?

ANNE. Yes.

NICOLE. Someone told me God must be on vacation. Maybe there is no God. Maybe we made him up so we wouldn't all just go crazy.

ANNE. I don't believe that.

NICOLE. Then nothing makes any sense. My best friend, Mimi, died because she tried to save our lives. And my boyfriend died because he felt betrayed by my father and so he betrayed us in return. My father died to save Jewish lives, but he ended up killing innocent people. All that suffering and death. I can't make any sense of it. So I really want to know, where is God now?

ANNE. Right here, beside us.

NICOLE. *(Bitterly.)* We're in a cattle car.

ANNE. *(Pointing up to the tiny window.)* But we can still see the stars.

NICOLE. Are you scared?

ANNE. Yes.

NICOLE. Even though you have faith in God?

ANNE. Yes.

NICOLE. I'll be with you, no matter what happens.

ANNE. And I'll be with you. *(A few beats of the rumblings of the train.)*

NICOLE. It will be a work camp, won't it?

ANNE. Yes.

NICOLE. David was wrong, I'm sure of it.

ANNE. David?

NICOLE. Never mind.

ANNE. *(Both scared and brave.)* Nicole, if you're from the future and you really read my diary … then you know what happens to me.

NICOLE. No –

ANNE. Yes. You can tell me.

NICOLE. *(Chagrined.)* I never finished it.

ANNE. You never – *(She bursts out laughing.)* Peter put you up to this!

NICOLE. But I did read a very juicy part about you and him, how you loved him and didn't think you needed to wait until you were "a suitable age" –

ANNE. I'm a free thinker!

NICOLE. You sound like my little sister. She's planning to run away with Clark Gable.

ANNE. Don't tell Peter, but I don't think he's the perfect boy for me after all. I'd like to break a million hearts, wouldn't you?

NICOLE. Oh, yes!

ANNE. And see the whole world –

NICOLE. And have a million adventures …

ANNE. I want to see Paris!

NICOLE. Oh, it's wonderful – after the war I'll take you everywhere. The Louvre, and the Eiffel Tower –

ANNE. Where do you want to go?

NICOLE. Oh, I don't know … Palestine, maybe.

ANNE. Really?

NICOLE. I think a friend of mine is there.

ANNE. Then we'll go there. Everything is possible. Don't you see?

Verbatim testimony historical narratives

1. From the testimony of Erna Anolik – "Camps (Labor/Concentration)"

(https://iwitness.usc.edu/SFI/BrowseTopics.aspx?TopicID=7&ClipID=112)

Born: December 15, 1923, in Uzhorod, Czechoslovakia
In a November, 1996 interview, Erna Anolik recalls arrival and intake procedures at Auschwitz-Birkenau concentration camp.

ERNA

When we first came to Auschwitz, we were taken to an area where – we were marched in an area where they shaved our heads, we were undressed, and given grey dresses. No underwear. Just a grey dress. And wooden shoes. Then, we were taken back to these barracks. On the way to the place where they shaved our heads and took our clothing, there was a big ditch where apparently people from the train who were too sick to move were put into these ditches with the dead – the living with the dead … just left there. (*Crying.*) And every morning, about four o'clock, we went out to what was called the appell,* where they counted us. Lined up and they counted us. We stood there for several hours, until somebody came and went through the whole camp counting. Then we would go back into our barracks. We didn't work. We were not assigned any work. But I remember I volunteered to go and pick up the coffee or bread, whatever there was, at another camp, because I always thought that maybe (*crying*), maybe I'll see my parents. Of course, I never did.

*ah-PELL. Meaning "roll call." Literally "the counting"

2. From the testimony of Ellis Lewin – "Camps (Labor/Concentration)"

(http://iwitness.usc.edu/SFI/BrowseTopics.aspx?TopicID=7&ClipID=160)

Born: May 22, 1932, in Łódź, Poland*
In this December, 1996 interview, Ellis recalls the scene during arrival at Auschwitz-Birkenau death camp and the separation of families that took place.

ELLIS

When we arrived to Auschwitz, the minute they opened the wagons, it was just total, complete misery. Beatings and screamings and beatings and barking of dogs and growling of dogs and whistles of trains, and screaming and beating and screaming and commands given. It was just like you open the doors, and all of a sudden you find yourself in this inferno, in this, in this unimaginable horror that you, as an adult or a child, would see in nightmares … And we were just holding onto each other. And I don't know, within minutes, my mother and my sister were dragged to one side and I was dragged with my dad to another. We were told to go to another side. And, uh, I never had a chance to say goodbye to my mother. Never had a chance to say goodbye to my sister. The pace, the speed of this thing. It was done by design. It was done for the person to not be able to comprehend or understand or in any way be able to think for a second what was happening. It was just incredible. It was just an incredible situation. And as I tell it to you now, it's difficult for me even to describe it, because it was happening on a minute-to-minute situation.

And I got into this line. It was this big line. And I saw my mother on another side, where the women went. And I never saw her cry. I never saw her reach out. Last time I saw her, she was just hanging onto my sister. And my dad hollered to her, "You take care of her, I'll take care of him!" in Yiddish. "And whatever we have to do!" This was the last word I heard. Then, my dad threw me in front of him, and he says, "Keep walking very tall." Because we were observing what was going on in the front, you know, in the front of the lines. And the one thing you didn't want is for the Germans to see that you were holding onto your child, because that was the whole idea – to break up the family, murder the whole family. That was the genocide of the whole thing. So, by not identifying that this is your child, there was a little bit of an edge you had to possibly survive. The fact that you were on your own and you sort of didn't belong to any family.

LUHDJ

3. From the testimony of Itka Zygmuntowicz – "Camps (Labor/Concentration)"

(http://iwitness.usc.edu/SFI/BrowseTopics.aspx?TopicID=7&ClipID=163)

Born: April 15, 1926, in Ciechanów, Poland
In this March, 1996 interview, Itka describes a day of her life in the Auschwitz II- Birkenau death camp in Poland.
(NOTE: This testimony has been edited slightly for clarity, with additional words in parentheses, and omitted words indicated by ellipses.)

ITKA

I'd like to describe a day in Auschwitz. We would get up in the morning. To begin with, we slept and worked and wore the same clothes all the time. Every few months, they would disinfect. Every day, we had to stand and they counted. And that made us responsible. So say that … let's say one would want to run away. And if you had a heart, you would say, "How can I endanger all?" Because then we would all suffer. You could sometimes stand for hours or for days. Dead or alive, everybody had to be accountable. After the appell,* we would always march in five: "Eins, zwei, drei, vier, funf, links! Ein, zvie, drei…!"** Still I hear it in my … on both sides, the guards with dogs and marching. When you marched out – sometimes we never knew who would come back, because sometimes, at random, there were selections at the gate. They would take [people] away.

I remember there were instances where if one of us looked pale, the other would (*Makes gesture of pinching her cheeks.*). Sometimes, I would do it to Bina.*** Sometimes she'd say "Yitkele,**** you look so pale." And she would pinch my cheeks to make it look redder. First of all, they did everything to make us sick … Then, they would take you out because you were sick.

…

And then at work, we carried the gravel or the stones from one place to the other. Sometimes, they would mock us. And I remember, they would point to the gas chamber (and say): "Where is your God now?" And inside myself, I said (*Hand on heart.*), "Our God is *here*. But where is yours?"

*ah–PELL
**AYn, zvy, dry, veer, foonf, links! Ayn, zvy, dry… Meaning: One, two, three, four, five, Left! One, two, three…
***BEE-nah. Itka's friend in the camp
****YIT-kuh-luh. A nickname for Itka

4. From the testimony of Itka Zygmuntowicz – "Resilience"

(https://iwitness.usc.edu/sfi/BrowseTopics.aspx?TopicID=164&ClipID=1228)

Born: April 15, 1926, in Ciechanów, Poland
In this segment of Itka's 1996 interview, she explains that when she was on the brink of giving up, a new friendship with a fellow Auschwitz prisoner probably saved her life.

ITKA

I didn't care at that time about anything. In Auschwitz, when they made the appell* – the counting – if you weren't accountable, or if you didn't stand, or if you looked sick or you sat down, you would go to the gas chambers. And I was sitting. I didn't want to go out. They gave bread, and I was hungry, but I couldn't eat. How can you eat when you feel …? And I saved the piece of bread. I couldn't eat it. And in the morning, I woke up, it was gone. That was the final pushing that I needed. And a girl – Esther, I don't remember her last name – she came from a prison, so she must have done something before the war. Or maybe … I don't know. I didn't know her. And she said to me, "Poor Yitkele,** somebody stole her bread." And I was so grateful for that little compassion that she showed.

The next day, I didn't eat. I just couldn't, I just … I woke up in the middle of the night, and to my horror, Esther is eating my bread. And I was just shattered to pieces. I couldn't understand. She was the one who said "Poor Yitkele, somebody stole your bread." She was the one who stole it! That was the last straw. At that point I said, "I don't care what's happening anymore." I didn't intend at any point in my life to commit suicide, but I just was ready to give up. And as I was sitting, crying and everything, a girl came over, and she asked me: "Why are you crying?" I didn't answer her. But there was something urgent in her voice; something caring, it sounded. And she didn't know why I was crying. So she thought maybe I'm hungry. So she took a piece of bread from hers and she broke off (*makes gesture of breaking off a piece of bread*). She said, "Take it." I was afraid to accept the bread, because knowing what's happening to us there, that we were brought here to die either in the gas chambers or of sickness or fatigue or whatever, I was afraid to have a friend. I couldn't afford to lose anyone. But there was something in her voice, in her face. And maybe the need in me. Because I always *loved* people and I cared. I always had friends. And I knew if I accepted bread, she was offering more. So finally, I took the piece of bread. And Bina*** and I became inseparable. Bina became like more than a sister. Because under those conditions, you might not think a lot of a piece of bread, but in Auschwitz, a piece of bread means prolonging life. And maybe another day could mean liberation or just another day of survival.

*ah-PELL
**YIT-kuh-luh. A nickname for Itka
***BEE-nah

5. From the testimony of Eva Kor – "Auschwitz"

(https://iwitness.usc.edu/sfi/BrowseTopics.aspx?TopicID=5&ClipID=459)

*Born: January 31, 1934, in Port, Romania
In this March, 1995 interview, Eva discusses her arrival at Auschwitz-Birkenau and how she and her twin sister Miriam were brought to Josef Mengele's* medical experimentation barracks as 10-year-old girls.*

EVA

I thought for a while it seemed like I am watching something that's not really related to me. I was numb. I closed my eyes and I said, "Maybe this is a nightmare, and if I close them and open them up again, maybe the whole thing will disappear." It didn't. We sat there naked in the company of complete strangers for the better part of the day. Later on in the afternoon, we were lined up for registration and tattooing. They cut our braids down and the so-called barber explained that we are privileged because we are twins and we are permitted to have our own hair. Then we were lined up for registration and tattooing. And when my turn came, I decided I was going to fight back. That I was not going to let them do to me whatever they wanted without fighting back. And so, they started the number and I began screaming and kicking. And my number never came out clear. Two SS** and two women prisoners had to restrain me. And I said to myself, "Well, I need to find some kind of an excuse, because nice girls do not do that." And I said, "I will cooperate with you if you bring my mother here." And I remember they said, "Well, you could see her tomorrow." And I would think, "Really, how on earth will they reunite us tomorrow when they just ripped me apart from her earlier this morning?" It seemed to be such a bold lie, that I couldn't really accept it. Unfortunately, my poor sister believed it. She kept waiting for us to see my mother. She never told me about it until 1985.

They had a very tough time with me. I decided that I was not going to be a very cooperating victim. And so, I kicked, screamed, and it's very difficult, because the way they do that number, they heated a pen, like an old-fashioned writing pen – they heated it over open flame. Then, they dipped it into ink and then dot by dot, they had to make out the letter "A, dash, 7063." So, if you keep wiggling your arm, it is very difficult to make a good number. Miriam tells me that I bit the SS who was holding my arm. I still don't remember. But I was a nice little girl, right? I wouldn't do something like that.

*Joseph Mengele – known as "The Angel of Death" of Auschwitz, conducted horrific medical experiments on over 3,000 twins during the Holocaust, supposedly in the name of medical science. Eva and her sister Miriam were among only a very few of his victims to survive
**SS – "Schutzstaffel" – the foremost Nazi agency of terror. One branch of the SS was specifically tasked with running the concentration/extermination camps

Suggested props/costumes for Chapter 4 historical narrative scenes

- Women's sweaters
- Men's sweaters, jackets
- Men's and women's hats
- Small suitcases (1930s/1940s look)
- Red cloths for armbands (NO insignias)
- A loaf of bread (real or fake)
- Several pieces of hard bread (edible)
- Tin coffee can
- Rocks: gravel and larger rocks
- Scissors
- Ink pen (old fashioned)
- Battery-operated candle/flame

Devised theater activity

Create a scene which juxtaposes the de-humanization of entire segments of mankind, detailed in the verbatim testimony of a US soldier, with Shakespeare's words of adulation for the human form and mind.

Scene components

1   Portions or all of the *verbatim testimony* of liberator Howard Cwick
2   *Hamlet's speech* from Act II, Scene 2 of Shakespeare's *Hamlet*
3   The *physical action* of "sculpting" a human being, as an artist would sculpt a human figure from clay
4   Two or more *tableaus*
5   *Musical underscoring*
6   *Choral Repetition* – of words, physical gestures, or both

Texts

1   Excerpted testimony of Howard Cwick,* a Jewish American who took part in the liberation of the Buchenwald concentration camp in Germany as a US serviceman in 1945.

*Zwik. *A longer version of this testimony appears in the Verbatim testimony historical narrative Activity in the chapter "Liberation"*

When we walked in the gates [of the camp], every so often there were one or two or three dead bodies on the ground. Alongside the buildings were large wooden wagons with bodies. Naked bodies stacked like cord wood where they were thrown. Arms, legs, skeletal heads. There had to be eight or nine high and maybe sixteen to twenty across. And there were three or four of these wagons right out in the open. And what struck me was the number of dead bodies we saw just lying around. Like wherever they fell, that's where they lay ...

We came across a bunk that was either dragged outside or was stored outside, and I photographed it. The people, the prisoners, were still in it. It was still burning. Which means, just moments before we came into the camp, it had to have been set ablaze with the people still in it. I guess it was [the Germans'] last act of bestiality that they could perform.

2   Hamlet's speech, from Act II, Scene 2 of *Hamlet*, by William Shakespeare

What a piece of work is a man!
How noble in reason, how infinite in faculty!
In form and moving how express and admirable!
In action how like an angel, in apprehension how like a god!
The beauty of the world. The paragon of animals.

Staging considerations, choices and tips

1   How can you stage your scene so that the juxtaposition of the texts is best emphasized? Should you stage it with a split stage? Or with the physical actions interwoven?
2   Decide whether you want to alternate lines between Cwick's testimony and Shakespeare's dialogue, or present one text in its entirety followed by the other.
3   Consider having one actor read Cwick's testimony, but potentially include multiple actors in the reading of Hamlet's speech.
4   Which lines will be repeated and/or spoken chorally? From which text will the repeated words and phrases come? One or the other, or both?
5   Select one or more actors to be the sculptor(s), and one or more to be the forms being sculpted.

CHAPTER

5
Fleeing and hiding

Context

During the Holocaust, approximately six million Jews were murdered. Of Europe's pre-war Jewish population of children, only six to eleven percent survived compared to thirty-three percent of adult Jews. According to statistics from the Jewish Virtual Library's article, "Jewish Victims of the Holocaust: Hidden Children," at the start of World War II, 1.6 million Jewish children lived in areas that Germany and its allies would control; by the end in 1945, between one and 1.5 million of these children had died (1). Options for surviving the Nazis' plan to exterminate the Jews were limited, difficult and dangerous. Survival for some was possible because they fled from targeted European areas prior to the beginning of the carnage. Others' lives were spared because of their decision to go into hiding. Neither option came with a guarantee of life.

Prior to the start of the war, there were Jews who sought to escape from Nazi controlled areas. Some 90,000 German and Austrian Jews fled to nearby countries between 1933 and 1939. Once the war began, it was harder to go. Although Germany allowed emigration until November 1941, the government made it difficult to leave. The problem was further complicated by the fact that few countries were willing to take Jews trying to escape. Some who had been fortunate enough to flee Germany found themselves in countries that were later taken over by the Nazis, putting them again in jeopardy. Nearly 30,000 Polish Jews were able to flee to the Soviet Union between 1939 and 1941 and, although typically exiled to the harsh interior of the country, many survived. Neutral countries such as Switzerland and Portugal also were desirable destinations, although not all Jewish refugees were granted entry. An escape route via the Balkans was used from 1937 to 1944 by the Zionist movement to carry Jews to Palestine. Perhaps surprisingly, in areas secured by Italian forces, such as southern France, Greece and Yugoslavia, the Italians gave safe-haven to Jews from mid-1942 to September 1943.

Helping Jews to flee were Jewish organizations such as the World Jewish Congress, the Jewish Agency for Palestine and the Joint Distribution Committee. Non-Jews who were sympathetic to the Jewish plight and those who were opposed to the Nazis also provided aid. Underground networks were active in southern France and able to smuggle Jews to safety in Spain, Switzerland and northern Italy. In the French village of Chambon-sur-Lignon, Protestants harbored between 3,000 and 5,000 seeking sanctuary. Elsewhere, Catholics saved Jewish lives. The resistance movement in Nazi-occupied Denmark launched a nationwide rescue, helping nearly 8,000 people, most of whom were Jews, to escape by boat to Sweden. There, over a two-week period, small boats carrying between 12 and 14 passengers crossed narrow waters on a life-saving mission.

For those who could not get away, an alternative was hiding, although this was not an easy choice. Making the decision to go into hiding could be agonizing. Parents and children might be separated because it was not always possible for families to hide together. Separation brought additional worries as parents and

IMAGE 5.1 Group portrait of youth hiding in LeChambon

children were each concerned about what might happen to the other and if their loved ones would survive. An additional worry was whether family members would be able to find each other again if they had to hide separately because concealment often involved moving multiple times and loved ones not being told of the new locations. Some adults felt that hiding was not a viable option because they could not leave elderly or sick relatives behind. Others hoped to stay in place until the threat passed or the Allies were victorious. Sadly, there were those who simply did not have the means to go into hiding as it required money that rescuers sometimes needed or was necessary to pay for false documents. In addition to financial considerations, there were connections crucial to finding safe places and those willing to rescue others. For both Jews and those who might save them, the risks were tremendous and the punishments, if caught, severe. A wrong word, ill-prepared false documents, trusting the wrong person or even rumormonger could have dire consequences.

It might be surprising that more people were not willing to save Jews, but in addition to the dangers that they would face in doing so, there also was the history of antisemitism and the Nazis' negative portrayal of Jews that fostered fear and resentment, if not hatred, of those needing help. In addition to negative propaganda about Jews, the Nazis offered rewards such as money or food to those willing to turn in Jews. Another reason for not harboring Jews was support for the government's actions. Additionally, in places such as Poland, blackmailers were able to profit from the Jews' plight by demanding money or property in exchange for not turning in those under

IMAGE 5.2 Postcard photo of two men showing their wartime hiding place

threat. Even Jews might betray other Jews as was the case in Germany when the Gestapo (the German secret police) offered some an opportunity to avoid deportation if they would turn in others who had gone underground.

There were basically two ways to hide for those who elected to do so. If one's physical appearance allowed for it, a person might hide in plain sight. In other words, if the person did not look too Jewish and could pass as a non-Jew, with a new name and false identity papers, they might remain in the open. If, however, they needed to erase their existence to evade deportation or death, then they would have to find refuge where they would not be detected. Hiding places included, but were not limited to attics, basements, crawl spaces, sewers, barns, haystacks, chicken coops, forests, convents, parochial schools and orphanages. Those in hiding might not be able to move during bombing raids, making them more vulnerable to the attacks. Further, depending upon where they were concealed, they might not see daylight for months or years. For those in better circumstances, opportunities to move more freely might exist. The conditions encountered when hidden were as varied as the shelters provided.

Hiding was fraught with limitations. It was easier to conceal girls than boys. The Jewish custom of circumcision meant that Jewish boys could be identified as non-Christians. Families sometimes could hide together, but more often they had to do so separately. If a parent could accompany a child, it was likely to be the mother, as fathers had been sent to the camps. Children separated from their families might find themselves in the care of strangers, far from home, and enduring frightening travel to places of concealment. Further, hiding might require multiple moves. If a place became too dangerous or if the rescuers decided that they would no longer keep the Jews in their protection, it was necessary to find sanctuary elsewhere.

The Nazis searched diligently for hidden Jews, and children were especially vulnerable as there were actions targeted specifically at finding the young. The Nazis considered them useless mouths to feed and feared their ability to reproduce if they were allowed to live and grow to adulthood.

> Only 11 percent of the approximately 1.7 million European Jews under the age of sixteen alive in 1939 survived the Second World War. In other words, 1.5 million young Jews were killed during the Holocaust … But there were thousands of other Jewish children – somewhere between ten thousand and one hundred thousand of them – who were hidden during the Holocaust, who were not caught and who survived.
>
> (Greenfeld 2)

For a child, life in hiding meant learning to lie, suppressing emotions, remaining vigilant and giving up many of life's normal activities. If a hidden child became ill, it might be impossible to call a doctor as that could arouse suspicions. As a child grew, new clothes might have to be made from scraps of material or from the hand-me-downs of other youngsters. Food and water might be difficult to find, and it could be nearly impossible to bathe or to launder one's clothes. If a child was secreted by a Christian family, he or she might have to learn the rituals of their faith and practice it, giving up the observances of their Jewish religion. If in peril of discovery, a child might have to think quickly and speak convincingly; to do otherwise could be fatal.

Some of the groups that helped to save or hide children included Christians, members of resistance groups, humanitarians, organized rescue groups and religious parties. Their efforts included finding hiding places, moving children around, keeping records in code to elude discovery, as well as providing money and false papers. Those who rescued children had to, at times, concoct elaborate explanations as to why there was an unfamiliar child with them. They had the additional burdens of knowing that they could be denounced and punished at any time. Penalties included arrest, deportation or even death, and these could be applied to family members as well. Finances also were a consideration, as a child in hiding was an additional expense. One of the greatest worries was that of knowing that their charge was completely dependent upon them for everything – for life itself.

When the war was over, and children no longer remained hidden, life presented new challenges. Some had no parents or family with whom to reunite; some had been so young when they were hidden that they did not even know their biological parents. Some parents could not find their children. Some rescuers demanded money for the return of the child in their keeping. Other rescuers had grown fond of the child they protected and refused to surrender the youngster, making it necessary in certain cases for courts to decide custody. In some instances, those who had survived in hiding found that former homes had been plundered. Another problem was that simmering hatred for and blame of Jews for the war by non-Jews made it too dangerous to return to places that the survivors once had lived, leaving some stateless as well as homeless. In addition, there were those who experienced survivor guilt; they could not deal with the emotional repercussions of having lived when so many others had not. And although they had not had normal childhoods, some hidden children were told that they were too young to have really suffered. Nothing could be further from the truth.

Perhaps the best-known hidden child was Anne Frank. She was born Annelies Marie Frank on June 12, 1929, to Otto and Edith Frank in Frankfurt, Germany. The family fled to Amsterdam from Germany. Otto went first, followed by Edith and Anne's sister, Margot. Anne joined them in 1934. The Germans took over Amsterdam in 1940 and two years later began to send Jews from the Netherlands to the Westerbork transit camp and then to the extermination camps of Auschwitz-Birkenau and Sobibor. Along with four others, the Van Pels family and Fritz Pfeffer, the Franks hid in the Secret Annex at Prinsengracht 263 in central Amsterdam. The eight were helped by Johannes Kleiman, Victor Kugler, Bep Voskuijl and Miep Gies who brought them food, supplies and news. They survived in hiding for two years, but they were arrested by a Gestapo official and two Dutch police collaborators on August 4, 1944. The Franks were sent to Westerbork on August 8 and on September 4 they were sent to Auschwitz-Birkenau. Anne and Margot were selected for labor and moved to Bergen-Belsen in October 1944. The sisters died of typhus in March 1945.

Scripted scenes and monologues

1. Monologue – *The Diary of Anne Frank* by Francis Goodrich and Albert Hackett, newly adapted by Wendy Kesselman

> *ANNE FRANK, a Jewish teenager in Nazi-occupied Amsterdam, lives in hiding in the "Secret Annex" of an office building, along with her family and four others. She chronicles their daily lives in her diary.*
> *(Alone in her bed, ANNE wakes with a start, her shadow, enormous, illuminated on the wall. She speaks out.)*

ANNE. Just as I was falling asleep, my friend Hanneli* appeared, dressed in rags, her face thin and worn. She looked at me with such sadness in her eyes I could read the message in them: "Oh Anne, why have you deserted me? Help me, help me, rescue me from this hell!" If only I could. Why have I been chosen to live, and you die? Oh Hanneli, Hanneli, if you ever return, I'll take you in, share everything I have with you. Are you still alive? I keep seeing your enormous eyes, keep seeing myself in your place. You're a reminder of what my fate might have been.

IMAGE 5.3 Anne Frank at 11 years of age

What will we do if we're … no I mustn't write that down. But the question won't go away. It looms before me in total absolute horror.

HAH-nah-lee

SPOTLIGHT ACTIVITY

The Diary of Anne Frank

"Dreams"

In Anne's brief monologue from *The Diary of Anne Frank*, she recounts an image that she saw just as she was falling asleep. In this activity, students will create and stage a dream that Anne might have had while in hiding. The dream could be pleasant, such as her wedding or playing with childhood friends, or it might be dark or disturbing.

1   Divide students into pairs or small groups.
2   Allow students time to create and rehearse their scenes.
3   Have each group perform their scene for the rest of the class.
4   Allow each group to share why they thought that Anne might have this dream.

---

2. Monologue – *The Survivor* by Susan Nanus, based on the memoirs of Jack Eisner

> *LUTEK is a 15-year-old aristocratic boy from a rich Warsaw family. In this monologue, he speaks as if speaking to his friend Jacek, and recounts what happened to them both as they took part in the Warsaw Ghetto uprising and then attempted to flee.*

LUTEK. It was the best music we ever made. Better than Verdi. Better than the chorus in Beethoven's ninth. The sound of our guns and German screams and our laughter when we saw them run.

When you said it was time to get out of the ghetto, I followed you. Those sewers disgusted me, but I knew it was the only way out. The water was filthy and full of rats. The smoke pouring in from the burning ghetto was so thick, we could hardly breathe. But in spite of everything, we had hope. Maybe there was still a way to get out alive.

But then the thing I was scared of most finally happened. We were caught and beaten and locked into a cattle car.

I cut my hands raw pulling the barbed wire off that window. And I held you by your heels so you could crawl out and pull off the seal and break the lock. And then we opened the door and we could see the trees and the fields rolling by in the night. We were so close to being free.

I was scared to jump, but I was ready. Other kids were jumping from other cars, too. But the Germans guarding the roof started shooting. So you told me to throw my coat out first, so they'd shoot at that, and then jump.

That was a really good idea, Jacek.* But it didn't work. There were too many guards, and they saw me. And they shot me. And I sang Sh'ma Yisroel** as I bled to death on the gravel next to the railroad track. Somewhere between Warsaw and the gas chambers.

YAH-tzek

**(Shə-MAH Yis-ro-ALE)* the most important prayer in Judaism, proclaiming that there is one God

3. Scene for two actors – *The Diary of Anne Frank* by Francis Goodrich and Albert Hackett, newly adapted by Wendy Kesselman

> *ANNE (15) and PETER (17) are two Jewish teenagers hiding from the Nazis in a "Secret Annex" in Amsterdam along with their families. After two years in hiding together, the teens have developed a close relationship which is evolving into a romance.*
>
> *ANNE and PETER have just gone up to the attic, ANNE stumbling in the red high-heeled shoes that Miep (a Dutch friend who assists them) has given her.*

ANNE. They're so old-fashioned! I guess they don't realize how much more advanced we are.

PETER. You look nice.

ANNE. Really?

PETER. I like the shoes. I've always liked the shoes. (*ANNE holds out her feet.*)

ANNE. Miep always does everything just right.

PETER. She likes you a lot.

ANNE. I love her. But I hate having to ask for absolutely everything. Doesn't it make you miserable to be so dependent on people?

PETER. (*Lighting a candle on top of a crate.*) I'm not miserable anymore. I mean … even bumping into you on the stairs sometimes. I feel … (*He stops.*)

ANNE. I feel the same. (*PETER holds out a chair for her.*)

PETER. (*Grinning.*) You've changed. I use to think you were a real pain in the neck.

ANNE. My life before seems so unreal – nothing to do with who I am now. I see myself then as an utterly superficial girl. I wouldn't go back to being her for the world.

PETER. You sure know a lot about yourself, don't you? I guess it comes from all that writing you do.

ANNE. If I didn't – I mean write what I think, what I feel – I'd suffocate! (*He is silent, staring at her.*) I want to be a real writer one day. I know I can write – I'm my harshest critic – but who knows if I truly have talent or not. (*She pauses.*) What do you want to do?

PETER. (*Pulling up a crate, sitting down.*) I don't know. Some job that doesn't take much brains. Maybe if I had your drive –

ANNE. That's ridiculous.

PETER. No. It's true. I'm a complete idiot.

ANNE. You're too hard on yourself.

PETER. I didn't have much going for me on the outside.

ANNE. But don't you miss – Oh Peter, I miss so many things … (*Going to the window.*) Sometimes I dream I'm back in our old apartment. I wake up and wonder …why can't I run outside? (*She stops.*) Oh! You can see the moon from here – just like you said. How beautiful! (*Turning back into the* attic.) Look at our attic. The moonlight coming in.

PETER. (*Coming up behind her.*) Are you cold?

ANNE. No. Well, maybe just a little.

PETER. (*Putting his jacket around her shoulders.*) Here. (*Slowly he lifts his hand, touches a lock of her hair. She remains still.*)

ANNE. (*Turning toward him.*) Peter … have you ever kissed a girl?

PETER. I guess so.

ANNE. You have? When?

PETER. It wasn't a big deal or anything.

ANNE. Tell me.

PETER. On my birthday. I was blindfolded. I don't even know who the girl was. (*ANNE laughs.*)

ANNE. (*In a rush.*) There's nothing wrong with being kissed or anything. Though I'm sure Margot would never kiss a boy unless she were engaged to him. And I know Mother never touched a man before she met Pim.* My girlfriends would say, "Anne, how shocking!" But who cares what they'd say anyway? Everything's different now … here.

PETER. You called it our attic before. Do you really think it's ours?

ANNE. (*Quiet.*) I do.

PETER. You won't let them stop you coming here, will you?

ANNE. No. I promise. (*A pause.*) Maybe I'll bring one of my stories and read it to you sometime.

PETER. You'll come tomorrow night?

ANNE. If you want me to.

PETER. I do.

(**MR. FRANK** calls up to the attic: It's 9:50!)

ANNE. (*Smiling.*) I will then. (*She turns to go. Silence. Behind her, PETER holds his breath, then quickly, awkwardly kisses the back of her head. She doesn't move. Suddenly she turns, throws her arms around his neck, kisses him on the mouth. The kiss grows longer. In a daze they embrace. ANNE gazes at him, enraptured, then tears down the stairs without looking back. PETER blows out the candle.*)

*Pim is Anne's nickname for her father

4. Scene for two actors – *Angel in the Night* by Joanna Halpert Kraus

> *MANIA* is a Jewish teenager who has escaped from the ghetto. PAWLINA** is a Polish teenager who is secretly hiding MANIA and other Jews in her family's barn.*
> *PAWLINA is outfitting MANIA to look like a Polish country girl (blouse, long skirt, apron, bare feet, hair in long braids wound around her head) so that she can come out from hiding by pretending to be a non-Jew. PAWLINA places a large cross around MANIA's neck. MANIA recites Pater Nostra in Latin.*

MANIA. Panme nostrum quotidianum da nobis hodie et
Dimette nobis debita nostra, sicut et now dimittimus debitoribus nostris
Et ne non inducas in tentationem.
Amen.***

PAWLINA. (*Corrects her.*) You forgot the last line. "Sed libera nos a malo." Then, "Amen."

MANIA. (*Repeats correctly.*) Sed libera nos a malo. What does that mean?

PAWLINA. Deliver us from evil. Remember to cross yourself a lot too. Like this. (*Demonstrates touching with the three fingers of right hand, the forehead, heart, left shoulder, right shoulder. MANIA repeats.*) It's the little things like that that could give you away. Now here are your papers, put them in your pocket.

MANIA. (*Reads.*) Cecylia Kozlowski.

PAWLINA. She died three months ago.

MANIA. (*Frightened.*) What if they know that?

PAWLINA. The church records burned in a fire. They can't check. It wasn't easy to get.

MANIA. (*Whirls around.*) OUTSIDE! I'm going outside. Thank you, Panna Pawlina. Thank you.

PAWLINA. You can thank me by not doing anything foolish.

MANIA. What do you mean?

PAWLINA. Don't look frightened. Walk with your head up, straight back, walk as if you worked in the fields. A country girl walks like this. (*There is a slight sway to her walk.*) Her feet are tough. Let's see you. (*MANIA walks.*) Too much of the city in that. Swing your arms. And talk back to them.

MANIA. Talk back to them! Are you sure?

PAWLINA. Sure I'm sure. A farm girl would.

MANIA. You'll be with me, won't you?

PAWLINA. Yes. But you have to know what to do in case. I wish you weren't so pale.

MANIA. In case of what?

PAWLINA. Trouble. Any kind of trouble.

MANIA. Why do you have to work for the Germans?

PAWLINA. There's no choice. They took all the young Polish men to Germany. The women they've kept here. But it's still the same. Forced labor.

MANIA. Where are we going?

PAWLINA. Zoborow. A kommandant's home.

MANIA. You mean a home they took over?

PAWLINA. Probably.

MANIA. A Jewish home?

PAWLINA. I don't know. I haven't seen it. We'll go through the woods, so you can drink in the fresh air. Remember, you're a cousin on my mother's side. They haven't seen you before, because you just came. What's your new name?

MANIA. Panna Pawlina, couldn't I just go outside without all this fuss?

PAWLINA. Mania, if you want to go out, the safest place in the world is right under the enemy's nose. A Jewish girl would never be working for the Nazis! But if the soldiers see a pretty face they haven't seen before, a girl who says she's just out for a walk, they'll be suspicious. Now do you want to go out or not?

MANIA. Yes! What are we going to do there? Cook?

PAWLINA. Clean. His wife is coming, and he wants it spotless by tonight, so I said I needed help and I'd bring my cousin.

MANIA. Did you say clean?

PAWLINA. Yes. Clean. Sweep, mop, dust, scrub the floors, wash the windows, beat the rugs. Whatever has to be done, we'll do.

MANIA. (*As they exit.*) But Pawlina, I've never cleaned before!

PAWLINA. It's easy. I can't show you here; but when we get there, I'll explain everything. (*Reassuring her.*) Don't worry. If my little sister Bronia can clean, so can you. That part's simple.

*MAW-nya
**Paw-LEENA
***Translation: "Give us this day our daily bread, And forgive us our trespasses, As we forgive those who trespass against us, And lead us not into temptation"

5. Scene for two female actors – *Kindertransport* by Diane Samuels

> *HELGA is a German-Jewish woman in her early thirties. EVA is HELGA's nine-year-old daughter.*
>
> *In this scene, HELGA is preparing her daughter to leave Germany on a Kindertransport, a safe passage out of Nazi Germany organized by an organization called the Movement for the Care of Children from Germany, which was formed immediately after Kristallnacht in November 1938. The group was responsible for rescuing almost ten thousand unaccompanied children in the nine months prior to the outbreak of war, with most being relocated in Britain. EVA is too young to understand what is really happening, as her mother attempts to remain stoic while holding to a decision which she believes will save her daughter's life.*
>
> *(EVA is sitting on the floor, reading. The book is a large, hard-backed children's storybook entitled Der Rattenfänger.* HELGA enters. She is holding a coat, a button, needle and some thread.)*

EVA. What's an abyss, Mutti?**

HELGA. (*Sitting down and ushering EVA to sit next to her.*) An Abyss is a deep and terrible chasm.

EVA. What is a chasm?

HELGA. A huge gash in the rocks.

EVA. What's a ...

(*EVA puts down the book.*)

HELGA. Eva, sew on your buttons now. Show me that you can do it.

EVA. I can't get the thread through the needle. It's too thick. You do it.

HELGA. Lick the thread ...

EVA. Do I have to?

HELGA. Yes. Lick the thread.

EVA. I don't want to sew.

HELGA. How else will the buttons get onto the coat?

EVA. The coat's too big for me.

HELGA. It's to last next winter too.

EVA. Please.

HELGA. No.

EVA. Why won't you help me?

HELGA. You have to be able to manage on your own.

EVA. Why?

HELGA. Because you do. Now, lick the thread.

(*EVA licks the thread.*)

That should flatten it ... and hold the needle firmly and place the end of the thread between your fingers ... not too near ... that's it ... now try to push it through.

(*EVA concentrates on the needle and thread. HELGA watches closely.*)

See. You don't need me. It's good.

EVA. I don't mind having my coat open a bit. Really. I've got enough buttons.

HELGA. You'll miss it when the wind blows.

EVA. Can't I do it later?

HELGA. There's no "later" left, Eva.

EVA. After the packing, after my story ...

HELGA. Now.

(*EVA gives in and sews.*)

* *"The Ratcatcher"*
** *Mama (in German)*

6. Scene for two actors – *Kindertransport* by Diane Samuels

> *EVA is a nine-year-old German-Jewish girl who is escaping Nazi Germany, heading to England as part of the Kindertransport (see description in scene above). OFFICER is a Nazi border officer. (The ellipses indicate lines that have been omitted from the original script.) (The sounds of the railway station become louder and louder. Another train whistle.)*

EVA. Mutti! Vati!* Hello! Hello! See. I did get into the carriage. I said I would. See, I'm not crying. I said I wouldn't. I can't open the window! It's sealed tight! Why've you taken your gloves off? You're knocking too hard. Your knuckles are going red! What? I can't hear you!
(*Sound of long, shrill train whistle.*)
Louder! Louder! What? I can't hear! I can't … See you in England.
(*Sounds of train starting to move. EVA sits.*)
I musn't stare at the cross-eyed boy.
(*Train whistle blows.*)
What if he talks to me?
(*Sounds of children chattering. Suddenly a young child cries and cries.*)
You musn't cry. There's no point.
(*The crying continues.*)
Stop it.
(*The crying continues.*)
We'll all see our muttis and vatis soon enough.
(*The crying calms slightly.*)
And don't look at that cross-eyed boy.
…
(*The crying calms. Sounds of children laughing.*)
(*Announcing to all around her.*) Did any of you know? In England all the men have pipes and look like Sherlock Holmes and everyone has a dog.
(*Enter a Nazi border OFFICER. He approaches EVA.*)
OFFICER. No councillor in here?
EVA. She's in the next carriage.
OFFICER. (*Picking up EVA's case.*) Whose case is this?
EVA. Mine.
OFFICER. Stand up straight.
(*EVA stands.*)
Turn your label around then. It's gone the wrong way. Can't see your number.
EVA. (*Turning the label round. Quietly.*) Sorry.
OFFICER. Speak up.
EVA. Sorry.
OFFICER. Sir! Sorry, Sir.
EVA. Sorry, Sir.
OFFICER. No one will know what to do with you if they can't see your number.
(*Silence.*)
Will they?
EVA. No, Sir.
OFFICER. Might have to remove you from the train.
(*Silence.*)
Mightn't we?
EVA. Yes, Sir.
OFFICER. D'you know it at least?
EVA. Pardon, Sir?

OFFICER. Know your number. If you don't know it you might forget who you are.
EVA. 3362, Sir.
OFFICER. (*Taking out a pen.*) Don't want you to forget who you are now, do we?
EVA. No, Sir.
OFFICER. Let me remind you.
(*He draws a huge Star of David on the label.*)
There. That should tell 'em wherever it is you're going. Best to keep them informed, eh?
EVA. (*Terrified.*) Yes, Sir.
(*OFFICER opens and searches the case, throwing everything onto the floor. He finds the mouth organ.*)
OFFICER. You can't take valuables out of the country. Can't take anything for gain.
EVA. I wouldn't sell it, Sir.
OFFICER. What's it for then?
EVA. For music, Sir. I play it, Sir.
OFFICER. You any good?
EVA. I suppose so …
OFFICER. Go on then. Prove it's not just to make money.
(*EVA takes it and plays nervously, badly.*)
You need more practice. Better keep it. What money have you got? (*He digs into EVA's pockets and takes out a few coins, which he takes and pockets.*)
Better clear up the mess.
(*EVA starts to clear up. OFFICER feels in a pocket and produces a toffee.*)
OFFICER. (*Giving the toffee to EVA.*) Here kiddie. A sweetie for you.
(*OFFICER ruffles EVA's hair and exits. EVA grips the toffee tightly and tidies up the clothes into the case.*)
(*Sounds of a train speeding along. Children's excited chatter. In German, "The border, the border, the border."*)
EVA. It is the border! The border! Can't get us now! We're out! Out! Stuff your stupid Hitler. Stuff your stupid toffees! (*She throws down the toffee.*) Keep them! Hope your eyes fall out and you die the worst death on earth! Hope you all rot in hell forever and ever! Hope no one buries you! Hope the rats come and eat up all your remains until there's nothing left!

* *German for Mother! Father!*

Verbatim testimony historical narratives

1. From the testimony of Aaron Elster – "Hiding"

(http://iwitness.usc.edu/SFI/BrowseTopics.aspx?TopicID=29&ClipID=280)

Born: February 4, 1933, in Sokołów Podlaski (Lublin, Poland)
In a November, 1995 interview, Aaron describes hiding in an attic in a Polish apartment building when he was an 11-year-old boy. (The phrase in parentheses has been added for clarity.)

AARON

You sit in the attic and you really have – I can't read, I have nothing to read, I have nothing to do. So you're trying to figure out how to spend some time. And sometimes I would separate the thin sheets (hanging over the window) to be able to look down into the yard. And one of the tenants had a little girl. And I remember her. She always used to be in the backyard. And she would stand there and eat out of a dish, some kind of food. And I would be so envious of her and so I would actually curse her for having what she had, and me being in my situation. And I guess sometimes I used to go stir crazy in the attic. I used to run around – it was a bare attic – I used to run around and she would hear me. The little girl insisted that there was somebody up there. And the parents told her, "No. It's rats or mice up there." So one day, she insisted that she wants to go and look, and her parents brought her up to convince her that there was nobody up there. And I hid in the extreme corner where it was totally dark, hoping that they wouldn't see me. But one of the tenants saw me. And he turned around and told his daughter, "See, there's nobody here." And they left. And I thought that perhaps that was going to be the end. That they were going to turn us in. He was a school teacher, I later found out. But nobody said a word.

2.　From the testimony of Claire Boren – "Children"

(https://iwitness.usc.edu/sfi/BrowseTopics.aspx?TopicID=8&ClipID=247)

Born: July 8, 1938, in Mizocz, Poland
In an August, 1996 interview, Claire describes her experience of hiding in Poland with her mother when she was a very young girl.

CLAIRE

Apparently, (my mother) knocked on the door and they took us in. And they were religious people. They were some sort of evangelical sect. And they took us in. They were very poor. They hid us in a barn where they dug out a hole, on top of which a pig stood. The hole was long enough that my mother and I could lie down. Just if one of us was at the back, the other one had to be on the side. We could not stand up. I think we could sit up. And at night, they would let us come out. It was totally pitch black (in the hole). It was like a grave. And at the beginning, my mother would tell me stories. She afterwards told me she would tell me every book she ever read, every movie she ever saw … But after a while, I guess, she started sort of running out of stories. Whatever the reason was – they also lowered food to us once a day – my days and nights got mixed up. So when she was awake, I was asleep, and when I was awake, she was asleep. So, I retreated into this total fantasy world, you know. I just lived in this make-believe world. It got to the point where I lost all touch with reality. I just … I just left this world. I think it started out where I was thinking mostly about my father. You know, I was gonna find him, he was gonna come get me out of here … There was that kind of thinking. And after a while, I don't know what I was thinking of … I was out of it. We were there a few months. And it got to the point where – this my mother tells me – that the people, these peasants, said to her that the devil possessed me – that she should kill me or something. But she decided that she just had to get me out of there. I wasn't eating, and I uh, I didn't know where I was.

So we left. And we went to some village – it was all in the same area – a village where my mother ran into someone who had been a former maid of ours. And they kept us. And we were up in an attic. But the best part of it was I was just let loose. They just let me run with the kids, with the farm children, the peasant children. And, you know, I went with them to the fields to take care of the animals and just run around. And I just … I came back to myself.

3. From the testimony of Kristine Keren – "Hiding"

(http://iwitness.usc.edu/SFI/BrowseTopics.aspx?TopicID=29&ClipID=173)

> *Born: October 28, 1935, in Lwów, Poland*
> *In a June, 1998 interview, Kristine details her father's preparations to escape with his family from the Lwów* Ghetto in Poland by creating a hiding place in the city's sewer tunnels. Her father was anticipating that the ghetto would soon by "liquidated" – or emptied – by the Nazis, with all of its occupants being sent to concentration camps. One day, while secretly working on his construction project in the sewer, he was startled to run into workers, unsure if they would turn him in, ignore him, or help him.*

KRISTINE

[The sewer workers] asked my father "What are you doing here?" And he said, "I am trying to find a hiding place for my family." And they looked at him and they said "Let us check the work, what you did." And they checked the work and they said, "Not bad. Not bad. But it can be done better." And one of them said, "You know, we can help you, but it will cost you a lot of money." The time when they were supposed to meet, my father went down through this tunnel that he built. He went down and he brought the money. And then one of them, his name was Socha,** he came with my father up to the basement where we were hiding. He helped my father to make this tunnel more professional, you know. And he said that the night when the liquidation of the ghetto would come, he would wait for us in the sewer. And in a few days, I remember, my father came and he said, "That's it. We have to leave right now." And I asked my father, "Where are we going?" And he said, "Don't be scared, don't be afraid." He took me on his back and he told me, "Hold me tight and go with me." And every second I was asking him, "Daddy, where are we going? Where are we going?" And then I remember that my father took us to some small side tunnel and he said that we would stay there. And we walked through this tunnel and it was – it was a sewer! Then we were walking through this. And the rats! The spiders' webs. We had to pull it back – the spiders' webs. It was terrible. And the smell?! And we were sitting there and waiting. My father left because he was going to look for Socha. Socha brought some blankets – one or two blankets. And we started to organize. We had a carbide lamp that we could cook something, warm water, and cook something. And in this place, we were eleven people in this place. And this was our last place that we stayed. And in this place, we stayed 14 months. 14 months we stayed in this place.

*Luh-VOV
**SŌ-ha

4. From the testimony of Marion Pritchard – "Hiding"

(https://iwitness.usc.edu/sfi/BrowseTopics.aspx?TopicID=29&ClipID=375)

Born: November 7, 1920, in Amsterdam, the Netherlands
In a May, 1998 interview, Marion Pritchard, a former member of the Dutch Resistance, recounts her experience of hiding a Jewish man (Freddie) and his three small children in 1942, and the shocking action she took to save them from being discovered. She was assisted by a man named Karl Poch, a Jewish, gay man who had been a friend of Marion's when they were dancers in the ballet. Karl, who was in hiding in a nearby structure, heard the commotion, and came over to help.
(NOTE: this testimony has been edited slightly for length and clarity. Additionally, three sentences from Pritchard's full testimony that are not in this clip, have been added for clarification.)

MARION

Miek* is the one who asked me to find a place. And he and his brother built a hiding place underneath the living-room floor. And at night, I'd open it up. 'Cause when you heard a motor vehicle come, or a truck, you knew it wasn't somebody Dutch, you knew, most likely, it was the Nazis looking for Jews. So we practiced, and I could get him and the kids in there and cover it all up in about thirty seconds. And this one particular night, a Dutch Nazi policeman brought three German Nazi officers to the house. Then they left. I heaved a sigh of relief and went about my business. And (the family was) in the hiding place, but I let them out. I let the kids out after half an hour, because I hadn't had time to give the baby her sleeping powder and she began to cry. And Freddie decided to stay in the hiding place, 'cause he was working on his PhD thesis and he was in the middle of an important chapter. Some people know how to concentrate!

So then, the Dutch policeman came back. And I couldn't think of anything else to do except to shoot him. Miek – the gentile who had asked me to find a place for them – had given me a gun, and I had put it behind the books on the shelf above the bed, never intending to use it. I'm basically against capital punishment and killing in general. Yet your unconscious is quite powerful. And when it was a choice, most likely between the kids and him, I chose him. And I didn't wait to see what he was gonna do or what he was going to say. But then, obviously, if he had gone into the other room he would have seen the kids. He might have known the kids were around anyway. My instinct was, that if I didn't get rid of him, those kids were doomed.

So (afterward), we talked briefly, and we decided that Karl would go walk to the village, which of course was strictly against the rules. You're not supposed to be out during curfew. Especially if you're a Jew. And I suggested that he stay with the kids and that I go to the village, but he wasn't having any of that. And he went to see the baker, who in normal times brought his wares around in a wagon with a horse. And the baker agreed that as soon as curfew ended in the morning, he would come with his horse and wagon and get the body. And before Karl came back, together they went to see the local undertaker. And the local undertaker agreed to bury the body in a coffin with somebody who was having a funeral the next day.

MEEK

Suggested props/costumes for Chapter 5 historical narrative scenes

- Men's and women's sweaters, jackets
- Women's head scarves and aprons
- Boys' and girls' caps and hats
- Sheet (window covering)
- Bowl and spoon or fork
- Dark fabric (hole in ground)
- Hard hat(s)
- Money (bills)
- Lantern or flashlight
- Spider web (such as that sold for Halloween décor)
- Old blanket(s)
- Pot or pan
- Stick (to be used as gun stand-in)
- Red armbands
- Policeman's hat
- Baker's hat and/or apron
- Baby doll

Devised theater activity

Devise a scene combining the format of the game "hide and seek," with verbatim testimonies of survivors. The game will begin as the classic children's game, but will morph into something much more serious and consequential.

Scene material

1 The format of the children's game *hide and seek*.
2 Lines of *verbatim testimony* from people who went into hiding and/or escaped from Germany and its occupied countries during the Holocaust.
3 Musical underscoring (optional).

Texts

1 While there is no exact "text" for hide and seek, there are a number of steps typically associated with playing the game.

1 The designated "Seeker," sometimes referred to as "It," should close his/her eyes and count to a certain number – perhaps 100 – while the "Players" find a place to hide.
2 Once the Seeker has finished counting, s/he should call out "Ready or not, here I come!"
3 At this point, the Seeker may begin searching for the Players.
4 While the Seeker is searching, Players may attempt to run to safety by arriving at "home base," where they can no longer be tagged out.

2 The following testimonies have been transcribed from online videos on the Shoah Foundation's IWitness site. Some of these testimonies appear in the verbatim testimony activity earlier in this chapter.

AARON ELSTER. You sit in the attic and you really have – I can't read, I have nothing to read, I have nothing to do.
AARON ELSTER. And I hid in the extreme corner where it was totally dark, hoping that they wouldn't see me. But one of the tenants saw me.
CLAIRE BOREN. They hid us in a barn where they dug out a hole, on top of which a pig stood. The hole was long enough that my mother and I could lie down.
CLAIRE BOREN. We could not stand up. I think we could sit up. And at night, they would let us come out. It was totally pitch black. It was like a grave.
KRISTINE KEREN. And every second I was asking him, "Daddy, where are we going? Where are we going?" And then I remember that my father took us to some

small side tunnel and he said that we would stay there. And we walked through this tunnel and it was – it was a sewer!

KRISTINE KEREN. And in this place, we were eleven people in this place. And this was our last place that we stayed. And in this place, we stayed 14 months.

IRENE ABRAMS. We bicycled a good part of the night to a place where there was a river. The river was the demarcation point.

IRENE ABRAMS. And there was a little boat there. And there were already about five, six people in the boat. And he said goodbye to us. And he put us in the boat and we crossed.

ESTHER BEM. In 1943, the Germans occupied Italy. And then, everything changed. In the middle of the night on September 8th of 1943, an unknown person arrived to our door, knocked at night and said "Run! Disappear!"

ESTHER BEM. My parents and I took what we could. Very little. And we left. We started climbing mountains. There were mountains behind that village. It was a picturesque, beautiful village. And we climbed, and we climbed.

Staging considerations, choices and tips

1   Choose one actor to be the Seeker.
2   Have the other actors portray the survivors above: Aaron Elster, Claire Boren, Kristine Keren, Irene Abrams and Esther Bem. These will be the "Players." If you do not have enough actors to play all five roles, you may eliminate one or more. (None of the testimonies is gender-specific, so gender should not be a consideration in who plays which person.)
3   Some dialogue may be invented in order to begin the game. Play the beginning of the scene as a simple childhood game rather than as anything ominous.
4   After each Player goes into his/her hiding spot, have each deliver his/her first line of dialogue (while the Seeker is still counting).
5   After the Seeker announces "Ready or not, here I come," have each Player deliver his/her second line of dialogue. As they do, they will either return to "home base" and exclaim "Safe!" or they will be captured.
6   Decide which of the Players will be captured and which will be able to make it to safety.
7   It is very important that the capturing be portrayed as something very dangerous and sinister. Keep it simple. You may involve other actors to assist the Seeker in this task. You may have them wear a red cloth armband to denote that they are Nazis, but there is no need to use any additional Nazi symbolism, which could be offensive and triggering. A red armband will be enough to identify who the actor(s) is/are portraying. Again, make this staging very simple and very clean. This can be done by "tagging" those who are out and having them leave the stage, or by holding their hands behind their backs and leading them offstage or to another area of the stage.

8   If you choose to use musical underscoring, search for music which conveys darkness and/or danger without being too overpowering. You may not want to use underscoring until the tone of the scene changes from innocent to dangerous.

9   As with Chapter 2's devised theater activity, the use of a childhood game in this instance, when paired with life or death consequences, can bring about interesting theatrical results. By juxtaposing an innocent childhood pastime with dangerous and often deadly real-life scenarios, how does that change the nature of the way you view the game? the idea of hiding or fleeing from danger? How do you want your audience to feel when they watch your scene?

6 Resistance

Context

Why didn't the Jews fight back is a question that students often ask when studying the Holocaust. While it is true that in many situations resistance did not take place, it is also true that, when possible, resistance was undertaken in countries, in ghettos and in camps. It also is important to note that there were many kinds of resistance practiced, by both individuals and by groups, and many challenges and dangers associated with trying to fight back.

There were a number of reasons why resistance was difficult. One was the might of the German armed forces. By contrast, Jews often found it difficult to obtain weaponry and ammunition. They had to look at endeavors such as purchasing or smuggling to arm themselves. In certain cases, guns had to be taken apart and then reassembled to get them into the hands of those who needed them. In addition, Jews did not have the backing of military forces from other countries. The United States, for example, did not prioritize freeing prisoners from the camps or bombing the railroad lines that transported them to their incarcerations or deaths.

Another tactic that kept resistance in check was known as collective responsibility. The Germans would kill entire families or entire communities to punish the acts of anyone who engaged in resistance. Similar to this was the penalty that a person faced if caught helping a Jew; giving aid could cost someone their life.

A different deterrent to resistance was the use of lies and secrets by the Germans. Jews who were being deported were told that they were being "resettled." They did not realize the fate that awaited them. Tactics were implemented which furthered the deception. In Auschwitz, for example, prior to being gassed, prisoners had to write postcards to friends and family telling the recipients that they were fine and all was well. The inability of those targeted to fathom the horror also played into Nazi ploys. Some Jews who had served their country in World War I found it inconceivable that the same country would murder them. There also were those who found it impossible to believe that things would get worse and that their extermination would be government policy. The decision to resist came often only after those destined to be murdered realized the inevitability of their fate and decided that it did not matter if it was futile to struggle against their oppressors. For them, it was more noble to die fighting.

Isolation of the Jewish population was another barrier to resistance. Jews in ghettos, for example, were largely cut off from the rest of the world. It is worth remembering that, unlike today, communication with the outside world during this period was slow and difficult, hampering efforts to make others aware of what was happening and to solicit aid. In addition, the Nazis had many supporters among local populations. It was difficult to know who to trust. Collaborators, Nazi sympathizers and anti–Semites were dangers to those who might try to resist. Additionally, other groups that had opposed Hitler had been, for all practical purposes, eliminated. Opposition from Socialists, Communists and trade unionists had been harshly suppressed; by mid–summer 1933, the Nazi Party was the only legal party. Conformity was mandated.

Unarmed and armed resistance, however, did exist and took many forms. Included in the former were educational, cultural and spiritual practices. Examples included staging concerts and theatrical performances, creating artwork that depicted Nazi atrocities, publishing and disseminating underground newspapers, running underground schools which taught either secular or religious subjects to young people, and maintaining undisclosed libraries. Additional practices included recording the horrors inflicted by the Nazis by keeping diaries and hiding documentation in forbidden archives as well as listening to the BBC or other broadcasts and then disseminating the information. Spiritual resistance included activities which helped those persecuted to maintain their dignity despite Nazi attempts to disgrace, demean and dehumanize them. This included engaging in prayer or holding secret religious services in defiance of their oppressors' ban on such activities and giving aid to or rescuing others. Escape, too, was in a sense considered an act of resistance.

Two examples of corps of young Jews known for their resistance efforts are the Herbert Baum group and the White Rose group. The former, which included Jewish Zionist members of the Communist Party, had some limited success in Germany, but ultimately they were executed for their activities. The White Rose student opposition movement founded in 1942 by Hans Scholl, Sophie Scholl, Christopher Probst, Willi Graf and Alexander Schmorell eventually expanded to include students in Hamburg, Freiburg, Berlin and Vienna. They undertook to distribute leaflets in which they denounced the Nazis and urged action against the arms industry. The Scholls, brother and sister, were turned in by a janitor and executed.

Engaging in both unarmed and armed acts of resistance were partisan groups. In the forests of Eastern Europe, some 20,000 to 30,000 Jewish partisans were members of resistance groups. Partisan activity took place in both Eastern and Western Europe. Some partisan groups cut telephone, telegraph and electricity lines. They also

IMAGE 6.1 A Jewish partisan group in the Rudninkai Forest

destroyed transportation lines and power stations. They wrecked or sabotaged factories making materials for the German war effort as a way of subverting their production capabilities.

Armed resistance included both organized efforts and guerilla tactics. Some of the most dramatic acts of armed Jewish resistance took place in "5 major ghettos, 45 small ghettos, 5 major concentration and extermination camps, and 18 forced labor camps" ("Resistance during the Holocaust" 4). Armed attacks were staged by inmates at the infamous Treblinka, Sobibor and Auschwitz–Birkenau camps. Of the ghetto uprisings, the most famous occurred in the Warsaw Ghetto and lasted from April 19, 1943, through May 16, 1943. Members of separate underground groups within that ghetto formed the Jewish Fighting Organization (ZOB) and were led by 23-year-old Mordechai Anielewicz. To quell the uprising, the Nazis blew up buildings and burned the ghetto to the ground. Resistance leaders committed suicide; remaining ghetto residents were sent to Treblinka.

Teens and young adults bore much of the responsibility for underground resistance. They were daring and less encumbered by responsibilities than their parents. This also was true in the ghettos where young fighters, motivated by a desire for revenge or by desperation, preferred to take on their oppressors rather than be shot in mass executions, gassed or worked to death. To whatever degree they were or were not successful, their efforts were examples of heroism.

Scripted scenes and monologues

1. Scene for three actors – *The White Rose* by Lillian Garrett-Groag

Sitting in her brother HANS' room at the University of Munich, SOPHIE SCHOLL has just made the discovery that a group of college students has begun circulating a publication challenging the Nazis and their philosophies. She immediately knows who those students are, and she very much wants to join them.

As the scene begins, SOPHIE is sitting ram-rod straight on an armchair clutching an open book to her chest. Somebody outside approaches whistling the "Wiener Blut Waltz." The door opens and HANS and his friend ALEXANDER SCHMORRELL enter. It's very late at night.

HANS. Sophie! What are you doing up?

SOPHIE. Waiting.

HANS. Oh, good. Are you hungry? We brought –

SOPHIE. No.

SCHMORELL. What's the matter? No letter from Fritz?

SOPHIE. I don't write to Fritz anymore.

SCHMORELL. (*Beat.*) I'm glad.

SOPHIE. Someone has been passing around a leaflet. It's very interesting. Whoever they are, they call themselves "The White Rose." Imagine, my favorite flower!

HANS. Really?

SCHMORELL. It sounds like a perfume advertisement.

SOPHIE. (*Without taking her eyes off them, she pulls a crumpled piece of paper from her cardigan pocket. She reads.*) "The Spartan code of law was based on the dangerous principle that human beings are to be considered means and not ends – thereby destroying the foundations of morality and natural law."

HANS. (*Uncomfortable.*) That's Schiller, isn't it?

SOPHIE. (*Picking up the book from the chair.*) I found the passage underlined in your book. (*Pause.*)

HANS. I couldn't – go on just *talking* … about it. Making jokes because we feel helpless. I don't like to feel helpless. I want to take them on!

SOPHIE. You mean … we go at them? Just like that?

HANS. Not you. Just us.

SOPHIE. Why not me?

HANS. It's dangerous!

SOPHIE. For you, too.

SCHMORELL. We're men.

SOPHIE. Don't' worry, I'll carry smelling salts.

HANS. I don't want you in this.

SOPHIE. Too late.

HANS. Stay out of it, Sophie!
SOPHIE. I can't!
HANS. You mean you won't!
SOPHIE. Can't! I can't just … knuckle under.
SCHMORELL. Hubris.
SOPHIE. Nobody asked *you*!
SCHMORELL. Right.
HANS. Aren't you afraid, Sophie?
SOPHIE. I'm terrified. But the worst of it is, I'm so afraid, I think if I don't *do* something right now … I'll start going along with them.
SCHMORELL. Nonsense.
SOPHIE. It isn't. We're no better than anybody else. Fear is the great mind killer.
HANS. We could be found out any moment and –
SOPHIE. They won't catch us! We're smarter, quicker – we're younger! And we're right! They can't catch us!
HANS. I won't let you –
SOPHIE. You used to take me everywhere with you.
HANS. (*Peevish.*) Don't remind me. "Me too, me too!"
SOPHIE. Hansel …
HANS. Don't call me Hansel in front of people!
SOPHIE. Alex is not *people*.
SCHMORELL. Oh, fine.
HANS. What do we tell mom and dad? I'm supposed to be looking after you.
SOPHIE. Tell them we love them.
HANS. Don't get flippant with me Sophie!
SOPHIE. Then don't tell me what to do!
SCHMORELL. Hey, hey!
SOPHIE. Anybody talking to you?
SCHMORELL. No, no.
SOPHIE. (*To HANS.*) Do the others know?
HANS. No. And they never will.

2. Monologue – *The White Rose* by Lillian Garrett-Groag

21-year-old German student SOPHIE SCHOLL has been arrested by the SS for participating in resistance activities. She speaks to her interrogator, Robert Mohr, Head of the Munich Gestapo.

SOPHIE. The real damage is done by those millions who want to "survive." Those honest men who just want to be left in peace; who don't want their little lives disturbed by anything bigger than themselves. Those with no sides, and no causes. Those who won't take the measure of their own strength for fear of antagonizing their own shadows. Those who don't like to make waves or enemies. Those for whom passion, truth, freedom, honor, principles, are only *literature*. Those for whom everything is "relative," the excuse of the man with no values. Those who have no absolutes because their souls can't encompass them. Those who live small, mate small and die small. The reductionist approach to life. If you keep it small, you'll keep it under control. If you don't make any noise, the bogeyman won't find you. And it's an illusion, because they die too, those people who rolled up their spirits into tiny little balls to hide them under their puny lives to be safe. *Safe?* From what? Life is always on the edge of death. Narrow streets lead to the same place as the big, wide avenues, and the little candles burn themselves out just like the flaming torch. I choose my own way to burn. I don't want to survive, I want to live.

3. Monologue – *The White Rose* by Lillian Garrett-Groag

> *Twenty-five-year-old HANS SCHOLL is being interrogated by Robert Mohr, Head of the Munich Gestapo. HANS has been arrested for participating in resistance activities. (The ellipses indicate Mohr's responses which have been omitted.)*

HANS. Herr Mohr, if you believe Hitler, you believe anything. The war is lost. It will be months before we come to trial, and months before the appeals and the final sentence go through. By then you will be a bad memory in history and the world will know that there were Germans who refused to live dishonorably.

…

We had neighbors. A family called Nathan. Germans. German nationals, Mohr. In Germany for generations. In fact, you couldn't get any more "German" than that. But you know something? They've disappeared! Nobody knows where they've gone. Their house is empty. Their door, boarded up. I want them back, Mohr. Can you do that? Can you find them for me? Because until I see the Nathans again, until I hear their piano, see their milk bottles at their doorstep; until I see them turning their lights on in the parlor, until then, I will hold you accountable!

…

I want my neighbors back! I want my country back! Give me back my country, you son of a bitch!

4. Monologue – *And a Child Shall Lead* by Michael Slade

> *ERIK KOSEK is a young Jewish boy who is imprisoned in the Theresienstadt ghetto-camp. He idolizes his older friend Miroslav, who has started an underground publication called VEDEM, documenting daily life and atrocities in the camp. In this scene, ERIK has become disillusioned by Miroslav, no longer believing him to be the pillar of strength and morality that he once thought him to be. Here, ERIK reads the story he has written for VEDEM, which exposes the Nazis' attempt to pass Terezin off as a "model camp." (The ellipses indicate Miroslav's short interjections which have been omitted.)*

ERIK. (*Sarcastic.*) VEDEM* REPORT. "The Big Joke." Today the Red Cross visited the camp. Yesterday's final preparation was to ship over one third of Terezin's residents to Poland … so it wouldn't seem too crowded here. This morning, old Mr. Epstein was given a new suit and a top hat and named the mayor. He was the only Jew to tour with the Red Cross visitors. He was accompanied by his "Chauffeur." Of course his chauffeur was really an SS Officer in civilian clothes. The delegation had a lovely day. Photos were taken. Some of the younger children were given new clothes and got to ride on the carousel in the new play area … which was all specially built for the occasion. We got to go round and round on the carousel all day. For eight hours we got to go round and round without a stop … so the Red Cross wouldn't miss us. The Red Cross people were very happy to see that the rumors they had heard were false. That living conditions were fine. That there was no over-crowding. That food was ample. That we had our own independent government. They were careful not to open any doors they weren't shown. Not to touch the wet paint. Not to speak to anyone they weren't introduced to. Not to continue down the road to the crematorium. Everyone was very, very happy.
(*He crumbles up the piece of paper and throws it at Miroslav.*)
Why didn't you get our newspaper to the Red Cross? Why didn't you even try?
…
If you'd given the copies to me like I asked, I would've run straight at them, screaming "Read this!" I would have jumped off that damned carousel, waving the newspaper at them!
…
At least I would've died doing something. You were too scared to even try.

* *Vedem means "We Are Leading" in Czech*

SPOTLIGHT ACTIVITY

And a Child Shall Lead and *The White Rose*

"Monuments to Bravery"

A clear sense of the characters' bravery and determination is evident in the scripted scene and monologues in this chapter. In this activity, students will create a monument to their principles.

1   Divide students into small groups.
2   Instruct each group to come up with one noun that exemplifies one or more of the characters in the scripted scene and monologues in this section. (Sample words might include: bravery, courage, resistance, determination, strength, conviction, morality, justice.)
3   Instruct each group to physically create a monument which honors these young characters by making a tableau (frozen picture) which expresses their chosen word. All of the students in each group should be a part of the same "statue" or "monument."

4   Have each group present their tableau to the rest of the class. Allow the audience to guess what each group's word was.

5   Discuss the tableaus, encouraging each group to describe how their monument conveys the spirit of the young people in this chapter's scene and monologues.

Verbatim testimony historical narratives

1. From the testimony of Itka Zygmuntowicz – "Resilience"

(https://iwitness.usc.edu/sfi/BrowseTopics.aspx?TopicID=164&ClipID=1228)

Born: April 15, 1926, in Ciechanów, Poland
In this March, 1996 interview, Itka recalls the beatings she and her mother received from two Gestapo* for refusing to give them information about a man in their town. In doing so, she explains that "resistance" doesn't always have to be a physical act.

ITKA

What I heard – what terrible screams. I never heard anybody scream like this. So I realized that they must be torturing her. They wanted her to submit. Not to resist. To tell them. To betray another fellow Jew. And my mother was determined not to. And after a long time, screaming and screaming and screaming – it was tearing my heart – it became completely silent. Because while she was screaming, at least I had a sign that she's alive. But after it got silent, I no longer knew whether my mother's still alive or not. After what looked to me like an eternity, but in actuality, wasn't so long, the door swung open, and two Gestapo – one holding her under the armpit, the other, under the other armpit, dragging her across the floor. She was beaten horribly. And as they took her out, they took me in – that she should see. And I didn't know if she's still conscious or not. And I looked at her. And just with her face, she gave me a sign – not to tell. At that moment, I couldn't understand. I was too young. Why would she allow herself to be so beaten and even maybe killed to protect a stranger, practically? It was just an acquaintance … And now they take me in, she's gonna let them beat me? I couldn't understand, may she forgive me. But I knew that this was an important moment and I wasn't completely dumb. And I started to realize maybe she must have a good reason. So they took me in and I was next in line in beating … And I didn't say anything. I too was silent. I too would not betray somebody else. Because it's not menshleych**. So I didn't say. And after I was beaten, and they saw that neither my mother – even though she heard me screaming – she didn't tell and I didn't tell. So, I heard one of them saying that he doesn't believe that we know. And they let us go home.

I realized then that that was my mother's and my test of menschlekeyt.*** And that was the first time that I learned about spiritual resistance. That you don't have to take just a gun. That there's something else. And this story affected me very much.

*Gestapo: the official secret police of Nazi Germany and German-occupied Europe
**MENSH-lik. Meaning: in a humane way
***MENSH-lih-kite. Meaning: human decency

2. From the testimony of Anna Heilman – "Resistance"

(http://iwitness.usc.edu/SFI/BrowseTopics.aspx?TopicID=59&ClipID=269)

Born: December 1, 1928, in Warsaw, Poland
In this February, 1996 interview, Anna describes how she assisted with an uprising that took place at the Birkenau concentration camp by smuggling gunpowder from the munitions factory where she and her sister worked while imprisoned at the camp. They wrapped gunpowder in small rags and boxes which they stored in the hems of their dresses to bring to a unit of Sonderkommandos* in the camp.

ANNA

On the way from the factory – it was about three kilometers to Birkenau where we lived – we used to carry this on our bodies. From time to time there were searches. When we heard there was a search, we used to unwrap this gunpowder, throw it on the ground and mix it with our feet on the ground so it was not distinguishable from the dirt underfoot. (If there was no search) then we used to bring it into Birkenau. I gave it to my sister and my sister gave it to – I don't know. Either to … Roza Robota or somebody else. I don't know exactly who. Then it went to a special hiding place. Roza Robota had contact with a man from the crematorium. They had privileges to come into the women's camp. And at that particular spot, they used to come and pick it up and bring it into the crematorium.

In October, '44, there was a revolt in the crematorium. The Sonderkommando – those were the people who were manning the crematorium – knew that from time to time after a certain period of time, they were to be murdered so as not to bear witness. And that particular group decided that they are going to rebel. They used this gunpowder and manufactured little hand grenades made out of metal, round boxes of shoe polish with a wick and filled with gun powder. And when you lit it, it exploded. I don't know how much damage it did or it didn't do. This revolt, it took place on October 7th, 1944, and was aborted. Either they were betrayed or whatever. All the Sonderkommando people were killed. But the crematorium was destroyed as well. There were four crematoriums in Birkenau and one was destroyed by this. After the revolt, the Germans found this little handmade grenade and they identified the gunpowder, which of course, we didn't know that gunpowder has some special characteristics. They identified this gunpowder as coming only from the union. And only from pulverone** from where my sister worked. They started an investigation. They imprisoned four girls: Roza Robota, Ala Gärtner, Regina Saperstein and Ester Weisblum. They tortured them mercilessly, and eventually hanged them publicly on January 5th, 1945.

*Sonderkommandos (Special Commandos) were units made up of Jewish concentration camp inmates who were made to remove victims from the gas chambers and place them into crematoriums
**pulverone – an explosive black powder*

3. From the testimony of Mira Shelub – "Resistance"

(http://iwitness.usc.edu/SFI/BrowseTopics.aspx?TopicID=59&ClipID=168)

*Born: January 13, 1922, in Zdzięcioł, Poland
In this November, 1996 interview, Mira describes what it was like to live in the Lipiczany Forest in Poland with a group of Jewish partisans.**

MIRA

Let me tell you a little bit about the partisans. In the forest – where did we live in the forest? Where did we get our food? Our ammunition? And what was our goal? Okay. In the forest, during the summer we lived under trees. In the forest! During the winter, we would occupy peasants' homes. Where did we get our food? The food – we got our food from the friendly peasants. They would supply us with food and with ammunition. Now, the *un*friendly peasants would supply the Germans. They – (the friendly peasants) – would prepare food orders and we would stop at their places, and pick up the prepared food orders and leave receipts: "The partisans were here, and they picked up the food." Our goal: we were not interested in getting involved in open battle fights, because we were not equipped or trained for it. But, we were interested in getting involved in sabotage acts. To interrupt and disrupt the transportation and the communication at the front. The missions consisted to blow up a train, or to attack a local police station. And usually, when they would go on a mission, not too many – maybe about 20 people, you know, about 18 people. So the peasants would say "You know how many partisans were here? In the hundreds!" Because we would come and make a big noise, psychologically, so that they'll think that a lot of partisans were here. So they'd say "Do you know how many? In the 100s!" And the Germans would get scared.

Besides, it's very scary to get into the forest, because you have a feeling that each tree is shooting at you.

Partisans: Some Jews who managed to escape from ghettos and camps formed their own fighting units. These fighters, or partisans, were concentrated in densely wooded areas

4. From the testimony of Sol Liber – "Resistance"

(http://iwitness.usc.edu/SFI/BrowseTopics.aspx?TopicID=59&ClipID=169)

Born: December 3, 1923, in Warsaw, Poland

In this August, 1994 interview, Sol describes his involvement in the Warsaw Ghetto uprising of 1943* when he was 19 years old. While he was caught by the Nazis, miraculously, he was not immediately killed, but was sent to Treblinka with the other inhabitants of the ghetto.

SOL

They gave me a gun. And they explained to me what our duties would be. That we'll meet once a month. And if we need something, we could phone. Not to the organization's bunker, but to a private home, and they will relay the message. And I joined. And we were meeting every month. We were talking about what's going to happen. We stored gasoline for Molotov cocktails to make. And they knew where I lived, so they'd get some people from the same area – about 16 of us – and they said, "This is your area. If the uprising comes to be, if they're going to ship us out (to a concentration camp), the first thing you have to do is burn the factory that makes parts for airplanes – this is your first duty. To break the windows, throw in some Molotov cocktails and this will go …"

The first Passover night, the first Seder, the ghetto is surrounded. Ukraines (they were in the SS** also) surrounded, like every ten feet, an SS with a machine gun. Next day, they marched in, and we opened fire. The guard was right about ten feet from our house. We were sitting on the roof. They thought they'd march in like usual, like nothin' happened, ya know? We opened fire. And when we opened fire, a few fell. And they backed up. They backed out of the ghetto. They backed out. And in the meantime, a few of us had the order to burn this factory. They went to burn the factory, and the factory went up in flames. And then later, we fought and we fought. And there was a young kid, about 13 years old. A Jewish kid that was going around squealing to the Germans where the bunkers are. Every second building had a bunker. And he came to our bunker. And the SS came down and he opened the lid and he said, "If you don't come out, we'll throw in a few hand grenades and you'll be buried right here." So everybody figures, as long as we're alive, we have a chance. If he throws a few hand grenades – that's all gone. So, we all came out.

*Warsaw Ghetto Uprising – a revolt that took place in April 1943 in the Warsaw Ghetto when the Germans attempted to deport the remaining inhabitants to Treblinka concentration camp. The defense forces, commanded by Mordecai Anielewicz, fought the Germans for 27 days, before the ghetto was destroyed

**SS – a unit of Nazis, created as a group of bodyguards to Hitler and later expanded to take charge of intelligence, central security, policing action, and the mass extermination of those they considered inferior or undesirable

5. From the testimony of Leslie Banos – "Hiding"

(http://iwitness.usc.edu/SFI/BrowseTopics.aspx?TopicID=29&ClipID=175)

Born: August 16, 1923, Nyírbátor, Hungary
In a July, 1995 interview, Leslie describes how he was selected by the Nazis to be an officer's candidate in a Hungarian military school akin to West Point. He agreed to their terms, because he secretly wanted access to information that would allow him to help the Jews of Hungary. He then rescued Jews from the Budapest ghetto, and with the help of his aunt and cousin, hid them in his aunt's factory.

LESLIE

The first person I picked up – it was my cousin, who was a Jewish guy. Dr. Markowich. And I took him into my aunt's factory. Now, the first time, we never thought of it, to open the hole and put them in. You know, in the sewer system. We just told them "You just hide underneath the benches and sleep there and everything what you can do," you know? And then, the more and more people I picked up, my aunt became panicky. Because they had to feed these people. It wasn't just like leaving people right there, you know, on their own. They couldn't get out to buy food. Besides, there was no food available. And so, what happened was, we had to find a place for them to hide. So, as an experiment, I said, "Let's see what's behind the wall." What we thought at the time to be, honestly, we didn't know there was a sewer in between. We thought the wall only separated the two parts of her factory. Until we opened the wall, then we see that this was actually a big hole where the sewer system was. We said, "That's perfect. We can put the people right here." And my aunt set up a little kitchen and started to feed first two people, then three people, and more and more and more as I brought them in. And I had free rein in the ghetto because I had the German military car. I always wore my helmet, because it looked very impressive you know. And I went in and I took people out from the ghetto with no questions. Nobody asked questions. You know, I always told them I was taking them to headquarters for questioning. And instead of this, I took them to my aunt's place. You know, her husband was petrified. He wouldn't get close to the place. He just stayed in the home. He was afraid if any-body found out he would be the first one to be shot. So, he was a chicken, like I said. He had absolutely nothing to do with that. All the credit goes to my aunt and my cousin who helped. She was a young girl at the time, who I believe was 12 years old, who helped with the cooking and everything for the people.

Suggested props/costumes for Chapter 6 historical narrative scenes

- Men's and women's sweaters, jackets, hats
- Small bags (to hold "gunpowder")

- Shoe polish tins
- Baskets or burlap sacks (filled with "food")
- Scraps of paper with written notes
- Several sticks (stand-ins for "guns")
- Bottle and rag (Molotov cocktail)
- Benches
- Large soup pot with ladle
- Several bowls
- Military helmet
- Car steering wheel
- Women's aprons

Devised theater activity

Using the song "Zog Nit Keynmol," create a scene which celebrates the defiant optimism of the Jewish Partisans while acknowledging the dangerous conditions under which they operated.

Scene components

1   The *lyrics* to the song "Zog Nit Keynmol," commonly referred to as "The Partisan Song."
2   The *music* to the song "Zog Nit Keynmol."
3   Two or more *tableaus*, inspired by the photograph of Jewish Partisans on page 98.
4   No fewer than five *choral movements*
5   *Lighting effects.*

Texts

1   "Zog Nit Keynmol" – literally, "Never Say," has lyrics which were written in 1943 by Hirsh Glik, an inmate of the Vilna Ghetto. The song is better known by the title "The Partisan Song." Glik was inspired to write the song after hearing news of the Warsaw Ghetto uprising. "Zog Nit Keynmol" was adopted by a group of Jewish partisans who were conducting resistance operations throughout Eastern Europe. It later came to define the entire resistance movement of Jews against the Nazis. Hirsh Glik set his lyrics to music by Soviet Jewish composers Dmitri and Daniel Pokrass, who originally composed the melody for a Soviet film in 1938.

The Partisan Song: "Never Say That You Have Reached The Final Road"
(English translation by Bret Werb)

Never say that you have reached the final road,
Though leaden clouds conceal blue skies above,
The hour that we've yearned for now draws near,
Our steps proclaim like drumbeats: We Are Here!
From green and palmy lands, and countries white with snow,
We've come with all our suffering and woe;
And anywhere our blood has stained the ground
There our courage and our valor will rebound!
The morning sun will make the new day glow,
And our dark yesterday will vanish with the foe,
But should tomorrow's sun await the dawn too long,
Let this song ring out for ages yet to come!
Not with lead was this song written – but with blood;
It wasn't warbled in the forest by a bird!
But a people, trapped between collapsing walls,
With weapons held in hand, they sang this song!
So, never say that you have reached the final road,
Though leaden clouds conceal blues skies above,
The hour that we've yearned for now draws near,
Our steps proclaim like drumbeats: We Are Here!

Here are the song lyrics both in their original Yiddish (right hand column) and in transliterated Yiddish (left column).

---

zog nit keyn mol, az du geyst dem letstn veg,	זאָג ניט קיין מאָל, אַז דו גייסט דעם לעצטן וועג,
khotsh himlen blayene farshteln bloye teg.	כאָטש הימלען בלייענע פֿאַרשטעלן בלויע טעג.
kumen vet nokh undzer oysgebenkte sho,	קומען וועט נאָך אונדזער אויסגעבענקטע שעה –
s'vet a poyk ton undzer trot: mir zaynen do!	ס'וועט אַ פּויק טאָן אונדזער טראָט: מיר זיינען דאָ!
fun grinem palmenland biz vaysn land fun shney,	פֿון גרינעם פֿאַלמענלאַנד ביז ווייסן לאַנד פֿון שניי,
mir kumen on mit undzer payn, mit undzer vey,	מיר קומען אָן מיט אונדזער פּיין, מיט אונדזער וויי,
un vu gefaln s'iz a shprits fun undzer blut,	און וווּ געפֿאַלן ס'איז אַ שפּריץ פֿון אונדזער בלוט,
shprotsn vet dort undzer gvure, undzer mut!	שפּראָצן וועט דאָרט אונדזער גבֿורה, אונדזער מוט!
s'vet di morgnzun bagildn undz dem haynt,	טנייה מעד זדנוא וָדליגאַב ווָזנגראַם יד טעוו'ס,
un der nekhtn vet farshvindn mit dem faynt,	טנייַפֿ מעד טימ וָדניוושראַפֿ טעוו וָטכענ רעד וָא
nor oyb farzamen vet di zun in dem kayor –	ראָיאַק מעד וזוון וזי יד טעוו וָעמאַזראַפֿ ביוא ראָנ –
vi a parol zol geyn dos lid fun dor tsu dor.	רוד וצ רוד וָופֿ דיל סאָד נייג לאָז לאָראַפּ אַ יוו.
dos lid geshribn iz mit blut, un nit mit blay,	דאָס ליד געשריבן איז מיט בלוט, און ניט מיט בליי,
s'iz nit keyn lidl fun a foygl oyf der fray,	ס'איז ניט קיין לידל פֿון אַ פֿויגל אויף דער פֿריי,
dos hot a folk tsvishn falndike vent	דאָס האָט אַ פֿאָלק צווישן פֿאַלנדיקע ווענט
dos lid gezungen mit naganes in di hent.	דאָס ליד געזונגען מיט נאַגאַנעס אין די הענט.
to zog nit keyn mol, az du geyst dem letstn veg,	טאָ זאָג ניט קיין מאָל, אַז דו גייסט דעם לעצטן וועג,
khotsh himlen blayene farshteln bloye teg.	כאָטש הימלען בלייענע פֿאַרשטעלן בלויע טעג.
kumen vet nokh undzer oysgebenkte sho –	קומען וועט נאָך אונדזער אויסגעבענקטע שעה –
s'vet a poyk ton undzer trot: mir zaynen do!	ס'וועט אַ פּויק טאָן אונדזער טראָט: מיר זיינען דאָ!

2   The music: multiple recorded versions of this song can be found at: (https://
archives.savethemusic.com/bin/archives.cgi?q=songs&search=title&id=Zog+nit
+keynmol).

Staging considerations, choices and tips

1   Will you be singing the song or reciting the lyrics? If you are singing, consider
learning a portion of the lyrics in their original Yiddish by working with the
transliterated lyrics above and rehearsing with one of the recordings. Consider
alternating between English and Yiddish or between spoken and sung verses of
the song.

2   How can you capture the sense of danger that the Partisans must have felt?
Consider using lighting to help set the tone. Even in a traditional classroom
setting, lighting can be used to great effect. Turn out the overhead lights, close
any classroom blinds and use only handheld lighting sources such as flashlights,
lanterns or battery-operated candles. Try using the light of flashlights in criss-
crossing patterns like search lights, or having the actors hold flashlights under their
chins to create a shadowy effect.

3   Consider the volume at which you are singing. Are the people in your scene in
hiding? Do they move from being in hiding to being in the open? Fluctuate your
volume to indicate these different possibilities.

7

Liberation

Context

World War II was nearing an end in 1945 and, as the Allied and Soviet forces bore down on their Nazi foes, they encountered horrors beyond imagination. Concentration camps, mass graves, and sick, dehydrated and starving prisoners were evidence of Nazi atrocities. While liberation of the camps had not been a primary mission, American, British, French, Soviet and Canadian forces freed inmates, provided food and medical help, and collected evidence of Nazi brutality upon encountering these prisons. In efforts to hide their crimes and prevent prisoners from being liberated, the Germans had moved some captives to camps within Germany, but this effort did not prevent the rescuers from freeing thousands who had been dehumanized and burying countless more who had died. Even soldiers hardened by the battlefield were shaken by what they saw.

Prisoners housed in extermination, concentration, and slave-labor camps were liberated. These various camp populations included Jews, political prisoners, resistance fighters, activists and criminals, as well as Gypsies, prisoners of war and others. In certain cases, like at the Gunskirchen camp liberated by Americans in May of 1945, the emancipation seemed unreal and some inmates stayed in the camp an extra day. For those securing the captives' freedom, there was a strong need to document the crimes against humanity that they saw. American General Dwight D. Eisenhower, after encountering the camp at Ohrdruf, urged Congress and journalists to document the horrors of the camps for both the public to see and to serve as evidence in future war crimes trials. In addition, German citizens were made to visit camps and bury the dead, forcing them to be witnesses to brutal history.

The following chart provides an overview of when some of the camps were liberated and by whom.

Camp	Liberated by	Date
Majdanek	Soviets	July, 1944
Auschwitz	Soviets	January, 1945
Gross-Rosen	Soviets	February, 1945
Sachsenhausen	Soviets	April, 1945
Ravensbrueck	Soviets	April, 1945
Stutthof	Soviets	May, 1945
Buchenwald	Americans	April, 1945
Dora-Mittelbau	Americans	April, 1945
Flossenburg	Americans	April, 1945
Dachau	Americans	April, 1945
Mauthausen	Americans	May, 1945
Ohrdruf	Americans	April, 1945
Neuengamme	British	April, 1945
Bergen-Belsen	British	April, 1945

The Soviets found the first major Nazi camp, Majdanek, located near Lublin, Poland. Before troops got there, the Nazis tried to destroy the camp. The large crematorium was burned; however, the gas chambers remained as evidence of the mass executions that took place at this death camp. Belzec, Sobibor and Treblinka, all extermination camps, also were Soviet finds in 1944. In 1943, however, after killing most of Poland's Jewish population, the Nazis razed these sites, attempting to destroy evidence of their crimes.

While Chelmno was the first extermination camp located in Poland, Auschwitz was the last to cease operation. When this infamous death camp was liberated by the Soviets on January 27, 1945, they found more than 6,000 prisoners there, including children. The rescuers also found a treasure trove of evidence of Nazi crimes.

> Soviets found personal belongings of the victims. They discovered, for example, hundreds of thousands of men's suits, more than 800,000 women's outfits, and more than 14,000 pounds of human hair.
>
> ("Liberation of Nazi Camps" 3)

More than 1.1 million people had been murdered at Auschwitz from 1940 to 1945. Death was present before and after Soviets found the camp. As the Allies neared Auschwitz, the Nazis forced Jewish prisoners from there into concentration camps elsewhere, imposing death marches, and making these other camps more overcrowded and disease-ridden. After liberation, within a few days, more than half of those who remained at the death camp and were freed passed away. Health conditions caused by incarceration and harsh treatment had proven fatal.

American troops liberated Buchenwald on April 11, 1945. There they freed more than 20,000 prisoners. The concentration and slave-labor camps freed by Americans could best be described as living hells. In Dachau, for example, they found dead bodies piled like wood, one atop the other, and survivors who looked like skeletons.

The British found some 60,000 prisoners when they freed Bergen-Belsen, a camp where typhus wreaked such havoc that an estimated 13,000 inmates perished from the disease or from starvation within weeks of being saved. The camp where Anne Frank died had to be burned to the ground by the British to prevent disease from spreading. The conditions there were atrocious. The troops found thousands of unburied corpses. There were so many dead that the British had to use bulldozers to dig mass graves. At first, they made camp guards carry the corpses without protective gear, and some of the guards contracted and died from the illnesses that had killed their captives. When a faster method of burial was needed, the bulldozers were used. A Jewish chaplain attended to the dead.

Over three million Jews were murdered in the death camps established by the Nazis as they tried to rid Europe of Jews. Newsreels and photographs documenting the horrors of the camps made people in Western societies aware of what had really happened there. The result was a demand for justice and a revulsion of Nazis, Germans and Germany. Ultimately, much of the evidence found and documented at the camps was presented at the Nuremberg War Crimes trials.

Liberation brought new challenges to those who had been victims of the Nazis. There were issues of repatriation, rehabilitation, and reuniting with loved ones who had survived. An estimated seven to nine million people had been deported away from their homes by the end of World War II. Those from Western European countries were more likely to return to their homes than those from Eastern European countries. An estimated 1.5 to 2 million declined repatriation. Many did not want to return to places that held terrible memories for them. Some had no homes to which they could return. Some went home only to find their homes and property stolen by neighbors. Some encountered rampant antisemitism. In Poland, for example, anti-Jewish riots called pogroms were numerous. In 1946, one which occurred in the Polish town of Kielce claimed at least 42 Jewish lives. Whatever their reasons, those without homes were the people who ended up in Displaced Persons (DP) camps.

DP camps were run by the United Nations Relief and Rehabilitation Administration (UNRRA) and by the Allies in European areas under their control. These facilities were in Germany, Austria and Italy. According to Yad Vashem's Shoah Resource Center, "By the end of 1946, there were approximately 250,000 Jewish DPs – 185,000 in Germany, 45,000 in Austria, and 20,000 in Italy" ("Displaced Persons, Jewish" 1). The majority of Jewish DPs were Poles; others were from Czechoslovakia, Hungary and Romania. Many of the DP camps had been concentration camps or German Army camps. The first inhabitants were concentration camp survivors and they were faced with conditions similar to those that they had endured as prisoners. Originally, those in the camps were grouped by nationality and Jews could find themselves grouped with Nazi collaborators or worse. Later, their special status was recognized, and they were put in separate camps where they could engage in self-governance, taking responsibility for things like sanitation, hygiene, as well as cultural, educational and religious activities. The Jewish Joint Distribution Committee and the Jewish Agency helped financially. Most camp inhabitants were eager to try to return to normal living.

The UNRRA established the Central Tracing Bureau to help survivors as they searched for relatives who also had not perished. Newspapers and radio broadcasts communicated names and locations of survivors to help friends and family members to find each other. Many Jewish agencies helped DPs with resources, training and immigration, albeit the latter was sometimes illegal. Teachers came to the camps from the United States and Israel to foster education. Furthermore, religious schools were started, and religious holidays were observed.

Efforts to return to a normal life could be seen in many ways in DP camps. Jewish DPs wanted to marry, have families and repopulate their ranks. From 1946–1948, the highest birth rate in the world could be found in DP camps. Cultural life was established, including newspapers and magazines published in Yiddish, orchestras, theaters and commemoration projects. Sports clubs were created and competitions held, heralding the independence and will-power of the participants. There was political fervor as well, as Zionism grew as a movement which advocated for a Jewish homeland in what was then Palestine but what is now Israel.

Many of the Jewish DPs wanted to emigrate to Palestine but the British, who controlled it, were not particularly open to Jewish resettlement there because they were concerned about Arab reaction. The United States also had a rather restrictive immigration policy, but loosened it to give preference to DPs, especially widows and orphans. In 1948, Congress passed the Displaced Persons Act which authorized 200,000 DPs to enter the country, but the law was restrictive given its conditions. The bill was amended in 1950, making immigration easier for DPs.

In all, approximately 80,000 Jewish DPs went to the United States, 136,000 went to Israel, and 20,000 more settled in places like Canada and South Africa. When the state of Israel was established in 1948, the need for DP camps declined. By 1952, most of these camps were closed.

Scripted scenes and monologues

1. Monologue – *The Survivor* by Susan Nanus, based on the memoirs of Jack Eisner

> *JACEK* is 15 years old. He is The Survivor of the play's title. This speech takes place at the end of the play.*
> *JACEK is alone onstage. He addresses the audience.*

JACEK. Maidanek ** was first. I worked in a storage house searching for valuables in the clothes of the dead. The SS took the gold and diamonds, the clothes went back to Germany. One day I hid in a cattle car full of women's coats and I escaped.

The forests were next. I wandered around for three weeks until I found a Polish partisan group. They hated the Germans, but they hated the Jews more, and tried to kill me. I escaped from them, too.

The next camp was Budzin. I tried to escape again, but Ukrainian guards and their dogs chased me up a tree and marched me barefoot back through the snow to my punishment. Seventy lashes with a whip.

Then came Flossenberg. It was in Germany and there was nowhere to escape. We lived 500 in a barracks. We worked 12 hours a day. We were fed a cup of ersatz coffee in the morning and a bowl of watery soup and a slice of bread at night. We never bathed. We never changed our clothes. They called us subhuman. We were.

One day, they evacuated the camp and forced us deeper into Germany. We called it the Death March. Anyone who slowed down or tried to rest was automatically shot. Then the Americans caught up with us, and it was over. I weighed 80 pounds. I was bald. I had no teeth. But I was alive.

(*Pause.*) When I was in the camps, I was sure that the Germans would succeed with their plan. That by the time the war was over, there would only be about five of us left. Ten at the most, but probably just five.

And after we were found and fed, we'd be put into a museum. A huge brick building in the middle of Europe. A museum of Jews. Where people would file past to stare at the last remnant of an extinct species. More than five of us made it. But I still feel like I'm in a museum. Only the rest of the world is preserved behind glass while I stand here, separate and alone.

And I can't understand how it is that I'm still here and all of them are gone. Where did they go? When I went back to Warsaw, there was nothing left, not even a street sign. In Treblinka, only stones. In Auschwitz, nothing but chimneys and barbed wire.

And I can't stop asking the question: Why me?

* *YAH-tzek*
* *my-DAH-nek*

2. Monologue – *Dreams of Anne Frank* by Bernard Kops

> *OTTO FRANK (57) was the only one of his immediate family to survive the Holocaust. His daughter, Anne, posthumously became one of the most famous people in the world following the publication of the diary she kept while hiding from the Nazis with her family in Amsterdam.*
>
> *This monologue opens the play. A man enters … and speaks quietly without undue emotion.*

OTTO. I'm Otto Frank. Anne Frank was my daughter, and she was very special. I survived the war. Somehow. Anne didn't. Survival was random. Pure chance. That morning when our liberators arrived, I just sat there. Numb. The gates were open but I had no spirit to get up and run. I knew then that my wife was dead and my neighbors. And my children were God knows where. I was breathing, yet I was dead. We were all dead, those departed and those still there on that morning. The gates were open and everything was incredibly silent and peaceful. All the guards disappeared; as if they had been spirited away in the night, and that morning for the first time in ages I heard a bird singing. I think it was a blackbird because its song was so beautiful. It couldn't have been a nightingale. They avoided the skies above Auschwitz. Then we heard the sound of guns and great armored vehicles on the move. Getting closer. Russian soldiers appeared. With chocolate and cigarettes, liniment and bandages. We didn't cheer. We just sat there, slumped and staring. Nobody spoke. The sun was so bright and the heat soaked into my bones. And then one soldier started to play his accordion. Suddenly someone danced. In slow motion. Others joined in. More and more. Dancing. Dancing. Soon, everyone who could stand on two legs was dancing. And laughing. And crying. I watched. I just watched.

IMAGE 7.1 A soldier greets liberated prisoners

3. Scene for three actors – *Remember My Name* by Joanna Halpert Kraus

> *RACHEL SIMON is 13 years old. She is also known by the name Madeleine Petit.*
> *LÉON SIMON is Rachel's father. MARIE-THÉRÈSE BARBIÈRE is a 63-year-old*
> *war widow who has been hiding Rachel/Madeleine from the Nazis.*
> *This scene is set in Madame Barbière's kitchen in southern France, May, 1945.*
> *LÉON has just shown up at MARIE-THÉRÈSE's door. He has returned to France to*
> *get RACHEL at the end of the war, immediately following his liberation from a concentra-*
> *tion camp. (The ellipses between lines indicate lines from the full script that have been omitted.)*

RACHEL. Papa? (*Pulls away from MARIE-THÉRÈSE and crosses slowly to him. There is a long look.*) Papa! (*They embrace.*) I knew you'd come. They said – but I knew you'd come. (*Runs to the door.*) Maman.*

LÉON. She's not there.

RACHEL. Where is she?

(*LÉON doesn't answer.*)

RACHEL. Papa, where is she?

(*LÉON shakes his head.*)

RACHEL. Papa! Tell me!

LÉON. Typhus. She died of typhus in the camp.

RACHEL. No! Not Maman! NOT MAMAN. Maybe she escaped. Maybe –

LÉON. You can't understand. You weren't there. There was only one escape.

RACHEL. I made a lace tablecloth just for her. And every evening as soon as the first star appeared, I said goodnight. Just the way we said we would. (*Turns on him violently. All the pent-up rage and fear pours out.*) She can't be dead. She can't be. Why didn't you stop them?

(*MARIE-THÉRÈSE pulls her away.*)

RACHEL. I hate them. I HATE THEM! I HATE THEM!

LÉON. (*Drained.*) Hating won't bring her back.

MARIE-THÉRÈSE. But it helps. (*Gathers RACHEL in her arms.*)

...

(*RACHEL sobs.*)

MARIE-THÉRÈSE. (*To LÉON.*) When a river is swollen, it floods. Let her cry, monsieur, let her cry. Nature knows more than we do about healing.

LÉON. (*Far away.*) I ... can't ... cry.

...

RACHEL. (*Raising her head.*) Papa, where were you?

LÉON. Many places.

RACHEL. You were in one of those camps, weren't you?

(*LÉON nods.*)

RACHEL. In Poland?

LÉON. Poland, Germany. After a while, it doesn't matter. They can only kill you once. But you still have one of us left.

RACHEL. (*Crosses to him slowly.*) So do you, Papa. So do you. (*Looking at him.*) You look, so ... so ... so different?

LÉON. The Americans sent me to a hospital to fatten me up!

MARIE-THÉRÈSE. (*Dryly, bringing him some food.*) They didn't finish.

RACHEL. What about Maman?

LÉON. Too late. (*Touches her face.*) You're so healthy! Madame Barbière, you've given me my daughter! A reason to hope.

MARIE-THÉRÈSE. War is strange, monsieur. I could say the same.

LÉON. How can I thank you?

MARIE-THÉRÈSE. Don't take her away so soon. Stay with us … a few days.

LÉON. I owe you too much already.

MARIE-THÉRÈSE. We'll talk about that later. Later. Right now you need mountain air and rest. And more than a day of it. Even with our famous cabbage soup, I can't work miracles.

LÉON. (*Gazing at RACHEL.*) I think you already have.

RACHEL. Papa, stay. Until you're stronger … Please, Papa, stay.

LÉON. All right, Rachel. All right.

*Mother

SPOTLIGHT ACTIVITY

Remember My Name

"Reunion"

In the scene from *Remember My Name* above, Rachel is reunited with her father, Léon, after many years of separation. This activity will help students understand the degree of emotion which Rachel feels upon seeing her father by having them recall a memory in their own life in which they were reunited with someone they loved.

1   Ask students to recall a reunion. It can be with a lost pet, a friend that they haven't seen in a long time, a deployed parent, etc. They should recall the experience in as much detail as possible, either orally or in writing. (You might suggest that they close their eyes to remember the reunion before writing or speaking.)
2   Ask the students to list every emotion that they felt during the reunion.
3   Have some of the students enact the scene from *Remember My Name*, incorporating as many of their own recalled emotions as possible.

4. Scene for two female actors – *A Shayna Maidel* by Barbara Lebow

> LUSIA* *is a young woman (mid 20s) who has recently been liberated from a concentration camp.*
> HANNA** *is Lusia's best friend (mid 20s) who survived life in the camp with LUSIA. She is very ill.*

While the primary setting of the play is 1946, Manhattan, where LUSIA has recently been reunited with her father and sister after surviving the Holocaust, the following scene takes place in Poland in 1945, and is a flashback to the moments after liberation when LUSIA and HANNA discover a house in the Polish countryside.
(They are clutching each other, leaning on one another for physical support and warmth. HANNA breaks away, looks around.)

HANNA. (*Whispering.*) Now follow me. Into the house. (*HANNA moves toward the bedroom. LUSIA pulls back, frightened.*)
LUSIA. But we can't go in there! (*Both women are weak and cold. HANNA has the energy given by a fever.*)
HANNA. Yes we can!
LUSIA. No!
HANNA. But we're free!
LUSIA. I don't believe it.
HANNA. Liberated.
LUSIA. Liberated.
HANNA. He said it was all right. The Russian on his horse. He said the whole town belongs to us now.
LUSIA. (*Close to HANNA, whispering, terrified.*) But there might be someone in there.
HANNA. So what? Old women and babies only. They were left behind.
LUSIA. I wouldn't put my foot in a German house.
HANNA. It was a Polish house before they took it.
LUSIA. It's no good, Hanna. It had Nazis in it.
HANNA. We're free. We can go where we want to. We can take anything. Food. Clothes. Take back what they stole. He told us. The Russian on his horse. In Yiddish. Who would have guessed? In Yiddish.
LUSIA. But there's a grandmother in there, Hanna. And a little baby. We might frighten them.
HANNA. How can you say such a thing? Your mother wasn't frightened? (*As HANNA speaks, LUSIA covers her ears, humming to drown her out.*) Sprinze*** wasn't frightened on the way to the ovens? They took your sweet little girl. They took your mother. They took everything from us, but we can't take a warm coat or a piece of sausage from –
LUSIA. Stop! I don't want to hear! We can't be like them! We can't do what they did! And I don't want a warm coat. I want to be like the dead ones. I don't want –
HANNA. Shhh! See. She ran away. (*Leading LUSIA in.*) Took the baby out the window. Look. Lusia. It's empty. Come. There's nobody here. Look. A bowl of cereal. For the baby. Oatmeal. Still hot. And a sausage. Milk.
LUSIA. It will make you sick to eat all at once. Just take a little bit, Hanna! (*But HANNA is eating the imaginary food rapidly, insanely. Then she sees the doll. She picks it up and cradles it like a baby.*)
HANNA. This is for my baby.
LUSIA. It belongs to another child.
HANNA. It's for the future. For my baby.
LUSIA. You'd bring a child into this world? Anyway, we can't have children anymore.

HANNA. I can.

LUSIA. You can't, Hanna. I can't. We stopped our periods. We're not women anymore. We don't have women's bodies.

HANNA. We will. (*LUSIA turns away from her.*) Eat. And get round. Soft. Clean. Bleed. (*She is weakening, having difficulty breathing, crumples on the bed. LUSIA turns to her.*) Have babies. You and Duvid.

LUSIA. (*Moving to comfort HANNA.*) All right, Hanna. We'll have babies.

HANNA. (*Hugging the doll tightly.*) And me …

LUSIA. You with someone wonderful like Duvid.

HANNA. A handsome Russian soldier.

LUSIA. On a horse.

HANNA. Who, out of nowhere, speaks Yiddish.

LUSIA. (*Laughing.*) The horse?

HANNA. Even the horse speaks Yiddish. (*HANNA and LUSIA both start laughing wildly until HANNA begins to cough. She weakens greatly.*)

LUSIA. Shh. Soon you'll be better. Now there'll be doctors and medicine.

HANNA. (*Giving LUSIA the doll.*) I ate too much. You were right. But it's a good reason to be sick for a change. Overeating. What would your mama say? (*She rises with effort.*) Here, you take the doll.

LUSIA. But it's yours.

HANNA. You'll need it before I do. Don't even know the Russian's name yet. Let go of me. (*She pushes LUSIA away.*) Hold the doll. Protect it. I'm going to throw up and I don't want to get it dirty. (*LUSIA stands up as HANNA exits.*) Not dirty. Go away from me, Lusia. Gai avek fun mir.****

*LOO-sha
**HAH-na
***SPRINT-zah. Daughter of Lusia and Duvid who was murdered by the Nazis
****GAY a-VEK FOON MIR (Yiddish). Translation: Go away from me

Verbatim testimony historical narratives

1. From the testimony of Martin Aaron – "Liberation"

(http://iwitness.usc.edu/SFI/BrowseTopics.aspx?TopicID=40&ClipID=12)

Born: April 21, 1929, in Teresva, Czechoslovakia
In this April, 1997 interview, Martin tells of being transported from another concentration camp to Bergen-Belsen in Germany in April, 1945, and of his liberation the very next day, as the war was coming to an end and the German army was fleeing the camps.

MARTIN

We got in that train – I don't know how long we were on that train. And we came into what I know now was Bergen-Belsen. As far as – I was only half alive and half ... We were coming out of those railroad cars holding onto one another. We couldn't just walk off by ourselves. We were skin and bones. And two or three of us, holding on like drunks, just to be able to walk to – just to sit down. And I remember, I sat down on the steps of one of the buildings.

And the next day, we didn't see any more guards. There were just hundreds and hundreds of people dressed like I was dressed, in striped clothes. And we were on our own. So, the many people I've seen who were in better shape than I was were in the kitchens that the German Army had. They were already completely going in there and grabbing and completely tearing the kitchen apart for anything they could find, and eating it and distributing it and fighting. And I was too weak even to go into the building. So, I tried to get or catch anything. I was in the back of a building, picking some peels that were peeled, maybe days before, potato peels, and eating those things. Some had some dirt on it. You could feel it. But it was something you could put in your mouth. You could eat it. And we were left completely with some water in the back of the building that you could faucet, that you could get some water ...

And I crawled back to the building that I was at before, sitting down on the steps. And I don't know how many days I was there – two, three or four – I honestly don't know. And in that time – about a day or two – someone kept saying they saw some Red Cross panel trucks outside, some military trucks. And somebody said – it's British soldiers. And when I heard that, I couldn't ... (*choking back tears*). That's when I believe I – when I heard that, that's the first time that I felt that I was human. That somewhere ... That it's *over*. I was too weak to even stand up.

2. From the testimony of David Abrams – "Postwar Life/Return to Life"

(http://iwitness.usc.edu/SFI/BrowseTopics.aspx?TopicID=52&ClipID=178)

Born: December 8, 1928, in Dej, Romania
In this November, 1997 interview, David remembers returning to his hometown following his liberation from the concentration camps, and his subsequent search for his family members. Earlier in his testimony, David reveals that this interview marked the first time that he shared his survival story with anyone.

DAVID

I finally got home to my hometown in the middle of the night. It was about two o'clock in the morning at the railway station. After weeks of going from one train to another, from one city to another, I found my way home. And there was a welcoming committee from the town. People who were already there ...

Every night a train pulled in, they came to welcome survivors. Sure enough, they came and sang. Happy! And then they asked me to go on the wagon with them to go back to town. Here I am, a sixteen-year-old boy, a little over sixteen – and I refused to go with them, 'cause I wanted to walk on my own. I wanted to go to my home, to my house. It was crazy. So I walked at two o'clock in the morning. It was quite a distance in the dark. In the middle of the night, I get to my house where I lived. Number 9 Megyes Street ...

I start calling out names of my family, like I expected an answer, (like) "I'm home! I'm home from school!" you know? And it didn't take me long to realize there was no answer, nobody there.

So I woke up one of my neighbors, a gentile. And I asked him, "Do you know anything?" I told him, "I just arrived, and do you know what happened to my family?" So, he was telling me nobody came back except one sister came back. They told me where she stayed. So, I went there, and I knocked on the door. I yelled out my sister's name. This was Irene Heshowitz. This was my favorite sister who was three years older than me, that took me everywhere, that I adored. I called out, "Irene! Irene!" When she heard my voice, I heard screaming and crying, and she came down to meet me and brought me upstairs to stay there. It was really some reunion that I'll never forget ...

Then, later on, I had two more sisters – the one that was brought up in another town, she was in her own town. She went back there. And another older sister who also came after that. After I arrived, she arrived too. So, there were me and two sisters left in the whole family.

3. From the testimony of Bernard Bermack – "Liberation"

(http://iwitness.usc.edu/SFI/BrowseTopics.aspx?TopicID=40&ClipID=15)

Born: April 3, 1922, in St. Louis Missouri
In this March, 1998 interview, Bernard relates his experience as an American soldier liberating the Günskirchen concentration camp in Austria in May, 1945.

BERNARD

We had moved in quickly through Germany and we were heading toward the Austrian border. And we stopped at a little town called Günskirchenlager* which was a small concentration camp. That is the one that we liberated. That is, we were the first Americans in there. Horrible sight. It was not like Dachau or Buchenwald, not quite as big. But there were – the stench as you approached it was terrible. The stench of bodies, of dead rotting meat. And you saw corpses, just corpses. I'm sure you've seen pictures of them in magazines and TV. And it was a horrible sight. Some of the survivors were crawling on the ground out in the field, trying to dig up maybe a root to eat. Something to just keep alive. Skin and bones. Most of 'em were dead. They were just looking up at the sky. Horrible sights there. And, um, very few were still alive. The Germans knew we were coming, so they had abandoned the camp when we took it over there. So we – it was something you never forget. To see thousands of people with hundreds of bodies around there. And the living ones, just *barely*, barely living.

So we took some – the American commander said to go into town – so we took a truck into the main town. There was a bakery. It was closed. We broke the windows of the bakery, filled [the truck] up with bread, loaves of bread and everything. And we brought it back there. And we sort of distributed it. And when they saw, some of them couldn't even walk. They just crawled to us to try and get something to put in their mouth there. And we had to be careful, tell some of them, "Don't eat too much. You'll get sick." But listen, after starving to death, they stuffed whatever they could in their mouth there, you know. So, we felt we helped a little. Maybe we saved lives – If we saved the life of a dozen of them, we felt good about it, you see.

*Goonz-KEERK-chen-law-ger

4. From the testimony of Eva Kor – "Liberation"

(https://iwitness.usc.edu/sfi/BrowseTopics.aspx?TopicID=40&ClipID=461)

Born: January 31, 1934, in Port, Romania
In this April, 1995 interview, Eva recollects what happened in the days after the liberation of Auschwitz-Birkenau by the Soviet Army on January 27, 1945, when she was almost twelve years old.

EVA

We stayed in Auschwitz. The following day, they took us out, put on us striped uniforms and marched us between the barbed wire and took pictures of us with movie cameras. And I said, "Gosh, that's interesting. I guess we're movie stars – what?" I didn't understand why they were so interested. All I really wanted to do was go home. But I'm glad today that they did take those pictures.

We were taken from there to Katowice,* to a monastery, where we were supposed to – the rumor was, or maybe they told us, that we would wait there until the war ended. And then we would be taken to Palestine. And of course, I wanted to go to Palestine eventually, but I wanted to go home first. The first night there, I remember very clearly, because we were given nice small rooms with two beds and a white sheet. I have never ever seen anything so white! It was gleaming. I kept looking at that sheet.

And I couldn't sleep on it because I felt dirty. I was still filled with lice. I still had the clothes that I had in camp. And I was going to get these sheets dirty, so I had to remove the sheet and just sleep on the mattress. And they gave us toys, I remember. Dolls. And I felt very, very insulted. I realized that they have no idea that the child who survives life and death (*brief pause, shakes her head*) cannot play with dolls. I think the children, maybe I don't know at what age it starts, but I would say all children that are faced with life and death situations are no longer children. So, I just pushed the dolls to the side and I never wanted to look at them.

*KAT-oh-witz

5. From the testimony of Howard Cwick* – "Liberation"

(http://iwitness.usc.edu/SFI/BrowseTopics.aspx?TopicID=40&ClipID=179)

Born: August 25, 1923, in New York, NY
In this September, 1997 interview, Howard, a Jewish American, describes what he saw when he took part in the liberation of the Buchenwald concentration camp in Germany as a US serviceman in 1945.

HOWARD

When we walked in the gates [of the camp], every so often there were one or two or three dead bodies on the ground. The buildings were within twenty yards – twenty, twenty-five yards – from us. Alongside the buildings were large wooden wagons with bodies. Naked bodies stacked like cord wood where they were thrown. Arms, legs, skeletal heads. There had to be eight or nine high and maybe sixteen to twenty across. And there were three or four of these wagons right out in the open. People started to walk towards us. Some were wearing civilian clothes. Some were wearing these long black and white robes. Some had grey and black robes. It seemed like multiple kinds of uniforms. And what struck me was the number of dead bodies we saw just lying around. Like wherever they fell, that's where they lay. And when we started to approach – I started to approach some of these people – they backed away. They didn't know who we were. I think some of them were afraid that this was another trick that the Germans were performing. 'Cause some of them told me about some of the tricks the Germans played on them. And gradually, as I guess the word got out that the American soldiers were there, the yelling began. And from every corner of the field, or the place, people came running and yelling. And they ran to *this* bunch of GIs** and *that* bunch of GIs, and to us.

We came across a bunk that was either dragged outside or was stored outside, and I photographed it (*Takes off his glasses and rubs his eyes.*). The people, the prisoners, were still in it. It was still burning. Which means, just moments before we came into the camp, it had to have been set ablaze with the people still in it. I guess it was [the Germans'] last act of bestiality that they could perform. They hated us so. They hated the Jewish people so.

*Zwik
**GIs – another name for American soldiers

Suggested props/costumes for Chapter 7 historical narrative scenes

- Men's army uniform pieces: hats, shirts, jackets
- Pots and pans
- Potatoes
- Potato peels
- Man's night shirt or robe
- Men's and boy's hats/caps
- Several loaves of bread (real or fake)
- Pieces of bread (real)
- 1940s movie camera/and or still camera (or reasonable facsimile)
- Nun's habits/head wear (or reasonable facsimile)
- Long robes (black or white)
- White sheet(s)
- Doll(s) (1930s–40s looking)

Devised theater activity

Using verbatim testimony and news accounts, devise a scene about Liberation which demonstrates that the liberation of the camps was an event that was marked by shock and sorrow in addition to joy.

Scene material

1   *Verbatim testimony* from liberators and survivors who were liberated.
2   *Two news stories* filed in the days after the liberation of Auschwitz.
3   *Musical underscoring* and/or *sound effects*.

Texts

1   The following testimonies were transcribed from online videos on the Shoah Foundation's IWitness site:

ANTON MASON (Survivor. Liberated from Buchenwald.)

The Americans came in finally around 3:30 in the afternoon. People came in to look at the camp – some GIs. And I walked over to a GI and I asked him if he could give me some food. I was very hungry. So he gave me a Nestle bar and he gave me one of those paraffin packages that had cheese in it and it had some crackers in it. He also gave me a little can. I didn't know what it was, but later I realized it was Spam.

Then the Americans made the mistake of trying to feed the camp. They cooked up a bunch of food and there was no water in the camp, so they cooked it with shortening and fat and some people ate it. I didn't eat it, not because I didn't want to eat it. I couldn't get to it. They didn't have it for everybody. So those who got it, half of them died because they got dysentery from it. It was too much. Their stomachs couldn't take it.

LEON BASS (American soldier. Liberator of Buchenwald.)

So when the officer told us to follow him, and get on the truck, I did ask him, I said, "Where are we going?" He said, "We're going to a concentration camp." And I really was puzzled. 'Cause I didn't know a thing about that. No one had ever mentioned it in all the training I received. But on this day in April in 1945, I was gonna have the shock of my life, because I was going to walk into the midst of a concentration camp called Buchenwald. And you gotta believe me when I tell you, I wasn't ready for that. But you see, I can never forget that day, because when I walked through that gate, I saw in front of me what I call the walking dead. I saw human beings … human beings that had been beaten, starved, had been tortured, that looked like they had been denied everything, everything that would make anyone's life livable.

ROSE KAPLOVITZ (Survivor. Liberated from Ober Altstadt concentration camp.)

One of the girls approached the gate and pushed it open. We realized then that the war has ended. I cannot describe to you the feeling. All the girls ran towards the gate, ran into the street, where soon we were approached by the oncoming Russian Army. Liberation day was the greatest day in my life. We were jumping on top of the tanks, on top of their trucks, kissing them, hugging them, loving them. They were our liberators.

PAUL PARKS (American soldier. Liberator of Dachau.)

As we got inside, these people came out of these barrack-like buildings with their striped uniforms on, just in devastating shape. One of the fellows came out who spoke English, and he said, "Are you Americans?" And I said, "Yes." He said, "Thank God," and he hit the ground and started to pray.

CHARLOTTE CHANEY (US Army nurse. Liberator of Dachau.)

These were people, you have no idea, the skeletons, actually skeletons, how they could walk around. There were people from all over Europe. I remember taking a couple people from out of the compound. We would put them on cots and take them into the barracks. What we tried to do is to give plasma to these people … Now, if you ever saw an arm as big as a circle of your (fingers) … to get into a vein …

Food, we had to be careful. They could not digest meals. We would start off with a gruel. Try and start with that. There was tuberculosis, there was typhoid, there was dysentery – rampant.

JAMES HAYES (American soldier. Liberator of a concentration camp in the German city of Kassel.)

I walked into the building. The sight that greeted me was my first view of the Holocaust. It had these wooden bunks that we've all seen so often in perhaps four or five layers. And in these bunks, on the floors, and scattered around the room, were people dead, dying, getting ready to die, in a total stupor … some dressed, some undressed. And the stench was just awful. And this is the part of pictures that doesn't come through, because what you encounter in these places is the stench of the dying.

2   News Reports
Reported in The New York Times, February 2, 1945
This was one of the first reports published about the liberation of Auschwitz in an American newspaper. The story is credited to the wire service UP, and consisted of only three sentences. Oswiecim is the town in Poland where Auschwitz is located.

Saved from the "Murder Factory"

MOSCOW, February 2 (U.P.) – The newspaper *Pravda* reported today that the Red Army had saved several thousand tortured, emaciated inmates of the Germans' greatest "murder factory" at Oswiecim in south-west Poland.

Pravda's correspondent said fragmentary reports indicated that at least 1,500,000 persons were slaughtered at Oswiecim. During 1941, 1942 and early 1943, he said, five trains arrived daily at Oswiecim with Russians, Poles, Jews, Czechs, French and Yugoslavs jammed in sealed cars.

Reported by the BBC in England, January 27, 1945
(Source: http://news.bbc.co.uk/onthisday/hi/dates/stories/january/27/newsid_3520000/3520986.stm)

1945: Auschwitz death camp liberated

The Red Army has liberated the Nazis' biggest concentration camp at Auschwitz in south-western Poland.

According to reports, hundreds of thousands of Polish people, as well as Jews from a number of other European countries, have been held prisoner there in appalling conditions and many have been killed in the gas chambers.

Few details have emerged of the capture of Auschwitz, which has gained a reputation as the most notorious of the Nazi death camps.

Some reports say the German guards were given orders several days ago to destroy the crematoriums and gas chambers. Tens of thousands of prisoners – those who were able to walk – have been moved out of the prison and forced to march to other camps in Germany.

Details of what went on at the camp have been released previously by the Polish Government in exile in London and from prisoners who have escaped.

In July 1944 details were revealed of more than 400,000 Hungarian Jews who were sent to Poland many of whom ended up in Auschwitz. They were loaded onto trains and taken to the camp where many were put to death in the gas chambers.

Before they went, they were told they were being exchanged in Poland for prisoners of war and made to write cheerful letters to relatives at home telling them what was happening.

According to the Polish Ministry of Information, the gas chambers are capable of killing 6,000 people a day.

Since its establishment in 1940, only a handful of prisoners have escaped to tell of the full horror of the camp.

In October last year, a group of Polish prisoners mounted an attack on their German guards. The Germans reportedly machine-gunned the barracks killing 200 Polish prisoners. The Poles succeeded in killing six of their executioners.

When the Red Army arrived at the camp they found only a few thousand prisoners remaining. They had been too sick to leave.

The capture of Auschwitz comes as the Red Army has made important advances on three fronts: in East Prussia to the north, in western Poland as well as Silesia in eastern Germany. Fighting is continuing around the historic Polish western city of Poznan.

The Polish capital, Warsaw, was liberated a week ago after five-and-a-half years of German occupation.

(BBC)

Staging considerations, choices and tips

1   You do not need to use all of the texts provided; however, you should incorporate at least some text from each of the following: a liberator, a survivor, a news report.
2   Find ways to interweave the texts so that they are not recited as monologues; rather, have each actor deliver only a few lines of text at a time. Mix the news

reports in with the testimonies. Discover the most impactful ways of ordering the lines.

3   Will you include props or costume pieces? Select these carefully.

4   Will your scene include any interactions between actors? Or will each actor deliver his/her lines isolated from the other actors? There is validity in both choices.

5   Consider how you will use sound. Does musical underscoring help or hinder your emotional narrative? Are there sound effects that will help you tell your story? Consider using literal sound effects, such as the clicking of typewriter keys for the journalists, or the recorded sound of tanks rolling in to enhance the stories of the liberators moving into the camps.

8

Nazi war crimes and judgment

Context

Bringing to justice those who were responsible for mass murder and other crimes would span both years and geography and would sear the Holocaust into the annals of jurisprudence and history. The most well-known trials were those of the major Nazi war criminals held at Nuremberg and the trial of Adolf Eichmann held in Israel. These were not, however, the only ones. In addition to the trial of major war criminals, from 1945 to 1949 there would be 12 more trials at Nuremberg alone, involving more than 100 defendants and multiple courts. More trials would follow in other parts of the world.

As World War II was winding down, the Allies had to consider how to find justice for those who had suffered and lost so much. This would not be easy. The Allies – the United States, Great Britain, the Soviet Union and France – did not have the same legal systems. Questions of law would have to be addressed. So, too, would the question of where trials should be held and who should be accused. It was decided that not all Germans would be held responsible, only those accountable for wrongdoings, including mass murder. By October of 1943, the Allies supported asking the United Nations War Crimes Commission "to collect evidence of crimes and to identify those responsible" (Fireside 17). In addition, at the end of 1944, the legal office of the United States War Department directed the military to form units to gather evidence of criminal behavior by Nazi perpetrators and collaborators. In May 1945, Samuel Rosenman, representing the United States, and British, French and Soviet ministers agreed to establish an International Military Court (IMC). President Harry S. Truman tapped Supreme Court Justice Robert H. Jackson as Chief Prosecutor for the United States. Jackson also was charged with drafting the rules for the trial. The charter of the IMC, which framed how the trials would be held and the laws associated with them, was signed on August 6. The initial proceeding would be held in Nuremberg, Germany.

IMAGE 8.1 Defendants in the dock

The first to be tried would be those deemed major war criminals, men whose crimes extended beyond borders. These were the political and military upper echelon whose actions propelled death and destruction. Selecting Nuremberg for the trial was significant for several reasons. First, Adolf Hitler had held numerous rallies in the city. Second, the Nuremberg Laws, which took rights and property away from Jews, were announced there. Third, while much of the city had been destroyed in the war, the Palace of Justice was relatively intact and could serve as the trial's venue. In addition, it was a complex of five buildings that included a prison that could house 1,200 inmates. Before the trial could begin, however, the courtroom had to be enlarged. Furthermore, translators had to travel to Nuremberg, as did reporters from around the world.

Charges were filed against Nazi leaders as well as against Nazi organizations. The indictment against the former contained four counts: "(1) crimes against peace (i.e., the planning, initiating, and waging of wars of aggression in violation of international treaties and agreements), (2) crimes against humanity (i.e., exterminations, deportations, and genocide), (3) war crimes (i.e., violations of the laws of war), and (4) 'a common plan or conspiracy to commit' the criminal acts listed in the first three counts" (Ray 1). A defendant was entitled to legal counsel, a copy of his indictment and the right to examine witnesses. The original plan had been to try 24 individuals. However, Martin Bormann had to be tried in absentia because he had been killed and his body found in Berlin, Gustav Krupp von Bohlen was deemed senile and excused, and Robert Ley hanged himself in his cell. The 21 remaining are identified in the chart that follows as well as the verdict in his case.

Defendant	Role	Verdict	Noteworthy defense strategies
Hermann Goering	Head of Germany's Air Force and Hitler's chosen successor	Death by hanging; he committed suicide the night before his execution	Represented by Otto Stahmer, a lawyer, judge and Nazi
Hans Fritzsche	Chief Nazi radio broadcaster	Acquitted	
Rudolf Hess	Hitler's Deputy	Life in prison	Amnesia; did not testify
Hjalmar Horace Greeley Schacht	Economics Minister	Acquitted	Claimed he was innocent
Wilhelm Keitel	Head of the Wehrmacht Supreme Command for five years; passed along Hitler's orders	Death by hanging	Fulfilling his duties
Alfred Jodl	Chief of the High Command Operations Staff	Death by hanging	
Erich Raeder	Naval commander accused of trying to sink both commercial and war ships	Life in prison	
Karl Doenitz	Naval commander accused of trying to sink both commercial and war ships	Ten years in prison	
Hans Frank	Governor of Nazi-occupied Poland	Death by hanging	
Arthur Seyss-Inquart	Governor of Nazi-occupied The Netherlands	Death by hanging	

Defendant	Role	Verdict	Noteworthy defense strategies
Fritz Sauckel	Appropriated slave laborers	Death by hanging	Claimed he had worshipped Hitler
Albert Speer	Used slave laborers in factories	Twenty years in prison	
Joachim von Ribbentrop	Foreign Minister; duped countries into a false sense of security before they were invaded	Death by hanging	Claimed failing memory; doctors disagreed
Constantin von Neurath	Had been a Foreign Minister; served Hitler in the 1930s	Fifteen years in prison	
Ernst Kattenbrunner	Head of the Reich Security Office	Death by hanging	Used lies and denials
Franz von Papen	Former Chancellor; helped Hitler to gain power in 1933	Acquitted	
Wilhelm Frick	Interior Minister; helped Hitler to gain power in 1933	Death by hanging	
Baldur von Schirach	Head of the Hitler Youth	Twenty years in prison	
Julius Streicher	Spread hatred through publications such as *Der Stürmer*	Death by hanging	
Alfred Rosenberg	Spread Nazi racist ideology; helped move stolen artwork from Vichy France to Germany; helped to overthrow the government of Norway	Death by hanging	
Walter Funk	Served as Economics Minister; replaced Schacht as President of the Reichsbank	Life in prison	

The defendants were brought to Nuremberg by cargo plane and transported by ambulance to the Palace of Justice. To ensure their protection, the complex was surrounded by barbed wire and guarded by American military personnel and equipment. To prevent suicides like Ley's, the accused had to give up their neckties and shoelaces and were under constant watch.

The trial started on November 20, 1945, and lasted for 315 days. The presiding judge was Lord Justice Geoffrey Lawrence. There were eight judges, with two each from Great Britain, the United States, France and the Soviet Union; four of the eight were alternates. The verdicts against individual defendants were read on October 1, 1946. Appeals were denied. Ten died by hanging on October 15, 1946. The ashes of 11, including Goering, were taken to Dachau, cremated and then thrown into a river. Those with jail sentences served time at Spandau prison in West Berlin. Of those, Raeder, Frank, and von Neurath were given early release due to poor health; Hess was the only remaining prisoner there from 1966 to 1987. He committed suicide.

Several noteworthy firsts are associated with this trial. Before this, crimes against humanity had never been prosecuted. Simultaneous translations had not been used. And the term "genocide" originated here.

More trials followed at Nuremberg. These are known as the Subsequent Nuremberg Trials. These included the Doctors Trial, the Einsatzgruppen Trial, and trials for Reich Ministry officials, German judges, Krupp Armaments executives, and other civilian, military, legal and government personnel. Because of the politics of the Cold War, these proceedings had only American judges. Lasting from December 1946 to April 1949, these trials yielded convictions of 177 people.

The British set up courts as well, but they only tried those accused of crimes against British soldiers and Allied citizens in British zones. Most notably, a British military court tried the staff of the Bergen–Belsen concentration camp, and in a 1946 trial the accused were executives of Tesch and Stabenow, makers of Zyklon B gas.

Trials were held elsewhere as well. In Poland, a special court, in existence from September 1944 to 1949, tried Nazi war criminals. Rudolf Höess, Commandant of Auschwitz, was tried here as were a total of 5,450 war criminals. Of the nearly 40,000 suspected of war crimes in Hungary, 19,000 were found guilty. Norway tried Nazis and collaborators, including the Prime Minister. Courts in The Netherlands convicted 14,562 people from 1945 to 1950. Trial outcomes in Romania resulted in the execution of Prime Minister Ion Antonescu. In West Germany, 1958 saw the establishment of the Central Office of Judicial Administration. More than 90,000 were tried and 6,400 received harsh punishments. Other countries holding trials included Croatia, Israel, Austria, the United States, Canada, Italy and France. Trials were held for decades and brought to justice even perpetrators who had escaped to North and South American countries.

One of those was Adolf Eichmann, who was captured on May 11, 1960, by the Israeli secret service (the Mossad) in Argentina where he was living under an assumed name. He was spirited back to Israel by force nine days later. Eichmann had been responsible for "the identification, assembly, and transportation of Jews from all over occupied Europe to their final destinations at Auschwitz and other extermination camps

IMAGE 8.2 Defendant Adolf Eichmann on trial

in German-occupied Poland" (Berenbaum 1). He had been considered very capable of getting scarce resources, such as cattle cars to transport Jews. Trying Eichmann in Israel was controversial, but the Israelis used the 1950 Nazi and Nazi Collaborators' Punishment Law as the legal basis for the charges. As described by Deborah Lipstadt in her book, *The Eichmann Trial,*

> On April 11, 1961, the theatre of Beit Ha'am, Jerusalem's brand new cultural center, was packed. Over seven hundred people filled the room for the trial of a man accused of being the chief operational officer of the Final Solution. Newspapers worldwide carried news of this event. American television networks broadcast special telecasts. This was not the first Nazi war-crimes trial. Yet there were more reporters in Jerusalem than had gone to Nuremberg.
>
> (xi)

The cultural center's theater was converted into a courtroom and a glass booth was constructed for Eichmann. There were 15 counts in the indictment against him and these were classified as crimes against humanity, war crimes, crimes against the Jewish people and belonging to a hostile organization. Gideon Hausner, Israel's Attorney

IMAGE 8.3 Adolf Eichmann listens to the proceedings through a glass booth during his trial in Jerusalem

General, was the prosecutor. The attorney for the defense was Robert Servatius. Israel paid Servatius' fee because the Eichmann family could not afford it and West Germany, which had paid for the defense of other accused war criminals in foreign courts, refused to do so for this defendant. The presiding judge was Moshe Landau. Joining him were two other judges, Yitzhak Rauch and Benjamin Halevi. Most of the trial was conducted in Hebrew. Among other languages used were German, Yiddish, Hungarian and English. Witness testimonies were translated into Hebrew. Sometimes Eichmann was spoken to in German to be sure that he understood. There were simultaneous translations of the trial into English, French and German. When asked how he pled to the charges, Eichmann took the position that even if he had committed the crimes for which he stood accused, he was not guilty because he was following orders.

Witnesses against Eichmann spoke of his zeal and unrelenting determination to murder as many Jews as possible. Holocaust survivors told their stories, making the trial memorable and of major historical significance. The verdict was rendered on December 15, 1961. Eichmann was found guilty on all counts and sentenced to death. An appeal to the Supreme Court was unsuccessful. A few minutes before midnight on

May 31, 1962, Adolf Eichmann's punishment, death by hanging, was administered. His body was cremated and his ashes were scattered at sea.

There were important differences between the Nuremberg Major War Crimes trial and the Eichmann trial. The former had many defendants tried together whereas the latter had only one defendant. The Nuremberg trial was held in Germany right after World War II ended while Eichmann was tried in Israel a number of years later. The victors judged the Nuremberg defendants. In Eichmann's case, the judges acted for the state of Israel.

Regardless of where war crimes trials were held, the number of accused or the magnitude of the crimes, bringing the perpetrators of the Holocaust to justice helped the world to recognize the horrors that were designed to eliminate the Jews of Europe and claimed millions of lives. These trials put a human face to evil and those touched by it.

Scripted scenes and monologues

1. Scene for three actors – *Dark Road* by Laura Lundgren Smith

> *GRETA, 21, is a female guard in the Ravensbrück concentration camp. LISE, 19, is GRETA's younger sister. DAIMLER is a journalist in his 20s.*
> *The setting is Germany, 1946. GRETA has just been given a death sentence for her criminal actions as a guard at Ravensbrück. She is the youngest woman to receive this punishment. As she is being interviewed by DAIMLER, GRETA's memories come to life in flashback scenes with her sister, LISE.*

LISE. What's happened to you? What on earth has happened to you?

GRETA. I don't know what you mean.

LISE. Four months in this place, it's changed you so much.

GRETA. Don't be silly. I haven't changed.

LISE. You have changed, for the worse! Those are people, Greta. They're people.

GRETA. They're agitators, Gypsies, Jews, communists.

LISE. And they're human beings.

GRETA. If you say so.

LISE. If I say so? You don't see them as human?

GRETA. No, I don't.

LISE. Why not?

GRETA. Because it's easier that way!

(She storms away toward DAIMLER, where her demeanor changes. She leaves a shaken LISE, who puts her face in her hands and exits.)

DAIMLER. So, seeing them as less than human helped you cope?

GRETA. It was more than that. It isn't just that you see them as less. It is that they become less. We didn't use names. They were prisoners, numbers.

DAIMLER. Always? You never knew the names of any?

GRETA. They were the enemy. You know that. Names made them human. They weren't human to us. We made sure of it.

DAIMLER. Did you ever try to fight that idea?

GRETA. Does the butcher consider the lamb? It was a machine. People went in, we tore off their faces, and they became things.

DAIMLER. Things.

GRETA. Anyway, I wanted to do more than watch over that rabble. I had heard they were doing important medical research in the camp to help the soldiers.

(*LISE enters.*)

DAIMLER. You wanted to help with the research?

GRETA. Yes. But in the end, it was just part of the machine.

LISE. At least the research might help someone.

GRETA. Yes, I've heard they are doing amazing things.

LISE. But those stories … those poor people, locked away from their families. What if they took me away from you like that?

GRETA. Why are you so quick to defend them, Lise? They are enemies to the Reich.

LISE. In what way?

GRETA. They are dangerous.

LISE. Handing out handbills is dangerous?

GRETA. They are traitors to Germany.

LISE. Is just saying they disagree with Hitler's plans terrible enough to be put into a prison camp? Even I disagree with a lot of what the Reich is doing. With the war.

GRETA. So you say continually. You should be careful who hears you.

LISE. I'm not afraid. I'm more afraid of what I hear about that camp. Surely you could find a better job elsewhere.

GRETA. They're just rumors, Lise.

LISE. Promise me something.

GRETA. What?

LISE. (*Putting her arms around GRETA.*) Promise me you won't let them have you. (*GRETA extricates herself, and walks away. LISE calls after her.*)

LISE. Promise me!

2. Scene for two actors – *Dark Road* by Laura Lundgren Smith

> *GRETA was a female guard in the Ravensbrück concentration camp. DAIMLER is a journalist.*
>
> *The setting is Germany, 1946. GRETA has just been given a death sentence for her criminal actions as a guard at Ravensbrück. She is being interviewed by a journalist named DAIMLER, who has gained her trust by telling her that he, too, worked in a concentration camp – Auschwitz. He will later reveal that he was not a guard, but rather a prisoner, who was sent to the camp for writing articles condemning the Nazis.*

DAIMLER. The girls were treated like lab rats.

GRETA. The research was necessary. It was important.

DAIMLER. Some of the women, the bunnies as they were called, testified in the hearings. Showed those awful scars. Some were crippled.

GRETA. They survived, didn't they?

DAIMLER. And is that enough? Doesn't it matter that they suffered?

GRETA. Surely you know their suffering was for the greater good.

DAIMLER. And what of the ones who died?

GRETA. Death always takes his portion, Mr. Daimler.

DAIMLER. And those who died at your hands?

GRETA. (*Shrugs.*) The weak were culled.

DAIMLER. And you never questioned that your ideal Germany was going to be built on murder?

GRETA. Did you?

DAIMLER. Sometimes.

GRETA. (*Makes a disgusted "tsk" sound.*) Our conviction was to rid Germany of the vermin. Do you mind killing a flea? A rat? It's no different.

DAIMLER. And you were only doing your duty.

GRETA. Yes, just as we all did.

DAIMLER. No. I never harmed anyone.

GRETA. In the camps, we all harmed someone.

DAIMLER. Some more than others.

(*There is a pause as GRETA stares at him evenly.*)

And isn't saying it was your duty taking away personal choice? You did have a choice, didn't you?

GRETA. Would you embrace what all others detest? I had to choose, and I chose what was best for the future of this country. It became very clear to me there was no room for hesitation, for regret. (*Pins DAIMLER with a judgmental stare.*) Those things are signs of weakness.

DAIMLER. Was Lise aware of what you were doing at that time?

GRETA. Only some of it.

DAIMLER. And what did she think?

GRETA. Lise was gentle, like a child. She loved people. She fed strays even when we hadn't enough food for ourselves. And, she couldn't stand a bully.

DAIMLER. And the Nazis were bullies.

GRETA. We're all bullies, given the right situation.

DAIMLER. But not Lise?

GRETA. No. She hated the war, hated the Reich. Of Kristallnacht, she said, "All that broken glass? That's the soul of Germany."

DAIMLER. She didn't believe in the efforts against the Jews?

GRETA. No. She didn't believe in any of it.

DAIMLER. So one sister was a pacifist and one was a disciple of Hitler.

GRETA. What does it matter now?

3. Scene for two actors – *Dark Road* by Laura Lundgren Smith

GRETA served as a female guard in the Ravensbrück concentration camp. DAIMLER is a journalist who was imprisoned in Auschwitz for writing articles against the Nazis. The setting is Germany, 1946. GRETA has just been given a death sentence for her criminal actions as a guard at Ravensbrück. She is being interviewed by DAIMLER. We have just seen a memory of GRETA's – that of her sister being taken away by a Nazi Commandant. (The ellipses before DAIMLER's last speech indicate lines omitted from the full script.)

DAIMLER. You … you gave them your sister. You … You're …

GRETA. A monster? I've done what I've done. It cannot be undone. The road I've traveled goes only in one direction.

DAIMLER. And your sister?

GRETA. Did I change my mind? Did I save her?

DAIMLER. Did you?

GRETA. No. I did not.

DAIMLER. What happened to her?

GRETA. She was put in solitary confinement. In three weeks, the Russians liberated the camp. I was captured, tried, sentenced to hang.

DAIMLER. And Lise?

GRETA. I never saw her again. When we knew the Russians were coming, the gassings of prisoners were increased tenfold. Solitary contained the worst of the prisoners. They were gassed first.

DAIMLER. You sent your own sister to her death.

GRETA. I told you. I gave everything to the Reich.

DAIMLER. Your own sister.

GRETA. And I'd do it again. There is no room for the weak.

DAIMLER. Hitler said there was no truth, only victory. Tell me, is there victory for you, even in her death?

GRETA. *(After a beat, staring hard at DAIMLER.)* Yes.

DAIMLER. *(Leans on table in front of GRETA, staring at her, then, bitterly.)* Heil Hitler.

GRETA. So you want to gloat? To tell me how wrong I was? I won't believe you. *(Laughs.)* You should have died in Auschwitz.

DAIMLER. *(Laughs softly, after a moment.)* There was beauty in it for you, wasn't there? It was a hideous kind of art to you. You drew it all in blood, every twisted thing you did. Evil in effigy. Every human being you tormented, you beat, you murdered. Power over all, power like a sickness.

GRETA. I did it to empower Germany.

DAIMLER. No. To empower you.

GRETA. You know nothing.

DAIMLER. I know this: your sister watched as they took you, day by day, hour by hour. And you went. You chose. They showed you that dark road, and you went down it willingly. Evil isn't something that swallows you up. It's a choice you make, every day. Every time you see someone as less, as no longer human, as no longer worthy of dignity, of life. Evil becomes ordinary. It becomes routine. If you aren't careful, if you don't look it in the face every day, evil slips up beside you, puts its arm around you. It makes you a friend.

GRETA. (*After a slight pause.*) A friend? I was more than its friend. I was its confidante. Its servant. Its sister.

…

DAMLIER. (*Slight shake of head.*) Goodbye, Greta. And if there is a God in heaven, may He have mercy on your soul.

SPOTLIGHT ACTIVITY

Dark Road

"Character Traits"

1   To begin, have students form a circle. Each will use a word or phrase to describe Lise. The person next to him or her must repeat that word and then add their own. The activity continues with each player repeating all the words that have come before their turn and then adding their own. Continue going around the circle until every person has repeated the list and added their own word, such as in the example that follows.

First Person: Kind
Second Person: Kind, caring
Third Person: Kind, caring, sensitive

If someone has difficulty remembering the list, other students can help them. If a student truly cannot remember the list, ask them to simply add their word and continue with the next person. After all students have added to the list, their responses should be recorded on the board or on index cards or post-it notes.

2   Repeat the same exercise for Greta's character.
3   Pair students, with one playing Lise and one playing Greta. (Note: for this activity, the student's gender should not matter.) Each student will pick a word or phrase that describes their character from those that were recorded. The students should then create a scene, either with or without dialogue, in which they prominently display the trait selected for their character. Add the additional requirement that there must be a conflict in the scene. Once all pairs have performed their scenes, students should discuss how the traits were revealed. How did the nature of the conflict impact the actor's choices for the character? How can they apply the character development in these scenes to their understanding of these characters as they appear in the scenes in this chapter?

Verbatim testimony historical narratives

1. From the testimony of Dora Abend – "Jewish Survivor"

(https://iwitness.usc.edu/sfi/BrowseTopics.aspx?TopicID=69&ClipID=1286)

Born: May 5, 1927, in Lublin, Poland
*In this May, 1996 interview, concentration camp survivor Dora recalls returning to Germany
in the 1960s to serve as a witness in the war crimes trial of a female Nazi camp supervisor
named Brigitte.**

DORA

They had my name from the concentration camp and they came from Germany to
America and they called me up. And they told me, "We know you were there, in
Majdanek.** And we have two women that were Nazis in Majdanek and we want
you to come and you're going to testify against them." I didn't want to go. I was scared
to go to Germany. They know that I'm a witness, an eyewitness, and they're gonna kill
me. He says, "No. It's not gonna happen. We're gonna watch over you. You must do it.
You must go, because we don't have too many survivors like you. You were in seven
concentration camps. You can tell us. And you're going to identify these two women."

So I went. To Dusseldorf. And then [the trial] started. And the two women were
there. One was named Brigitte. With a dog she used to come – when we worked in
the fields, she used to come with a dog. That was Brigitte. She was tall and very ugly
and very skinny. And the other one – I didn't testify for the other one – she was someplace else in charge. I said, this one, Mrs. Ryan, I don't know her. She wasn't in charge
with us. But Brigitte, I know.

The one judge asked me – he says "You didn't see her for maybe 17 years. How
are you going to describe her? How are you going to recognize her?" Brigitte I'm
talking about. She was always watching us with a dog, with a German Shepherd, and
hitting us over the head. I says "It's easy to recognize her. Number one – she was the
ugliest German woman I ever saw." (*Laughs.*) Everybody was laughing! I didn't know
that everybody's listening. So I says, "She was skinny and very tall and very ugly and
she looks like she was so angry at us." We were good-looking girls, we weren't looking
like her, so she took advantage of us. And then I remember she had big feet. She must
have had between 14 and 20 size feet.

So he says, "Alright. Can you go through the court and pick Brigitte out after so
many years? I want to see if you recognize her." And I'm walking in that court, and I'm
looking at everybody. And, that court was filled with people – German people from
all over towns. They brought people from colleges, from high schools, they brought
students to witness everything. And I walked and I looked. Then I saw Brigitte. At first
I saw her, but I wasn't 100 percent sure. And I was standing there, and I looked at her
and she looked down. And she cried. What I saw is another woman. She was so skinny
then, but now she was so fat. Like that (*spreads arms*). Swollen up. Not fat as from food,

but from sickness probably. And I looked and I says, "I think that this is Brigitte." So he says "How do you recognize her?" I says, "She had a very big mouth with very thin lips and her feet was very big." So he says, "Brigitte stand up and show her your feet." So she stood up. And I says, "Yeah. Yes, that is Brigitte. I recognize her. That's her big feet and I know for sure it is." And he says, "Yes, you are right. That is Brigitte."

Bri-GEE-ta
**my-DAH-nek – *a concentration camp in Poland*

2. From the testimony of Allen Caine – "Jewish Survivor"

(https://iwitness.usc.edu/sfi/BrowseTopics.aspx?TopicID=69&ClipID=1287)

Born: May 5, 1924, in Ciechanów, Poland
In this October, 1995 interview, Allen Caine describes returning to Germany to give testimony in the war crimes trial of a Nazi Commandant and reveals his disappointment that his testimony, and that of other survivors, was not enough to convict the man.
(NOTE: several non-italicized parenthetical phrases have been added for clarity.)

ALLEN

I was subpoenaed. First a DA came here [to my home in the United States]. He interviewed me. The guy from Golleschau,* the Commandant, he was on trial. He was a half-breed. Half Polish, half German. And I went to Germany. Frankfurt am Main. And the next day I come in [to the courtroom]. And as I stick my head in, I turn right around, and I'm running out. [The Commandant] recognized me. Well, he didn't recognize me, but he figured that's me. The interpreter – I asked for an interpreter. I didn't want to speak fluently by myself German – he begged me "Please!" I said, "Germany doesn't have a hall of justice. Never had!" He said, "Well, this time we do!" And we were almost fighting together. And finally, I went in. I sit down. They all come in. They all greeted me. And they want me to look around, see if I see anybody. As I was talking to them, the Commandant was sitting like that (*cups hand around ear*) and listening. And I had a swivel chair. They wanted me to point him out. As I turned around, I pointed out like that (*swivels and points*). He thought I had a gun or something. He went like that (*raises both hands in the air*). That happened to be on a holiday. That's why the kids from school – German kids – used to come around and listen to the whole thing.

There were seven judges, one lady judge. [The lawyers] kept asking me, a few times, the same thing, to get me off the line: "What hat was he wearing? Did he wear a helmet?" See, I used to shine his shoes. I used to clean his motorcycle. "Did the motorcycle have heavy tires or thin tires?" Okay. I gave 'em the answer. Another guy – see he had two lawyers – asked me the same question. I said to the interpreter, I said, "You tell them I'm not talking to them. I gave them one answer and that's it." And then I broke down. I started to cry. [A judge] banged on it with that thing (*makes a motion like banging a gavel*). He said "Recess!" We came back. The first thing they did, they stood up and apologized to me. And I told 'em, "If you gonna ask me twice the same thing to confuse me, I'm not talking to you anymore." Because I knew the Germans. After the war, they were scared. Scared. Terrible.

And people from Israel came and testified against him and Argentina (too). And we couldn't do a damn thing. Because I testified that I saw him, that he killed two Christian Hungarians and he said he didn't. I couldn't testify that I'd *seen* it. I didn't. I was locked up. I heard the shots. I saw him coming in with a machine gun. Because he never usually had a machine gun, he only had a little revolver. And ... there wasn't enough. See, as a democrat country, you had to see it to testify. And I didn't see it. I didn't want to lie to get as low as they were. So the end was, years later, a friend of his, he was also an SS man,** he saw him killing a guy ... uh, one of *our* people.*** His friend – also an SS man. That's when he got jail. But when *we* testified, he didn't get jail. (*Sighs. Is silent.*)

*A concentration camp in Poland
**Schutzstaffel, or Protection Squads – originally established as Adolf Hitler's personal body-guard, and later, the elite guard of the Nazi Reich, overseeing the concentration camp system
***Meaning a fellow Jew

3. From the testimony of Jack Robbins – "War Crimes Trial Participant"

(https://iwitness.usc.edu/sfi/BrowseTopics.aspx?TopicID=69&ClipID=1288)

Born: November 1, 1919, in Flemington, New Jersey
An American attorney, Jack Robbins was unable to serve in World War II due to a medical condition. He felt a duty to serve his country in some way, and when the United States government was looking for lawyers to work as prosecutors at the Nuremberg Trials, Robbins enthusiastically signed on.

JACK

As General Taylor's legal aid, I worked very closely with him on everything he was doing. I traveled with him all over Europe, to various cities, collecting evidence. I also worked with him on drafting the indictments and drafting the opening statements in the first half dozen cases that were tried in Nuremberg. I'm talking about the first six of the Subsequent Proceedings. I was one of several prosecutors in the first case, the Medical case. There were twenty-three SS doctors who were charged with war crimes and crimes against humanity for conducting medical experiments in the con-centration camps, and then taking part in the euthanasia* program. We prepared the indictments and made the opening statement in that case.

The most important part of the prosecution's case in every situation depended on the German documents. As you know, the Germans were very meticulous record keepers. And the US Army, after the end of the war, had captured literally millions of documents. All of the cases involved witnesses as well as documents, but I would say the documents were the most important part.

(The main defendants in the Medical case were) Dr. Karl Brandt, who was the personal physician of Hitler and was head of all the German medical services ... the top doctor in Germany. And Himmler's** personal physician was also a defendant. Other defendants were other SS generals headquartered in the concentration camps. These defendants conducted unusually cruel and murderous experimentation in the concentration camps. They consisted of infecting concentration camp inmates with malaria, typhus and other diseases to determine the effectiveness of various kinds of vaccines. There were high altitude experiments in which a very high altitude was simulated and many inmates died in those experiments. Also, inmates were exposed to freezing experiments. They were subjected to extreme cold and extreme weather conditions. All of this was done in the name of trying to determine how the SS and German soldiers would fare in conditions like this. In the process, thousands of inmates were killed. I recall that Justice Musmanno*** described some of that in his opinion. And I recall that he said that there was not one single thing learned from these experiments that was useful. This was a part of the program that was undertaken by the Nazis and by the medical profession to "cleanse" the German population of persons they considered to be "not worthy to live." And that included Jews, Gypsies, Poles ... And this philosophy actually pre-dates Hitler. The "super race," the Aryanization of the race, goes back years before Hitler. And the medical profession enthusiastically followed Hitler and Himmler's pronouncement in this regard. There were more doctors that joined the Nazi party ... the representation of doctors was much higher than any other profession – than teachers or lawyers for example.

*The goal of the Nazi Euthanasia Program was to kill people with mental and physical disabilities. In the Nazi view, this would cleanse the "Aryan" race of people considered to be genetically defective and a financial burden to society
**Himmler – the second most powerful man after Hitler in Nazi Germany, responsible for conceiving and overseeing implementation of the "Final Solution"
***Judge Michael Musmanno – member of a tribunal of American judges appointed by President Truman who presided over the Subsequent Nuremberg Trials

Suggested props/costumes for Chapter 8 historical narrative scenes

- Men's and women's jackets, sweaters and hats – 1950s
- Large pair of women's shoes
- Judge's gavel
- Black robe (judge's)
- Briefcases
- Legal pads and pens
- Calibrated medicine droppers/glass pipettes (stand-ins for injection needles)

Devised theater activity

Devise a scene in which the text is the word-for-word transcript of the Nuremberg testimony of Rudolf Höss, Commandant of Auschwitz.

Scene components

1   The Nuremberg Trials *verbatim testimony of Rudolf Höss*, Commandant of Auschwitz
2   One additional line of dialogue: *"I was just following orders."*
3   *Choral repetition* of speech
4   *Choral percussion* sounds
5   *Choral movement* (optional)

Text

1   From the Testimony of Rudolf Höss, Commandant of Auschwitz, delivered at the Nuremberg Trials on Monday, April 15, 1946. Höss was being questioned as a defense witness by Dr. Kauffmann, who was the lawyer for Nazi General Ernst Kaltenbrunner.

Exactly one year later, HÖSS was executed by hanging after being tried and sentenced to death by the Polish Supreme National Tribunal. He was responsible for the deaths of 1.1 million Jews at Auschwitz. (The number he gives in this testimony – 2 million – was later discovered to be largely inflated. By his own admission, HÖSS did not know the actual number of deaths at Auschwitz when he delivered this testimony.) (The ellipses note places where lines of testimony have been removed for brevity and clarity.)

DR. KAUFFMANN. From 1940 to 1943, you were the Commander of the camp at Auschwitz. Is that true?
HÖSS. Yes.
DR. KAUFFMANN. And during that time, hundreds of thousands of human beings were sent to their death there. Is that correct?
HÖSS. Yes.
DR. KAUFFMANN. Is it true that you, yourself, have made no exact notes regarding the figures of the number of those victims because you were forbidden to make them?
HÖSS. Yes, that is correct.
DR. KAUFFMANN. Is it furthermore correct that exclusively one man by the name of Eichmann had notes about this, the man who had the task of organizing and assembling these people?
HÖSS. Yes.

DR. KAUFFMANN. Is it furthermore true that Eichmann stated to you that in Auschwitz a total sum of more than 2 million Jews had been destroyed?

HÖSS. Yes.

DR. KAUFFMANN. Men, women, and children?

HÖSS. Yes.

…

DR. KAUFFMANN. Is it true that in 1941 you were ordered to Berlin to see Himmler? Please state briefly what was discussed.

HÖSS. Yes. In the summer of 1941 I was summoned to Berlin to Reichsführer SS Himmler to receive personal orders. He told me something to the effect – I do not remember the exact words – that the Führer had given the order for a final solution of the Jewish question. We, the SS, must carry out that order. If it is not carried out now then the Jews will later on destroy the German people. He had chosen Auschwitz on account of its easy access by rail and also because the extensive site offered space for measures ensuring isolation.

…

DR. KAUFFMANN. And after the arrival of the transports were the victims stripped of everything they had? Did they have to undress completely; did they have to surrender their valuables? Is that true?

HÖSS. Yes.

DR. KAUFFMANN. And then they immediately went to their death?

HÖSS. Yes.

DR. KAUFFMANN. I ask you, according to your knowledge, did these people know what was in store for them?

HÖSS. The majority of them did not, for steps were taken to keep them in doubt about it and suspicion would not arise that they were to go to their death. For instance, all doors and all walls bore inscriptions to the effect that they were going to undergo a delousing operation or take a shower. This was made known in several languages to the internees by other internees who had come in with earlier transports and who were being used as auxiliary crews during the whole action.

DR. KAUFFMANN. And then, you told me the other day, that death by gassing set in within a period of 3 to 15 minutes. Is that correct?

HÖSS. Yes.

DR. KAUFFMANN. You also told me that even before death finally set in, the victims fell into a state of unconsciousness?

HÖSS. Yes. From what I was able to find out myself or from what was told me by medical officers, the time necessary for reaching unconsciousness or death varied according to the temperature and the number of people present in the chambers. Loss of consciousness took place within a few seconds or a few minutes.

DR. KAUFFMANN. Did you yourself ever feel pity with the victims, thinking of your own family and children?

HÖSS. Yes.

DR. KAUFFMANN. How was it possible for you to carry out these actions in spite of this?

HÖSS. Strict order, and the reason given for it by the Reichsführer Himmler.

2   Additional line of dialogue: "I was just following orders"

In German, the phrase was befehl ist befehl *("an order is an order"), and it was used so frequently by Nazi trial defendants that it came to be known as "the Nuremberg defense." In slightly different phrasing, it is the very defense given by Höss in the final line of his testimony which appears above.*

Staging considerations, choices and tips

1   Consider having a single actor portray/read Dr. Kauffmann, and a single actor portray/read Höss, along with a small group of additional actors performing the choral repetition, sounds and movements that will give the piece more theatrically. Make a choice about these additional actors – who are they "playing?" judges? other witnesses? trial observers? Or are they not literal characters, but more of a symbolic Greek chorus, giving moral commentary on the action?

2   Which words and phrases would you like to highlight by having the "Chorus" repeat them?

3   How will you make the percussive sounds? Will they be created solely through a physical action of the body – such as stomping or clapping? Or will you use some sort of tool or instrument? Will the sounds be germane to the setting – such as a judge's gavel? Or will they be less literal and more atmospheric?

4   How will you use the phrase "I was just following orders?" How often will it be repeated?
Consider using the German translation of the phrase as well.

5   What does the scene look like? Is the Chorus integrated into the stage picture with Dr. Kauffmann and Höss? Or do these actors appear in a different area of the stage? Will you be incorporating movement? Or will the piece be very still, emphasizing the words and sounds?

9

Survivors and subsequent generations

Context

The end of the war did not mean the end of suffering and strife for survivors of the Holocaust. The lives which they had once known were gone and they were faced with starting anew. They had, in effect, two lives – the one lived before the war and the one lived after. Some were so ill and malnourished that even liberation could not save them and they perished. Others had long recoveries from their illnesses and injuries. In addition, survivors faced continuing hatred of Jews by former Nazis and Nazi sympathizers, ill-treatment even from some American forces, and a lack of needed food and medicines for those trying to mend physically and emotionally. They encountered pogroms, stolen property, betrayal by trusted friends and long waits for emigration.

Survivors who returned to countries such as Poland, Czechoslovakia, Austria, Romania, Yugoslavia and Hungary often found strangers living in their homes. Former neighbors or others had kept or stolen their property. Jewish communities had been decimated and survivors had no homes, no work, no places of worship and no safe havens in their countries of origin.

> In Poland, particularly, survivors came home to open enmity. Hundreds of men and women returning from the concentration camps were shot by Poles. In July of 1946, the scattered, random killing turned into a full-scale pogrom in Kielce, Poland, where nearly fifty Jews were slaughtered.
>
> (Epstein 94–95)

Learning what had happened, Jews fled Eastern Europe for western areas under Allied control.

Liberation brought the establishment of Displaced Persons (DP) camps to house survivors. According to the United States Holocaust Memorial Museum, "From 1945

IMAGE 9.1 Portrait of teenagers in the Feldafding Displaced Persons Camp

to 1952, more than 250,000 Jewish Displaced Persons lived in camps and urban centers in Germany, Austria, and Italy. These facilities were administered by Allied authorities and the United Nations Relief and Rehabilitation Administration (UNRRA) ("Displaced Persons"). A priority for most was to see if any family members had survived and, if so, to locate them. The UNRRA, public radio broadcasts and newspapers were tools used to aid DPs in this search effort. Also assisting survivors was the American Jewish Joint Distribution Committee (JDC) which provided necessities such as food, clothing and job training for those in the camps.

DP camps were the sites of numerous weddings, as Jews were eager to begin new lives and families as well as to restore the Jewish population. Not all of these marriages were forged from love; rather they were a way to begin life again. Because having children was so important to survivors, a new generation had been born by the end of 1947.

Emigration opportunities for many DP camp residents came slowly, with some waiting years for visas. Helen Epstein notes that, "The last Displaced Persons camp – Foehrenwald in Bavaria – remained in operation until 1957" (95). Further, the "refugee problem," as the press called it, and the challenges faced by immigrants (called "greeners") to their new North American countries attest to how widespread the geography and trials associated with relocation could be. The United States, for example, saw 92,000 resettle within its borders and Canada saw more than 25,000 come there. Israel, Latin American countries and Australia also received their share of newcomers. There were, of course, those who tried to illegally enter Palestine, as

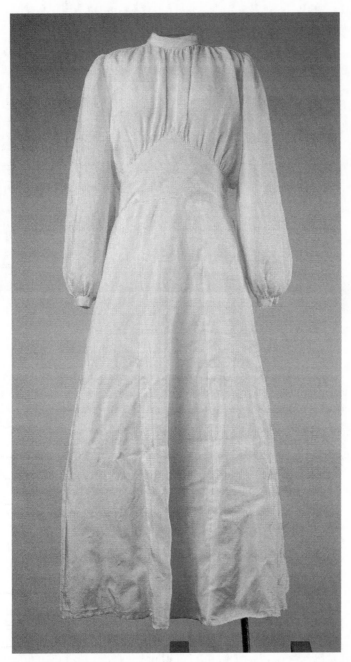

IMAGE 9.2 Wedding dress made from a parachute worn for a wedding in a Displaced Persons Camp

Israel was called before statehood. There also were those who opted to remain in their European countries of origin. Immigrants to new countries were not always welcomed with open arms. They could be perceived to be reminders of the Holocaust that other Jews wanted to forget, or as potential financial burdens, or as threats to Jews already in those countries.

Survivors tended to settle in neighborhoods populated by other survivors. There was a sense that only those who had gone through the Holocaust could really understand and that others did not want to hear about what they had lived through. In fact, these immigrants were originally considered to be refugees, rather than survivors. The latter term, which engenders respect and empathy, came into use quite some time later. Additionally, there also was a tendency for relatives to live near to each other. Their social circles largely consisted of kin and other survivors, perhaps reflecting a distrust of strangers, cynicism or emotional vulnerability.

Resettlement focused upon survivors' material needs; psychological needs at first were overlooked. The Hebrew Immigrant Aid Society helped survivors in the United States with finding work and housing. The Jewish Immigrant Aid Society fulfilled these functions in Canada. While these organizations tried to stay in contact with the refugees, many survivors simply opted to go it alone.

It was not uncommon for Holocaust survivors to suffer from physical and emotional problems. Resistance to disease for some was weaker than for nonsurvivors. Some survivors became hypochondriacs; others stoic in the face of illness. Depression, survivor guilt, anxiety and PTSD (post-traumatic stress disorder) could be seen in survivors and led some to commit suicide, in certain cases years after being liberated.

In order to seek reparations from Germany, survivors had to be examined by German doctors for physical and mental problems. There were those survivors who saw this as further humiliation and refused, choosing instead to forego compensation. Over time, survivors who were examined by mental health professionals helped to provide insight into psychological attributes that seemed to be common to those clients. Repressed emotions, preoccupation with or repressed mourning and exaggerated startle response (heightened fright or flight reactions) were a few of the noted issues. Of course, some survivors experienced no physical or mental trauma and painting all survivors with the same broad brush would be unwise.

Children of survivors, called Second Generation or 2G Holocaust Survivors were, not surprisingly, affected by their parents' experiences. When research on children of survivors started, one emerging point was that some of the trauma that the parents had experienced was passed, consciously or unconsciously, to their offspring. Children might, for example, be discouraged from standing out or not conforming. Children were encouraged to be healthy and safe lest their parents be worried about some harm coming to them. The children picked up on their parents' attitudes about Germany and about their Holocaust experiences, even if these weren't verbalized. They also may have learned not to ask about what family members had gone through during the war.

While surviving parents may have been overly protective of their children, their sons and daughters also felt protective of them. There was a sense that one could not be angry at parents, resulting in repressed feelings that negatively manifested themselves when these children were teens or adults. Difficulties that a child might experience could be trivialized by a parent as not measuring up to anything that the parent had gone through. Complaining might not be tolerated. Further, parents might have had little or no tolerance for their children's relationships with non-Jews.

While stereotyping is inadvisable, there are some findings that seem to be common. Early studies of children of survivors found that they had behaviors such as aggression or depression. Regarding being protective, not all parents were overprotective; there were those who were appreciative of their children's aggression because it represented something the survivors could not display if they were in the camps or in hiding. Other attitudes were similarly communicated from parent to child.

> The children of Jewish resistance fighters, for example, displayed a pride and a strength in their identity as Jews that was strikingly different from children of Jews who had spent prolonged periods of time hidden or living as Christians. Those children of survivors whose parents had sealed off their past responded by sealing off their own. Those whose parents had talked openly about their experience were most at ease with the subject while others, whose parents had tried to forget it, had little to say for themselves.
>
> (Epstein 137–138)

When children of survivors began reaching their teens, the ages at which their parents had been taken, they might have begun to have their own mental health issues or difficulties with their relationships with their parents. Children born of unions in which one parent was a survivor and one was not tended to have more anxiety than children whose parents were both survivors.

The feelings of 2G children could be complex and surprising. Some 2G had a sense that they were replacements for offspring who had been murdered. They felt a burden of expectation that they would fulfill the lives that had been cut short. They were aware that family loyalty was expected and of the pressure to erase parental losses. There were offspring who reported experiencing survival fantasies, with shower heads playing a role. Some reported testing their tolerance for pain and endurance. In so doing, they were attempting to replicate actual or imagined occurrences undergone by their parents.

Survivors wanted their children to be educated, seeing knowledge as something that could never be taken away. Many infused their offspring with moral integrity and a will to stand up to intolerance and oppression. A large percentage of 2G Survivors have applied these convictions to their own professional lives.

How will the Holocaust impact the children of the Second-Generation Survivors? It is hard to say. What is clear is that their parents want the Third Generation to live in a world that is unlike the one that allowed the Holocaust to happen.

Scripted scenes and monologues

1. Scene for two female actors – *A Shayna Maidel* by Barbara Lebow

> *ROSE/RAYZEL* is a young woman in her early 20s who has lived in the US since she was a young child. LUSIA** is ROSE's older sister. She recently arrived in New York after surviving the Holocaust. She speaks in halting English with a Yiddish-Polish accent. The scene takes place in 1946 in ROSE's West Side apartment in New York City. Separated since childhood when ROSE was able to leave Poland and come to America with her father at age four, and LUSIA was forced to remain behind with her mother after contracting scarlet fever, the sisters have recently been reunited. LUSIA has survived the horrors of a concentration camp, but other than creating lists of which relatives perished and which are still missing, she has shared little about her experience with her younger sister. As the scene begins ...*
>
> *LUSIA is seated on the sofa reading a magazine. ROSE is pacing.*

ROSE. (*Urgently.*) ... But I want you to tell me! Please, Lusia. How could you keep it from me? I have a right to know!

LUSIA. I got a right to study, listen the music, the words, so can talk more better. Get work, job. (*ROSE runs and turns off the radio.*)

ROSE. That's not going to help you, Lusia. Talk with *me*. I'll help you. That'll be much better. But, please, you've got to tell me what happened. (*LUSIA gets up and moves away to bedroom. ROSE follows.*)

LUSIA. You seen that list, Rayzel. That's all it was. What is says on that paper. (*LUSIA sits on bed, away from ROSE, who continues to pace.*)

ROSE. Lists. Lists! Your list, Papa's list. Like taking inventory of dry goods. Then, all through dinner, not a word out of place. Not a tear. Not a sigh. Papa is stone. But I'm not a baby and I want to know what happened. I see pictures in the newspapers I can't believe. And in the newsreels. I couldn't look, but I wanted to see. Is that what it was really like? Was my mother in one of those pictures? Were you? You're my family, tell me! (*LUSIA looks at ROSE before she speaks.*)

LUSIA. I cannot talk it. About it. Is all of living and dying. Is too much from the ... the *bainer* ...

ROSE. (*Quietly.*) Bones.

LUSIA. The bones. The *hartz*. The *flaish*. I want not talk it no more. OK?

ROSE. (*Sitting on bed.*) Not even about Mama?

LUSIA. About Mama I tell you this ... How was her *life*. Almost happy, only except for missing you. She was beautiful, skin like silk. Smooth and smells always from clean, like soap. And saying all the time things ... words ...

ROSE. Sayings.

LUSIA. Sayings to make things be better. She makes me laugh, and Hanna, my friend, too. She sings, not too good, like me. And cooks good, a lot, like you. She has

head in dreams, has dreams in head, forever. Things, no matter how bad, be going
better soon, says Mama. And just like Papa, whatever happens is the will of God.

ROSE. Even after –

LUSIA. Every day. The will of God. So that's Mama. What I remember. This I can
tell you. (*Pause, while ROSE considers something.*)

ROSE. (*Softly.*) Can't you get it off?

LUSIA. What?

ROSE. The number. The number on your arm.

LUSIA. Is forever. Get it off? No.

ROSE. How did they do it, Lusia? Did it hurt? What did you feel like when –

LUSIA. (*Going quickly into living room.*) Now pardon, please. I got to learn better
English. (*ROSE exits, distraught. LUSIA turns on radio.*)

*RAY-zel
**LOO-sha

2. Monologue – *2.5 Minute Ride* by Lisa Kron

> *In this monologue from her one-woman play, LISA recounts visiting Auschwitz with her
> 74-year-old father, who is going blind, has diabetes and a heart condition, and a family friend
> named Elizabeth. LISA's German-born father escaped the Nazis on a Kindertransport
> when he was a boy. Both of his parents were murdered in Auschwitz. LISA occasionally
> copes with the overwhelming emotions of the trip through dark humor. (The ellipses indicate
> places where lines from the full script have been omitted.)*

LISA. What month was it? October. It's so cold. Elizabeth's car has separate controls for
heating the driver and the passenger. On my side I've pushed the little lever all the way
over to hot. I don't think we listened to much music. Oh no. We did. Bach. Seems appropriate for the night before Auschwitz. Dinner at the Orbis Hotel. Dad says, "How funny,
tonight we're having a beer with dinner and tomorrow we'll be at Auschwitz." Dad and
I, we've been waiting for this our whole lives. We don't know how to feel. Tomorrow
we'll be at the place where his parents' bodies lie. No, they were burned. Will we step on
their ashes? Will we see a wooden palate where they slept? Will we kick a stone they also
kicked? Will they be hovering above the place, watching us? Are they waiting for their
boy? Have they waited all this time for their little boy to come and say goodbye to them?

...

What will I do, I thought, if my father cries. I've never seen him cry. What if he falls
to the ground and sobs and curses the heavens? On the one hand I feel like I have
these maternal feelings toward him and on the other hand I couldn't handle it if
I really had to hold him like I was his mother.

Oh. The room is full of hair. Is that my grandmother's hair? Is she here?

...

A room full of eyeglasses. They stumble off blind to their deaths. A room full of suitcases. The smell (*yuck*) the smell. A room full of artificial limbs. The Israelis are here. A big group with a huge Israeli flag. Huge enough for my father to easily see all day the big blue Mogen David.* What a blessing they're here today. He doesn't say too much but I know that these Israelis are his little safety valve. A reminder that the world of Auschwitz is no more.

The Star of David – the symbol on the Israeli flag and of the Jewish religion

3. Monologue – *2.5 Minute Ride* by Lisa Kron

> In this monologue from her one-woman play, LISA shares with the audience details about her emotional visit to Auschwitz with her aging Holocaust survivor father. (The ellipses indicate places where lines from the full script have been omitted.)

LISA. I'd been so afraid I wouldn't feel anything here.

I think that was my biggest fear.

But when I enter the crematorium for the first time in my life, I feel horror. Physical repulsion. I can feel my face contort, my lips pull back. In the gas chambers my father stops to take his 2:00 pill. This breaks my heart. I stand to the side and cry. Hard. I can feel … I can feel the bottom. It's clear to me now that everything in my life before this has been a shadow. This is the only reality – what happened to my father and his parents fifty years ago.

I don't know why I'm telling you this. You all already know what this looks like, right? You've seen these images before. You don't need me to describe this to you. You know, it's occurring to me that there's a fairly good chance there's someone sitting here who's been to Auschwitz before. And you don't need me to tell you what this looks like, do you? It's insulting really. It's upsetting and it's insulting. Even if you've never been there you've seen these images before, right?

…

Sometimes I feel like they show these images every fifteen minutes or something. You know the ones I'm talking about, the films from the liberation of the camps with the bulldozers and the bodies. Right? You all know what this looks like. I don't know what I'm doing. I feel like a cliché.

…

Do you know what (my Dad) told us when we were growing up? When we were growing up he told us many, many times, "If it weren't for the good fortune of being born a Jew I might have become a Nazi." And then he'd tell us this story: He'd gone to school with a boy named Lohmann who was the only other boy in his class at school who didn't wear a Hitler Youth uniform. My father wasn't allowed to wear one, of course, because he was a Jew and he was beaten by the other boys regularly for that but Lohmann didn't wear one because he refused. "I often wonder," my father would tell us when we were growing up, "I often wonder. If I had had the opportunity to wear that uniform if I would have had the courage of *Lohmann*? I'm lucky to be a Jew so I didn't have to *make that choice*."

4. Monologue – *Denial* by Peter Sagal

> *ADAM RYBURG is a bright, idealistic, government prosecutor in his 20s. He is the grandchild of Holocaust survivors, and an observant Jew who wears a kippah.* He is prosecuting a Holocaust denier (BERNARD COOPER) who is being represented by a Jewish lawyer named ABBY GERSTEN who has taken the case because of her absolute beliefs regarding the First Amendment.*
>
> *In this scene, RYBURG is meeting ABBY for the first time in her law office. (ABBY's lines are included in parentheses for context.) (The ellipses indicate lines that have been omitted from the full script.)*

RYBURG. How many did you lose?

[*ABBY. I don't …*]

RYBURG. During the war. (*Pause.*)

[*ABBY. My parents were born here. But they had some cousins in Poland … I've seen their letters, some pictures. But that shouldn't –*]

RYBURG. All my grandparents are survivors. They met in the refugee camps. They tend to marry each other; they say that no one else can understand. They all had families before the war, but nobody else survived. And the families back then – they were big. Aunts, uncles, cousins. Why is it? Why does this man and people like him attack us through our memory? And why are we so vulnerable there? You know the story of Samson, his hair? The rabbis asked, what does this text mean, what is it about hair, of all things, that gives us strength? *The time it takes to grow it*: the particular past of the individual, or the people. It's like I said, we Jews, we learn from the past, we change, we adapt, our past is our strength, no matter how horrible, no matter if it's drowned in blood. That's why language, words like "storm trooper," for example, are so important for us. We know not to use them lightly. Attack our past, or aid that attack, and you attack us.

…

You know what they were thinking, your cousins, as they were being herded into the chambers and the doors were screwed shut? "This can't be happening. It's against the *law*." And here's the irony: you'll appreciate this. They were wrong. It was perfectly legal.

**skullcap or yarmulke*

5. Scene for four female actors – *Kindertransport* by Diane Samuels

> *EVELYN is a middle-class English woman in her 50s. FAITH, in her 20s, is EVELYN's only child. HELGA is a German-Jewish woman in her 30s. EVA is EVELYN's younger self. She is the daughter of HELGA, and in this scene, is 17 years old.*
>
> *In this scene, near the end of the play, FAITH has discovered her mother's true identity as a German Jew who was sent to England as a young girl to escape the Nazis and was adopted by the British family that took her in. EVELYN's real mother – HELGA – appears in flashback, along with EVELYN's younger self – EVA. (EVELYN's adoptive mother LIL has one line in the scene which may be omitted.)*

EVELYN. Do you still want to know about my childhood, about my origins, about my parents?

FAITH. Yes.

EVELYN. Well, let me tell you. Let me tell you what little remains in my brain. And if I do, will you leave me alone afterwards? Will you please leave me alone?

FAITH. If that's what you want.

EVELYN. My father was called Werner Schlesinger. My mother was called Helga. They lived in Hamburg. They were Jews. I was an only child. I think I must have loved them a lot at one time. One forgets what these things feel like. Other feelings displace the original ones. I remember a huge cone of sweets that I had on my first day of school. There were a lot of toffees.

(Pause. EVELYN goes blank for a moment.)

I remember lots of books. Rows and rows. I imagine a whole house built of books and some of them were mine. A storybook filled with terrifying pictures: children's fingers being cut off; children being burnt in attic rooms and no one hearing them scream; children whose teeth fall out and choke them while they're asleep; children being taken away by a great ghoulish shadow with hooded eyebrows and a long hooked nose ... I can remember nothing else apart from a boy with a squint on the train I came away on. I kept trying not to look at him. Please believe me, Faith, there is nothing else in my memory from that time. It is honestly blank.

(Pause.)

FAITH. Did your parents die in a concentration camp?

EVELYN. Yes.

FAITH. Do you know which one?

EVELYN. Auschwitz.

(LIL. When did you find that out?)

FAITH. When did they die?

EVELYN. My father died in 1943. He was gassed soon after arrival.

FAITH. What about your mother?

EVELYN. My mother ... she was ... she was not gassed.

FAITH. What happened to her?

(HELGA enters. She is utterly transformed (from the beginning of the play) – thin, wizened, old-looking. Her hair is thin and short. EVELYN, LIL and FAITH all see her.)

(*EVA enters.*)

HELGA. Ist das Eva? (*Is it Eva?*)

(*EVA is speechless.*)

HELGA. Eva, bist du's wirklich? (*Is that you, Eva?*)

EVA. Mother?

(*HELGA approaches EVA and hugs her. EVA tries to hug back but is clearly very uncomfortable.*)

HELGA. Wie du dich varändert hast! (*How much you have changed!*)

EVA. I'm sorry. I don't quite understand.

HELGA (*English.*) How much you have changed.

EVA. So have you.

HELGA. You are sixteen now.

EVA. Seventeen.

HELGA. Blue is suiting to you. A lovely dress.

EVA. Thank you.

HELGA. You are very pretty.

EVA. This is a nice hotel. (*Pause.*) I can't believe you're here.

HELGA. I promised I would come, Eva.

EVA. I'm called Evelyn now.

HELGA. What is Evelyn?

EVA. I changed my name.

HELGA. Why?

EVA. I wanted an English name.

HELGA. Eva was the name of your great grandmother.

EVA. I didn't mean any disrespect.

HELGA. No. Of course not.

EVA. I'm sorry.

HELGA. Nothing is the same anymore.

EVA. It's just that I've settled down now.

HELGA. These are the pieces of my life.

EVA. There were no letters for all those years and then I saw the newsreels and newspapers …

HELGA. I am putting them all back together again.

EVA. I thought the worst.

HELGA. I always promised that I would come and get you.

EVA. I was a little girl then.

HELGA. I am sorry that there has been such a delay. It was not of my making. (*Pause.*) I am your Mutti, Eva.

EVA. Evelyn.

HELGA. Eva. Now I am here, you have back your proper name.

EVA. Evelyn is on my naturalization papers.

HELGA. Naturalized as English?

EVA. And adopted by Mr. and Mrs. Miller.

HELGA. How can you be adopted when your own mother is alive for you?

EVA. I thought that you were not alive.

HELGA. Never mind it. We have all done bad things in the last years that we regret. That is how we survive.

EVA. What did you do?

HELGA. I was right to send you here, yes? It is good to survive. Is it not, Eva?

EVA. Please call me Evelyn.

HELGA. Now we must put our lives right again. We will go to New York where your Onkel Klaus will help us to make a beginning.

EVA. All the way to New York?

HELGA. Who is here for us? No one. The remains of our family is in America.

EVA. I have a family here.

HELGA. These people were just a help to you in bad times. You can to leave them now behind. The bad times are finished. I know it.

EVA. I like it here.

HELGA. You will like it better in America.

EVA. Do I have to go away with you?

HELGA. That is what I came for.

IMAGE 9.3 Jewish refugee children from Children's Transport (Kindertransport) arrive in the United Kingdom

6. Scene for two female actors – *Kindertransport* by Diane Samuels

HELGA is a German-Jewish woman in her late 30s/early 40s. EVA is the daughter of HELGA. In this scene, she is 17 years old.
This scene picks up one week after the previous (flashback) scene left off.
Sounds of a quayside. A boat is about to leave. HELGA is waiting. EVA, very agitated, approaches her.

HELGA. Where have you been?
EVA. I said, in the lavatory.
HELGA. For half an hour in the lavatory?
EVA. I was being sick.
HELGA. Sick?
EVA. I'm all right now.
HELGA. Are you sure?
EVA. Yes.
HELGA. You should change your mind and come with me.
EVA. I haven't got a case.
HELGA. You could have your things sent on.
EVA. You said it was all right to come later.
HELGA. I said I would prefer you to come now. There is enough money from Onkel Klaus for a ticket.
EVA. I can't just leave.
HELGA. Why do you not want to be with your mother, Eva?
EVA. Evelyn. My name is Evelyn.
HELGA. Why are you so cold to me?
EVA. I don't mean to be cold.
HELGA. We have been together a week and you are still years away.
EVA. I can't help it.
(*Boat's hooter sounds.*)
HELGA. Boats do not wait for people.
EVA. I hope you have a safe trip.
HELGA. When is "later" when you are coming?
EVA. In a month or two.
HELGA. Just get on the boat with me. Do it now.
EVA. I'm not ready yet. Not at all.
HELGA. You're making a mistake.
EVA. You're making me –
HELGA. What am I making you do? I am your mother. I love you. We must be together.
EVA. We've not been together for too long.
HELGA. That is why it is even more important now.
EVA. I can't leave home yet.
HELGA. Home is inside you. Inside me and you. It is not a place.

EVA. I don't understand what you mean.

HELGA. You are wasting a chance hardly anyone else has been given.

EVA. I will come.

HELGA. Will you?

EVA. If you want me to.

HELGA. If I want you to?

EVA. Just not yet.

HELGA. Do you want to come to make a new life with me?

EVA. You keep asking me that.

HELGA. Do you?

EVA. It's hard for me.

HELGA. I lost your father. He was sick and they put him in line for the showers. I saw it. You know what I say to you. I lost him. But I did not lose myself. Nearly a million times over, right on the edge of life, but I held on with my bones rattling inside me. Why have you lost yourself, Eva? (*Ship's horn sounds out.*) I am going to start again. I want my daughter Eva with me. If you find her, Evelyn, by any chance, send her over to find me. (*HELGA embraces EVA who stands stock still. HELGA picks up her case and starts to walk away. EVA stands shaking silently.*)

SPOTLIGHT ACTIVITY

Kindertransport

"Hotseating"

There are two scenes in this chapter from the play, *Kindertransport*. Both explore the relationship between Evelyn (Eva) and her birth mother, Helga, who sent her to England in order to escape the Nazis.

Hotseating is a theatrical technique that allows an actor to learn more about a character.

1 Have the entire class read the scene(s) from the play *Kindertransport*.
2 If a student has been assigned to play the role of Evelyn, have her sit in front of the class and assume the role of Evelyn. (If no one student has been assigned this role, any student may take part in the activity.)
3 Classmates will take turns asking her questions about her experiences as related to the information they have learned about her and her circumstances through the *Kindertransport* scene(s). She must answer in character.
4 Follow the same steps with a student who will play Helga. She, too, must answer questions in character.
5 The activity can be replayed, with other students taking on the roles of mother and daughter. At the conclusion of the exercise, the class should discuss what new information about each character was revealed through hotseating.

Verbatim testimony historical narratives

1. **From the testimony of Leslie Altman, daughter of Brigitte Altman – "Jewish Survivor"**

(https://iwitness.usc.edu/sfi/BrowseTopics.aspx?TopicID=82&ClipID=1289)

Brigitte Altman: Born: August 15, 1924, in Klaipeda, Lithuania
In this August, 1997 interview, Leslie Altman, the adult daughter of Holocaust survivor Brigitte Altman, sits by her mother's side and shares the story of when she first learned of her mother's experience in the Holocaust, alternately addressing the interviewer and her mother.

LESLIE

I have never forgotten when I first found out about your experiences and your life. And I'd like to share this with you, because I don't know if you remember or not. But first of all, I'd like to say that my mother only provides information on an as-needed basis, and she does not lend herself to pontification. That being said, growing up in Texas, where, first of all, I hadn't a clue that my mother's life was different from any other mother's as a little girl, except for the fact that she was European … That was the only difference that I was aware of. I remember coming home from school one day, from the first grade. And as I would always do, I'd come home and chat with my mom as she was at her writing desk. And I remember telling you about my day and this funny little activity that I had seen other kids doing at recess. And I extended my arm above my shoulder and said, "Hal Hitler." And you were mortified. And you had stopped what you were doing and you were so astonished, and I couldn't figure out what I had done that had shocked you. And you immediately set me aside and explained to me, very briefly, the Holocaust and what it was and how it affected your life. And then I remember in the end, you corrected my pronunciation and said, "It's not 'Hal Hitler,' it was 'Heil Hitler,'"* and then you defined what "Heil" meant. This was first grade. So that was my introduction to this part of my mother's history. But it affected me in the sense that, when, as with other offspring – I hurt when my mother hurt. And to hear a sad story that affected my mother so deeply, it hurt me. Yet, in the 60s and 70s as I was growing up, this was not … the Holocaust was not discussed openly. So it was like I had this sad secret. So I always felt a little different as a result of that. And then, the other way I felt a little different was I always felt that, unlike other mothers, I never witnessed my mother ever looking or seeming carefree.

*Literally – "Hail Hitler," meaning a wish for the health and well-being of the Nazi leader, though the phrase came to be used as a standard greeting among Germans in a way that bestowed on Hitler the status of a Supreme Being

2. From the testimony of Ralph Abramovitch – "Jewish Survivor"

(https://iwitness.usc.edu/sfi/BrowseTopics.aspx?TopicID=82&ClipID=1262)

Born: April 16, 1923, in Kielce, Poland
In this August, 1997 interview, Ralph discusses the lasting impact of the Holocaust on his psychological condition.

RALPH

I used to tell [my children]. I used to tell them the stories. But most of the time, you know how teenagers are, they grow up, they have other interests. They were not too much involved in that. They tried to … If something came out, a film about the Holocaust or something, they always phoned me and said, "Daddy, don't watch." Because the dreams … that does not go away. We were liberated – physically. Mentally, we're not liberated. We're still in the camps, all day and all night we're in the camps. We're under the occupation, under the fear. You know, you cannot erase that. Day in and day out. I wish *one* night I could sleep through … Every time, something comes up from the camps. When I meet friends – any discussion – we play cards and we end up talking about the camps, about the war. Even now. *(Sighs. Takes a long beat.)* It wasn't easy. You can't erase that. It will always remain. I would give any amount to a doctor, he should help me to live without fear. Always thinking of what could happen. Whoever thought that things like that could happen? Civilized people. Europe was civilized! *(Sighs. Takes a long beat.)* I don't hate anybody. I would like to see harmony. *(Shrugs.)* You know the blame will always go on the minority. It always exists, in every country. When there's nobody else to blame, they're gonna blame the Jews.

3. From the testimony of Alan Brown – "Jewish Survivor"

(https://iwitness.usc.edu/sfi/BrowseTopics.aspx?TopicID=22&ClipID=1290)

Born: March 20, 1928, in Miskolc, Hungary
In this April, 1996 interview, Alan discusses the fact that the Holocaust is always present in his mind, and he speaks about the way he handled sharing his experiences with his children.

ALAN

Oh yes, [I think about the Shoah*] all the time. I take a shower, I think of gas chambers. Everything reminds me of the Shoah. Children. I see children, I start considering – "You wouldn't make it, you might make it …" Always.

I tried to go in between of telling [my children] too much and too little. My daughter says I didn't say enough, didn't tell enough. And one of my sons feels I was telling too much. The other one says probably I said enough. So it depends on who says it. I did not want them to feel the way I felt. At the same time, I wanted them to be aware of what kinds of things can happen, that they can transport it to their children, and that they will stand up for human rights.

Shoah – the Hebrew term for the Holocaust

Suggested props/costumes for Chapter 9 historical narrative scenes

- Men's and women's sweaters or jackets (1960s/1970s)
- Stationery and pen
- Girl's and boy's accessories: hairbows, headbands, baseball caps
- Deck of cards
- Telephone (1970s/1980s)

Devised theater activity

Devise a scene using the poem "Chorus of Orphans" *by Nelly Sachs, translated by Teresa Iverson.*

Scene components

1 "Chorus of Orphans" by Nelly Sachs, translated by Teresa Iverson
2 No fewer than *four tableaus*
3 Four *group breaths*
4 *Musical underscoring* (optional)

Text

The poem "Chorus of Orphans" was written by Holocaust survivor Nelly Sachs. Born in Berlin, Germany, in 1891, to upper-middle-class Jewish parents, Sachs survived by fleeing to Sweden in 1940, one week before she was scheduled to report to a concentration camp. She later became a highly regarded poet and playwright, winning the Nobel Prize in Literature in 1966. She died in 1970.

"Chorus of Orphans"
by Nelly Sachs, translated by Teresa Iverson

We orphans
We lament the world:

Our branch was cut down
And thrown into the fire –
Out of our protectors, they made firewood –
We orphans lie on the fields of Loneliness.
We orphans
We lament the world:
In the night our parents play hide-and-seek with us –
Behind the black folds of Night
Their faces study us,
Their mouths are saying something:
We were dry wood in a woodcarver's hand –
But our eyes have become angel-eyes
And look at you,
They see through the black
folds of Night –
We orphans
We lament the world:
Our toys have become stones,
Stones have faces, Father- and Mother-faces
They don't wilt like flowers, they don't bite like animals –
And they don't burn like dry wood, when one throws it in the oven –
We orphans, we lament the world:
World why have you taken our tender Mothers
And our Fathers, who said: My child, you resemble me!
We orphans, who no longer resemble anyone in the world!
O World,
It's you we accuse!

Staging considerations, choices and tips

1   Select the places in the poem where you want to create tableaus. Will these stage pictures be literal representations of what the poet is describing? Or will they be designed to represent the emotions that the poet is evoking? Or a combination of both?

2   Will the poem be voiced by one actor or multiple actors? If multiple – how will you divide the lines? Consider having the line "My child, you resemble me!" spoken by tableau actors who are representing "our tender Mothers/And our Fathers."

3   Where will the group breaths occur? How can you use these to the greatest effect?

4   Will you use any props in your piece? Select them carefully.

5   Try incorporating musical underscoring. As you are rehearsing your piece, decide if the music enhances or detracts from the words being spoken, and if the latter, perform the piece without the addition of music.

10

Deniers and denial

Context

Holocaust denial is a form of hate speech, and it is on the rise around the world. In an op-ed that first appeared in the *New York Daily News* and subsequently on the Anti-Defamation League's website, Holocaust denial is described as:

> a conspiracy theory which argues that Jews around the world knowingly fabricated evidence of their own genocide in order to extract reparations money from Germany, gain world sympathy, and facilitate the theft of Palestinian land for the creation of Israel. It is founded on the belief that Jews are able to force governments, Hollywood, the media and academia to promote a lie at the expense of non-Jews.
>
> (Greenblatt 1)

Deniers' tactics include promoting violence, using speeches and inflammatory rhetoric to further their cause, playing upon fear, infiltrating extremist groups, and blaming Jews for the economic difficulties of others. They take advantage of some people's inability or unwillingness to distinguish truth and reasoning from lies. They ignore evidence that does not support their claims. In short, deniers promote a revisionist history that argues either that the Holocaust did not happen or, if it did, that the number of those murdered is greatly exaggerated. A neo-Nazi interviewed on CNN said that he would never be convinced that six million Jews were killed in the Holocaust and claimed that the Nazis were misunderstood; he epitomizes the deniers' point of view.

Multiple arguments are used to support deniers' claims. One, for example, advances the concept that the Holocaust was so horrible that it seems like it could not have happened. They ignore mountains of evidence to posture that because it is so hard to believe, therefore it could not have occurred. Another of their strategies is to claim that the victims were the villains and that the Nazis should be absolved of any criminality.

After all, they claim, war is evil and the losing side always is mischaracterized as the wrongdoer when, in fact, there should be no moral equivalency since all sides are to blame. Killing Jews was akin to killing any other group or enemy in a war. They demand positive proof of Germany's guilt. Ironically, they do not hold themselves to this same standard when it comes to proof. Aligned with this argument is a similar claim that the United States and its allies were the aggressors and that a plan to exterminate the Jews did not exist. Another tactic that deniers engage in rests on manipulating evidence and drawing conclusions that are, in fact, invalid. If, for example, a Holocaust survivor misspeaks and makes an error in a statement, deniers will claim that since that one statement is incorrect, everything else that the person says must be false or incorrect. It is a tactic based upon faulty reasoning. Another approach that deniers use is aimed squarely at academia. Holocaust deniers argue that they are exposing the truth, putting Holocaust scholars in the position of having to refute the deniers' findings. Holocaust rebukers like this technique because it makes their falsehoods sound scholarly, as if they have academic validity and respect, and it puts real intellectuals on the defensive.

IMAGE 10.1 Auschwitz fence posts and Elie Wiesel quote on display at the United States Holocaust Memorial Museum

What motivates deniers? Root causes of Holocaust denial are antisemitism, hatred and racism. In certain countries, it is a way of easing guilt that stems from being sympathetic to or aligned with the Nazis during World War II. Contemporary targets for spreading messages of denial may be young people. Deniers realize that there is less awareness of the Holocaust among today's youth than among those older and the internet may be a contributing factor. Hate can be spread more rapidly online, making it easier to promote the fallacy that the Holocaust is a myth or a hoax. The number killed seems too large for a young person to imagine, making the lie that this mass murder did not occur easier for deniers to spread and for their youthful audiences to believe.

That the antisemitism, hatred and racism that undergird denial exist cannot be disputed. In 2017, Charlottesville, Virginia was the scene of a rally in which neo-Nazis carrying torches chanted, "Jews will not replace us." The following summer a rally in Berlin, Germany, commemorated the death of Rudolf Hess, one of Hitler's top officials. Here, neo-Nazis had police protection and carried banners with slogans such as "I regret nothing." Even Elie Wiesel, perhaps best known by students as the author of *Night*, could not escape this hateful thinking in life or in death. Although he passed away in 2016, in August of 2018, his childhood home in Romania was vandalized. Pink spray paint was used to deface the home with slurs and antisemitic messages. Not only was this horrible act aimed at Holocaust survivor and Nobel Laureate Wiesel, it was intended to insult the memory of those who perished in the Holocaust. To think that the animosity that spawns Holocaust denial has no impact in today's world is to risk a repeat of history.

Scripted scenes and monologues

1. Monologue – *Denial* by Peter Sagal

> BERNARD COOPER *is an academic in his 40s. He has recently written a book which denies the Holocaust. He is being prosecuted by the government, and hires a Jewish lawyer who is a First Amendment absolutist to defend him.*
>
> *In this monologue,* COOPER *is appearing at his own press conference. His responses are to various members of the press. (Note: no lines of dialogue have been removed from this speech. The questions from the press are not in the script;* COOPER *simply responds as if questions have been asked.)*

COOPER. Socrates. Galileo. Sir Thomas More. Tyndale … all punished because their truths were unacceptable to the orthodoxy. I ask you who am I that the government would try hard to silence me? Could it be that they are afraid that someone might listen to what I have to say? That's my question. What's yours? Oh, William Tyndale, T-Y-N-D-A-L-E, he was the first to translate the Bible into English. They burned him at the stake. Yes? No, not at all, I am not the least bit anti-semitic. Whatever that means. In fact, I feel that I am doing the Jewish people a great service: I bring them the news that their co-religionists didn't die after all. I don't understand why that makes them so upset. – Yes? Well, it's not surprising that he would say something like that. Noah Gomrowitz and his fellow exterminationists have a vested interest, as it were, in their version of the story. Compare his book sales to mine, and draw your own conclusions. – You there, with the lovely jacket. Oh, that's simple. Many of the Jews allegedly killed actually emigrated to the United States. The New York area. Well, have you ever been there? Would anyone notice a few thousand more? No, I'm very serious. Don't I sound serious? No, no, ask away. I've got all day.

2. Scene for two actors – *Denial* by Peter Sagal

ABBY GERSTEN is a civil liberties lawyer defending Holocaust denier BERNARD COOPER. Ironically, she is Jewish; but her virulent belief in the power of the First Amendment has led her to take COOPER's case. BERNARD COOPER is an academic in his 40s. He has recently written a book which denies the Holocaust. He is being prosecuted by the government, and hires ABBY to defend him.

In this scene, which takes place near the end of the play, ABBY informs COOPER that the prosecution is dropping all charges against him after learning that he has evidence that the Holocaust survivor, NOAH GOMROWITZ, who is suing COOPER, has included a false account of a death at Auschwitz – that of a man named NATHAN – in his book. COOPER was planning to exploit that account in the trial and to destroy GOMROWITZ's reputation. Though ABBY took COOPER's case willingly, she can no longer hide her extreme distaste for him, and in this, their last meeting, she turns his own twisted logic against him.

COOPER. The truth will out. He lied. I've caught him. *Falsus in partes, falsus in omnibus.* He tried to murder his own best friend!

ABBY. That saying of yours … false in part, false in whole, right?

COOPER. A legal term, I believe.

ABBY. So it is. Does it work in reverse, do you suppose? Truth in part …?

COOPER. What do you mean?

ABBY. Let's say you find Nathan again, force him to speak. He is a talkative fellow. What will he say?

COOPER. That his best friend, the great spokesman for the Holocaust, tried to murder him!

ABBY. By abandoning him to the gas chamber. At Auschwitz. But everybody knows that the gas chambers at Auschwitz were used for dry-cleaning only. And the ovens for warming leftovers.

COOPER. Immaterial. The point is we've caught Gomrowitz in a lie, one of many, and –

ABBY. Based on evidence from a man who, according to you, must be a liar because he says the Holocaust happened. To him.

COOPER. As you've told me a thousand times no one takes me seriously anyway. What do I care, if there appears to be an … inconsistency? It's a small price to pay.

ABBY. Let's talk price, then. You know what I'm going to do? I'm going to *jew it up*.* If you in any way make any sort of accusation against Noah Gomrowitz, I will file a class action libel lawsuit against you on behalf of every Holocaust survivor everywhere. Because by doing so, you will prove that you are not merely crazy and hateful, but that you know the truth and deliberately distort it.

COOPER. That's nonsense. Impossible.

ABBY. What the Jews have learned, the hard way, is that just because something is impossible doesn't mean it won't happen to you. You should learn from us, Mr. Cooper.

This is a twist on the antisemitic slur "jew down," which insinuates that Jews are cheap and always try to bargain for a lower price. ABBY is using the phrase ironically, playing into the notion that this is the kind of language that a bigot like COOPER would understand

3. Scene for seven actors – *Anne Frank & Me* by Cherie Bennett

JACK, EDDIE, DAVID, SUZANNE, CHRISSY, MIMI and NICOLE are all students in a 9th grade English class in a high school located in "a suburb in the American heartland." Their teacher, RENEE ZOOMS, who they have nicknamed "Bazooms," has assigned the class to read "The Diary of Anne Frank." As the scene begins, ZOOMS is questioning NICOLE about the book, which NICOLE has failed to read. Trying to worm her way out of explaining what the book is about, NICOLE mentions that some scholars don't believe Anne Frank actually wrote it. Just then, ZOOMS is called out of the class by URKIN, the school's principal, and the following scene unfolds.

JACK. Hey, you know what I heard? That Urkin was a medic in the Green Berets.

EDDIE. That a band, dude?

DAVID. Sure, Eddie, they open for the Smashing Pumpkins.

EDDIE. Righteous.

JACK. No, you know, Green Berets. Special Forces? Vietnam? They were like, tortured if they got caught.

SUZANNE. Well, at least they weren't sent to gas chambers.

CHRISSY. Neither were the Jews. That's what my friend said.

MIMI. Well, your "Friend" is just ignorant.

CHRISSY. I don't think so, he's pre-med. He told me the other side of the story.

DAVID. There is no "other side" of the story!

CHRISSY. There's two sides to every story.

DAVID. Oh, right, Chrissy. So if someone said, "Yo, the Earth is flat," you'd say "Whoa, guess that's the other side of the Earth-is-round story."

EDDIE. Ha! Dissed you!

DAVID. (*Shyly to NICOLE.*) You don't really believe what you said before, do you? You're too smart for that –

A BUNCH OF KIDS. (*Teasing DAVID.*) Ooooo –

NICOLE. I just couldn't think of anything else to say. I didn't get to finish the book. Quick, before Bazooms comes back, tell me what happened to Anne Frank.

CHRISSY. Who knows if there even was an Anne Frank.

SUZANNE. That's ridiculous.

CHRISSY. Do you really believe that Germans marched people into showers and turned on the gas? I mean, come on!

DAVID. I can't believe I'm having this conversation.

MIMI. Me neither.

SUZANNE. Me neither.

CHRISSY. Look, just because I have a different opinion from you guys is no reason to –

NICOLE. You guys, what difference does it make? It's ancient history! Now, please, tell me what happened to Anne Frank.

JACK. What bugs me is how we're not supposed to question anything they tell us, you know? We're not allowed to think.

EDDIE. Exactly, bro.

CHRISSY. Exactly. What are they so afraid of?

DAVID. Look, the Holocaust was genocide, get it?

NICOLE. Uh, Anne Frank?

JACK. No offense, Dave, but you're not exactly objective.

DAVID. Why, because I'm Jewish?

JACK. Look, it's no biggie, man.

DAVID. It's a real biggie.

NICOLE Hel-lo! What happened to Anne Frank?

MIMI. Well, I agree with David, and I'm not Jewish. I think –

SUZANNE. So do I.

SPOTLIGHT ACTIVITY

Anne Frank & Me

"Truth or Lies"

1 Divide the class into small groups.
2 Ask students to recall a time that a friend or a family member, such as a sibling or a cousin, asked them to say that they hadn't seen something that they had witnessed because admitting that they had observed the activity would result in the asker getting into trouble. How did they respond? Why did they make that choice? How did it make them feel? Why or why not would agreeing to the request be a form of denial?

If they honored the request and were later found to be lying, did they attempt to justify their choice? How?

3   Thinking about the above, have each group create a scene based upon the following set-up: A group of friends is studying the Holocaust in school. Getting together after class, one person says that he heard on the news that "According to a recent survey, 41% of Americans and 66% of millennials could not say what Auschwitz was" (Ross). Based upon these statistics, he tells his friends that the Holocaust must have been a hoax and that studying it in school is a waste of time. In the scene, the friends must counter this argument.

4   Have each group perform their scene.

5   Discuss the scenes. In which ones were the friends most persuasive? What made their arguments strong and effective?

Verbatim testimony historical narratives

1. From the testimony of Edith Baneth – "Jewish Survivor"

(https://iwitness.usc.edu/sfi/BrowseTopics.aspx?TopicID=31&ClipID=1291)

Born: November 7, 1926, in Opava, Czechoslovakia
In this January, 1998 interview, Edith relates how she did not speak about her experiences as a Holocaust survivor for 50 years. She was only motivated to share her story when Holocaust deniers started springing up after the Holocaust began to be talked about more openly in the 1980s and 90s.

EDITH

I have been quiet for 50 years. I shut the door on it, because that was the only way I could have started a new life. And the reason is because the films that came on television. I never can quite understand why it took the world thirty or forty years to bring those things all out. We were forgotten for thirty years. Nobody talked about it. Nobody knew about it. Even Jewish people living here were not quite informed about it. But then came suddenly Nazis – people with newspapers out [saying] "The Holocaust is a fiction. That couldn't possibly be that six million have died. That is all just … the Jews made it up." And that suddenly opened the doors for me again. The anger came in me. I, who have seen them daily going, seen the chimney burning after two hours of them being gassed, seen them arrive by the train, seen so many dead … How somebody possibly could say it isn't true. That's why I think I had to open my memory. Every time when I talk about it, I have to go through living it through. And believe me, it isn't easy. It takes me now quite a few days before I can sleep and come back to the day where I'm living today. But I do it out of anger that there could be somebody in the world who can say it hasn't happened. And I hope that these tapes will be kept for another three, four generations, and we'll avoid – that it should never happen again. And that lessons can be learned, especially for us, for Jewish people, that we should never be put in a position that we just get taken, that we have no way to do anything about it.

2. From the testimony of Paul Parks – "Liberator"

(https://iwitness.usc.edu/sfi/BrowseTopics.aspx?TopicID=31&ClipID=1292)

Born: May 7, 1923, in Indianapolis, Indiana, USA
Paul Parks served as a soldier in World War II and was one of the American liberators of Dachau concentration camp. Years later, he became active in the Civil Rights Movement, working alongside Dr. Martin Luther King. In this October, 1995 interview, Parks discusses the relationship between being a witness to the horrors of the concentration camps, his participation in the Civil Rights Movement, and his experience refuting Holocaust deniers.

PAUL

Since the war, I'd been involved with Dr. King. I think I've been in a jail in every state in the South. So I've been constantly fighting for people's rights. Dr. King and I sat up one night and he asked me the question: "Why are you here, Paul?" He said, "You're here. You're goin' with us to all these crazy places, people throwin' you in jail … Why?" And I said, "Dr. King, I saw a camp once where millions of people have been through and died." And I said, "Ya know something? I know what the end of bigotry looks like, the 'solution' to bigotry looks like from the standpoint of the bigot. Those people who we're fighting to change?" [This was] after they had killed the little kids in Birmingham and blown up the church. I said, "That is not an unusual activity for people who are haters, who believe that they're better than other people, who believe that the solution to those other people is to destroy them. And I've seen that, and I don't want that to ever happen again. And my commitment is to try to see that. And I really am a person of peace." And he says "You're learning." He said, "You've got to learn to put behind you a lot of things that's eatin' away at you. You really do." He said, "You gotta go to the mountaintop and think about yourself. And get yourself to a point where you can be a positive force for change."

And I've spoken before a group of people who said that they didn't believe that it was all [real]. And I said, "Look, let me tell you something. I don't have a picture except in my own mind, but I was there, and I saw it." They said "Are you sure you weren't just dreaming?" And I said, "No. I was there." And I'm gonna tell you something and I'm gonna tell *all* of you something – if you don't understand this and if you don't listen to what people are saying, we are doomed to repeat it again. And it makes no sense. There was a group out at the Charles Towne Army Veterans Home. And I said, "Most you guys in this room know exactly what the war was like. But you weren't there at Dachau or at any of the camps so you tell me. But I'm gonna tell you something – why did we fight the war in the first place? And who were we fighting? And what was that about? And think about it – it's a very short step between what you saw in the field and what happened at Dachau." Because I told 'em once again – "You saw the little kids blown up in England, you saw all of that. And that's because of the fact that one man and his followers believed they were better than anybody else in the world. And you heard them talk about that they were Aryans. I don't know what an Aryan is. But I heard Germans talk about they were important, they were somebody. But one human being can't be any better than another."

3. From the testimony of Alan Brown – "Jewish Survivor"

(https://iwitness.usc.edu/sfi/BrowseTopics.aspx?TopicID=31&ClipID=1293)

Born: March 20, 1928, in Miskolc, Hungary
Concentration camp survivor Alan Brown describes what led him to finally begin speaking publicly about his experiences in the Holocaust. A college professor, Alan was asked by a former student to write him a recommendation, at which time he learned that the young man was a Holocaust denier.

ALAN

Well, a revisionist* got me going [when I was] in my retirement. One of my former students who was a revisionist asked me to write him a recommendation, because he didn't proclaim revisionism in my class. He didn't know I was Jewish. And he said he had an open mind; he was racist, but he had an open mind. I said, "Alright, if you have an open mind then I can give you a better recommendation, but [you need to] show it. Let's go together to the Detroit Holocaust Memorial Center. I would like to watch you. And if you have an open mind, I could describe what I have seen." He was terribly surprised. But I was too. I was even more surprised than he was that I could talk to him. That I didn't break down. At that point I said – well, I offered him to come with me. But why do I have to do it [just] with him? Actually, this was the point that I called up a friend of mine at the Holocaust Memorial Center who was one of the speakers and to whom I'd many times said, "Martin, how can you get up there and talk about Auschwitz? How can you speak about it? I can't understand." And [then] I said to him, "Martin, could you help me do the same?" That's how I became a speaker. So, the point is don't ignore the revisionists. But react. These are the ones who persuaded me that I have a message to tell. So, I'm telling now. I meet some young kids who certainly couldn't have any knowledge about it. Their parents weren't alive, their grandparents, maybe, at the time. But I tell them. I tell them what happened to me. So, I would have probably become involved in Holocaust education anyhow. But it was a little bit faster and a bit more purposeful.

Another term for Holocaust denier. This terminology has fallen into disuse by everyone but the deniers themselves as it is intentionally misleading, giving an air of credibility to __in__credible falsehoods

Suggested props/costumes for Chapter 10 historical narrative scenes

- Television set (1970s/80s)
- TV remote
- Men's jackets (1960s/70s)
- Telephone (1970s/80s)
- Student backpack
- MLK dark suit jacket and skinny tie

Devised theater activity

Devise a scene which demonstrates the absurdity of Holocaust denial by juxtaposing the beliefs of deniers with texts from a reputable eyewitness (General Dwight D. Eisenhower) and an esteemed Nuremberg Trials lawyer (Justice Robert H. Jackson).

Scene components

1   *Two statistics* from the ADL's (Anti-Defamation League) 2014 *Survey of Attitudes toward Jews in over 100 Countries Around the World* concerning knowledge of the Holocaust and belief in the facts of the Holocaust.
2   *Definitions* of different types of Holocaust deniers.
3   Segment of a *letter* written by General (and later US President) Dwight D. Eisenhower describing what he saw when America liberated a concentration camp.
4   Portions of Justice Robert H. Jackson's *opening statement in the Nuremberg Trials*.

Texts

1   Statistics from the ADL Global 100: A Survey of Attitudes toward Jews in over 100 Countries Around the World (2014):
    - 35 percent of respondents have never heard of the Holocaust, and of those who have heard of the Holocaust, almost a third of them – 32 percent – believe it is either a myth or has been greatly exaggerated.
    - Throughout the world, people under the age of 65 are much less likely than older adults to believe its historical account.

2   Deniers and their beliefs:

- Truther: The Holocaust **was faked** – it was just propaganda created by the Allies to punish Germany.
- Denier: The Holocaust **didn't happen** – it was invented to generate sympathy for the Jews in order for them to create the nation of Israel.
- Revisionist: The Holocaust **wasn't that bad** – it's been greatly exaggerated. Especially the figure of 6 million Jewish victims.
- Victim Blamer: Jews and other victims **brought the Holocaust on themselves**.

3   From a letter written by General Dwight D. Eisenhower to George C. Marshall, 4/15/45 foreseeing the possibility of Holocaust deniers in the future. [The Papers of Dwight David Eisenhower, The War Years IV, doc Number 2418.]

The most interesting – although horrible – sight that I encountered during the trip was a visit to a German internment camp near Gotha. The things I saw beggar description … The visual evidence and the verbal testimony of starvation, cruelty and bestiality were so overpowering as to leave me a bit sick. In one room, where there were piled up twenty or thirty naked men, killed by starvation, George Patton would not even enter. He said he would get sick if he did so. I made the visit deliberately, in order to be in position to give first-hand evidence of these things if ever, in the future, there develops a tendency to charge these allegations merely to "propaganda."

4   From Justice Robert H. Jackson's Opening Statement of the Nuremberg Trials, given before the International Military Tribunal, November 21, 1945.

The wrongs which we seek to condemn and punish have been so calculated, so malignant, and so devastating, that civilization cannot tolerate their being ignored, because it cannot survive their being repeated.

We will not ask you to convict these men on the testimony of their foes. There is no count in the Indictment that cannot be proved by books and records. The Germans were always meticulous record keepers … Nor were they without vanity. They arranged frequently to be photographed in action. We will show you their own films. You will see their own conduct and hear their own voices as these defendants re-enact for you, from the screen, some of the events in the course of the conspiracy.

The most savage and numerous crimes planned and committed by the Nazis were those against the Jews.

The Nazi plan never was limited to extermination in Germany; always it contemplated extinguishing the Jew in Europe and often in the world.

The conspiracy or common plan to exterminate the Jew was so methodically and thoroughly pursued, that despite the German defeat and Nazi prostration this Nazi aim largely has succeeded. Only remnants of the European Jewish population remain in Germany, in the countries which Germany occupied, and in those which were her satellites or collaborators. Of the 9,600,000 Jews who lived in Nazi-dominated Europe, 60 percent are authoritatively estimated to have perished. Five million seven hundred thousand Jews are missing from the countries in which they formerly lived, and over 4,500,000 cannot be accounted for by the normal death rate nor by immigration; nor are they included among displaced persons. History does not record a crime ever perpetrated against so many victims or one ever carried out with such calculated cruelty.

Staging considerations, choices and suggestions

1   You do not need to use the full text provided by Justice Jackson. However, if you decide to use only portions of it, utilize the statements that your group finds most impactful.
2   Designate one actor to portray/read Eisenhower, one to portray/read Justice Jackson, and the others to deliver the lines involving the statistics and the deniers' beliefs.
3   Mix up the order of the lines from the various texts so that you are not delivering all of one, followed by another and another. Interweave the lines from the different texts/characters in a way that highlights the absurdity of the deniers' assertions. In doing so, make sure that it is clear to your audience which character is delivering which lines. Consider using small costume pieces such as: an army helmet or jacket for Eisenhower; a suit and tie for Justice Jackson; and, perhaps signs that can be worn by each of your actors representing the deniers.
4   How will you stage the piece? Will the actors playing deniers stand together, or will they be scattered around the stage?
5   Consider using choral speech elements such as repetition and echoing.
6   IMPORTANT NOTE: The subject matter of this chapter makes this devised theater activity the most delicate to create. It is extremely vital that the ideas of the deniers are clearly refuted by the facts expressed in Justice Jackson's speech and the verbatim eyewitness testimony of General Eisenhower.

About the plays

2.5 Minute Ride by Lisa Kron

This autobiographical one-woman play is about the playwright's relationship with her father, Walter, a Jewish Holocaust survivor who escaped Germany by Kindertransport in 1937 when he was 15. Growing up, Lisa's father insists on an annual family trip to an amusement park in Ohio. But it's a trip that Lisa takes to Auschwitz with her ailing father that helps her better understand Walter's personal history. Switching from the amusement park to the concentration camp, the darkly-humorous play embodies the author's statement that "humor and horror are flipsides of the same coin."

Published by Dramatic Publishing www.dramaticpublishing.com

A Shayna Maidel by Barbara Lebow

In 1946 Manhattan, Rose and her father Mordechai, who came to the United States prior to the Holocaust, welcome Lusia, Rose's sister, who stayed behind in Europe with her mother due to illness. Lusia, who survived a concentration camp, is now desperately seeking word of her husband's fate. Through flashbacks, details about the family's earlier life are revealed, and Rose begins to understand her connection to a mother and sister who she scarcely remembers. The title is Yiddish for "a pretty girl," and is a phrase that is used as a term of endearment, often by parents for their daughters.

Published by Dramatists Play Service www.dramatists.com

And A Child Shall Lead by Michael Slade

Based on the true story of children living in the Terezín ghetto who, despite the horrors of Nazi rule, used their creativity to write poems, make art, and produce an underground newspaper called "Vedem." The children's actual poems, stories and articles are interwoven throughout the play.

Published by Playscripts, Inc. www.playscripts.com

And Then They Came for Me: Remembering the World of Anne Frank by James Still

This is the story of Eva Schloss, a Jewish teenager who, like Anne Frank, is in hiding from the Nazis in an Amsterdam attic, and later ends up in a concentration camp. Anne Frank, who was Eva Schloss' real-life childhood friend, is a character in the play.

Published by Dramatic Publishing Company www.dramaticpublishing.com

Angel in the Night by Joanna H. Kraus

This play is based on the true story of Marysia Pawlina Szul, a Polish Catholic teen who saved the lives of four Jewish people during World War II and is honored in Yad Vashem, Israel. In the present, two survivors meet at a tree-planting ceremony honoring Pawlina's deed. In the past, in 1942, a fugitive family who has escaped from a Polish ghetto is hidden by Pawlina. At great peril to herself and without her family's knowledge, she becomes their sole protector and provider for two years.

Published by Samuel French, Inc. www.samuelfrench.com

Anne Frank & Me by Cherie Bennett

Modern-day American teen Nicole doubts the truth about the Holocaust and could not care less about it until she mysteriously finds herself on a train in a cattle car being transported to a concentration camp along with Anne Frank.

Published by Dramatic Publishing Company www.dramaticpublishing.com

Dark Road by Laura Lundgren Smith

German teenager Greta applies for a job as a guard at a nearby women's concentration camp believing that it will be an opportunity to provide for her sister, Lise. As she learns the reality of her duties, she also learns to justify her crimes, and heads further and further down the dark road of the Third Reich. Her kind-hearted sister, Lise, is shocked at what her sister becomes, and their once-strong sisterly bond begins to shatter.

Published by Playscripts, Inc. www.playscripts.com/play/2960

Denial by Peter Sagal

Abigail Gersten is a brilliant lawyer and a First Amendment absolutist. Though Jewish, she takes on the case of Professor Bernard Cooper, a Holocaust denier. Facing off against an idealistic government prosecutor and a well-respected Holocaust survivor, Abby's loyalties are called into question and she is forced to confront the differences between what is legal and what is right.

Published by Dramatic Publishing Company www.dramaticpublishing.com/denial

Dreams of Anne Frank by Bernard Kops

Using Anne's now-famous diary as a starting point, this play with music demystifies the iconic teenager by focusing on her imagination and creativity to retell the story of how two families hid from the Nazis in an Amsterdam attic.

Published by Samuel French www.samuelfrench.com/p/5035/dreams-of-anne-frank

East of Berlin by Hannah Moscovitch

As a teenager, Rudi discovers that his father was a doctor at Auschwitz. Trying to reconcile his inherited guilt, Rudi lashes out against his father and his friends, and eventually flees to Germany. While there, he follows in his father's footsteps by studying medicine and falls in love with Sarah, the daughter of a Holocaust survivor.

Published by Playwrights Canada Press www.playwrightscanada.com
orders@playwrights canada.com

Kindertransport by Diane Samuels

In 1938, Helga, a German Jewish woman, sends her nine-year-old daughter Eva to England on a Kindertransport in order to keep her from being captured by the Nazis. (Over 10,000 children were saved in this manner, with most being adopted by families in Britain.) And in the early 1990s, a young woman named Faith helps her mother, Evelyn, sort through boxes in a storage room in Evelyn's London home. In doing so, she uncovers items from her mother's unspoken past which reveal that Evelyn was in fact Eva, and not the Christian, British-born woman that Faith believed her to be.

Published by www.nickhernbooks.co.uk/plays-to-perform/kindertransport

Remember My Name by Joanna H. Kraus

During the war, Rachel Simon, a young Jewish French girl, is separated from her family and becomes a fighter for her homeland and her life. She survives with the assistance of a priest, a widow, and a teacher who is a member of the French resistance. At one point, she barely evades capture by a Nazi. Ultimately, she is reunited with her father at the war's end.

Published by Samuel French www.samuelfrench.com/p/5264/remember-my-name

T-Money & Wolf by Kevin Willmott and Ric Averill

Set in a Newark jail cell, the stories of an old man from Germany and a young gang member from New Jersey unfold, exposing similarities in the choices they made which brought them to their current situations. In flashback scenes, the man's history is revealed and we see how a typical German youth in the 1930s got swept up in Nazi ideology and became a murderous war criminal.

Published by Dramatic Publishing www.dramaticpublishing.com

The Diary of Anne Frank newly adapted by Wendy Kesselman from the play by Goodrich and Hackett

Based on the real-life diary of a now-iconic teenage girl, this is an impassioned drama about the lives of eight people hiding from the Nazis in Amsterdam. *The Diary of Anne Frank* captures the claustrophobic realities of their daily existence in "The Secret Annex" – their fears, their hopes, their laughter, and their grief. This play was the first widely-seen piece of theater in America that dealt with the Holocaust and those who suffered at the hands of the Nazis. Its original adaptation ran on Broadway for over 700 performances from October, 1955–June, 1957.

Published by Dramatists Play Service Inc. www.dramatists.com

The Survivor by Susan Nanus, based on the memoirs of Jack Eisner

A group of daring Jewish teenagers smuggle food, goods and, eventually, arms to the imprisoned Jews of the Warsaw Ghetto. One by one, they lose their lives as they valiantly struggle to fight back against the Nazis. That is, all of them except Jacek, "The Survivor," who promises to continue telling the stories of his friends as long as he lives.

Published by Samuel French, Inc. www.samuelfrench.com

The White Rose by Lillian Garrett-Groag

Based on the true story of a youth resistance movement against the Third Reich in Germany, 1943, this drama tells the story of Sophie Scholl and her brother Hans, who along with a number of other students at the University of Munich, begin publishing anonymous leaflets titled "The White Rose," protesting the atrocities of the Nazi regime. They are all eventually caught and arrested.

Published by Dramatists Play Service Inc. www.dramatists.com

Works cited

"Adolf Eichmann." *Trial International*, June 14, 2016, https://trialinternational.org/latest-post/adolf-eichmann/. Accessed June 18, 2019.

"The Aftermath of the Holocaust." *Holocaust Encyclopedia*, United States Holocaust Memorial Museum, https://encyclopedia.ushmm.org/content/en/article/the-aftermath-of-the-holocaust. Accessed December 26, 2018.

"Albert Speer." *Holocaust Encyclopedia*, United States Holocaust Memorial Museum, https://encyclopedia.ushmm.org/content/en/article/albert-speer. Accessed September 2, 2018.

"Anne Frank Biography." *Holocaust Encyclopedia*, United States Holocaust Memorial Museum, https://encyclopedia.ushmm.org/content/en/article/anne-frank-biography. Accessed December 28, 2018.

"Anti-Semitism: The Longest Hatred." *Holocaust Encyclopedia*, United States Holocaust Memorial Museum, www.ushmm.org/confront-antisemitism/antisemitism-the-longest-hatred. Accessed September 2, 2018.

Aroneanu, Eugene, comp. *Inside the Concentration Camps: Eyewitness Accounts of Life in Hitler's Death Camps.* Translated by Thomas Whissen, Praeger Publishers, 1996.

Axelrod, Toby. *In the Camps: Teens Who Survived the Nazi Concentration Camps.* New York: The Rosen Publishing Group, Inc., 1999.

Ayers, Eleanor H. *In the Ghettos: Teens Who Survived the Ghettos of the Holocaust.* New York: The Rosen Publishing Group, Inc., 1999.

Benz, Wolfgang. *The Holocaust: A German Historian Examines the Genocide.* New York: Columbia University Press, 1999.

Berenbaum, Michael. "Adolf Eichmann." *Encyclopedia Britannica*, May 27, 2019, *Britannica*. www.britannica.com/biography/Adolf-Eichmann. Accessed June 19, 2019.

Berenbaum, Michael. "Chelmno Concentration Camp." *Encyclopedia Britannica*, December 13, 2018, *Britannica*. www.britannica.com/place/Chelmno-concentration-camp-Poland. Accessed June 19, 2019.

Berenbaum, Michael. "Holocaust." *Encyclopedia Britannica*, March 20, 2019, *Britannica*. www.britannica.com/event/Holocaust. Accessed July 31, 2018.

Berenbaum, Michael. "Theresienstadt." *Encyclopedia Britannica*, December 20, 2018, *Britannica*. www.britannica.com/place/Theresienstadt. Accessed June 28, 2019.

Berenbaum, Michael. "Treblinka." *Encyclopedia Britannica*, December 11, 2018, *Britannica*. www.britannica. com/place/Treblinka. Accessed June 29, 2019.

Burnside, Daniel. Interview with Sarah Sidner. *Neo-Nazi Emboldened by Trump*, CNN, August 10, 2018.

"Bystanders." *Holocaust Encyclopedia*, United States Holocaust Memorial Museum, https://encyclopedia. ushmm.org/content/en/article/bystanders. Accessed September 2, 2018.

"Bystanders." *Yad Vashem*, www.yadvashem.org/yv/en/holocaust/resource_center/item.asp?gate=2–52 Accessed September 2, 2018.

"Collaboration." *Holocaust Encyclopedia*, United States Holocaust Memorial Museum, https://encyclo-pedia.ushmm.org/content/en/article/collaboration. Accessed September 2, 2018.

"Commemorating the 70th Anniversary of Liberation." *Holocaust Encyclopedia*, United States Holocaust Memorial Museum, www.ushmm.org/information/exhibitions/online-exhibitions/special-focus/ liberation-seventieth-anniversary. Accessed September 9, 2018.

"Concentration Camps, 1933–1939." *Holocaust Encyclopedia*, United States Holocaust Memorial Museum, https://encyclopedia.ushmm.org/content/en/article/concentration-camps-1933–39. Accessed September 9, 2018.

"Concentration Camps: List of Major Camps." *Jewish Virtual Library*, www.jewishvirtuallibrary.org/list-of-major-nazi-concentration-camps. Accessed June 28, 2019.

"Daily Life in the Ghettos." *Yad Vashem*, www.yadvashem.org/holocaust/about/ghettos/daily-life.html. Accessed May 19, 2019.

"Displaced Persons." *Holocaust Encyclopedia*, United States Holocaust Memorial Museum, https://encyclo-pedia.ushmm.org/content/en/article/displaced-persons. Accessed December 22, 2018.

"Displaced Persons, Jewish." Yad Vashem: Shoah Resource Center, The International School for Holocaust Studies, www.yadvashem.org/odot_pdf/Microsoft%20Word%20-%206273.pdf. Accessed December 21, 2018.

"Eichmann Trial." *Holocaust Encyclopedia*, United States Holocaust Memorial Museum, https://encyclo-pedia.ushmm.org/content/en/article/eichmann-trial?parent=en%2F10832. Accessed June 21, 2019.

Eisenstein, Bernice. *I Was a Child of Holocaust Survivors*. New York: Riverhead Books, 2006.

Epstein, Helen. *Children of the Holocaust: Conversations with Sons and Daughters of Survivors*. New York: G.P. Putman's Sons, 1979.

"Escape from German-Occupied Europe." *Holocaust Encyclopedia*, United States Holocaust Memorial Museum, https://encyclopedia.ushmm.org/content/en/article/escape-from-german-occupied-europe. Accessed December 28, 2018.

Fireside, Harvey. *The Nuremberg Nazi War Crimes Trials: A Headline Court Case*. Berkeley Heights, New Jersey: Enslow Publishers Inc., 2000.

"From Broken Glass: A Study Guide For High School Classrooms." The Anti-Defamation League, n.d.

Fuggle, Emily. "Ghettos in the Holocaust." *Imperial War Museums*, June 18, 2018. Accessed May 22, 2019.

"German Resistance to Hitler." *Holocaust Encyclopedia*, United States Holocaust Memorial Museum, https://encyclopedia.ushmm.org/content/en/article/german-resistance-to-hitler. Accessed August 6, 2018.

"Ghettos." *Holocaust Encyclopedia*, United States Holocaust Memorial Museum, https://encyclopedia. ushmm.org/content/en/article/ghettos. Accessed May 18, 2019.

"The Ghettos: 1939–1941." *A Teacher's Guide to the Holocaust*, Florida Center for Instructional Technology, College of Education, University of South Florida, 2005.

Greenfeld, Howard. *The Hidden Children*. New York: Ticknor & Fields, 1993.

Greenblatt, Jonathan. "Holocaust Denial is a Form of Hatred." *New York Daily News*, July, 20 2018, www. ADL.org. Accessed August 18, 2018.

Halleck, Elaine, ed. *Living in Nazi Germany*. Michigan: Greenhaven Press, 2004.

Hart, Stephen A. "*Liberation of the Concentration Camps*," History, British Broadcasting Corporation, February 17, 2011. Accessed December 28, 2018.

"Hidden Children: Daily Life." *Holocaust Encyclopedia*, United States Holocaust Memorial Museum, https://encyclopedia.ushmm.org/content/en/article/hidden-children-daily-life. Accessed December 29, 2018.

Hilberg, Raul. *Perpetrators, Victims, Bystanders: The Jewish Catastrophe 1933–1945*. New York: HarperPerrenial. 1993.

History.com Editors. "Alfred Rosenberg is Executed." *History.com*, www.history.com/this-day-in-history/alfred-rosenberg-is-executed, November 5, 2009 (updated June 7, 2019). Accessed June 24, 2019.

History.com Editors. "May 16, 1943: Warsaw Ghetto Uprising Ends." *History.com*, www.history.com/this-day-in history/warsaw-ghetto-uprising-ends. Accessed July 31, 2018.

"The History of the Holocaust." *Holocaust Memorial Center*, West Bloomfield, Michigan. n.d.

"The Holocaust Explained: How Were Camps Run?" *The Weiner Library*, www.theholocaustexplained.org/the-camps/how-were-the-camps-run/. Accessed June 26, 2019.

"The Holocaust Explained: Types of Camps." *The Weiner Library*, www.theholocaustexplained.org/the-camps/types-of-camps/. Accessed June 26, 2019.

"The Holocaust – Global Awareness and Denial." *Anti-Defamation League*, global100.adl.org. Accessed August 14, 2018.

"Holocaust Rescue: Rescue of Danish Jews." *Jewish Virtual Library*. www.jewishvirtuallibrary.org/the-rescue-of-danish-jews. Accessed December 28, 2018.

"Holocaust Survivor, Camp Liberator Share Memories." *All Things Considered*, NPR, May 5, 2005.

Höss, Rudolf. "Auschwitz: The Greatest Extermination Center." *The Holocaust: Death Camps*, edited by Tamara L. Roleff. Michigan: Greenhaven Press, Inc., 2002, pp. 149–161.

"Hundreds of neo-Nazis March in Berlin, Protected by Police." *U.S.A. Today*. August 19, 2018, p. 1.

"I Am My Brother's Keeper: A Tribute to the Righteous Among Nations – In Cellars, Pits and Attics." *Yad Vashem*, www.yadvashem.org/yv/en/exhibitions/righteous/hiding.asp. Accessed December 29, 2018.

"Introduction: The Nazi Death Camps." *The Holocaust: Death Camps*, edited by Tamara L. Roleff. Michigan: Greenhaven Press, Inc., 2002, pp. 11–34.

"Jewish Resistance." *Holocaust Encyclopedia*, United States Holocaust Memorial Museum, https://encyclopedia.ushmm.org/content/en/article/jewish-resistance. Accessed August 6, 2018.

Jewish Virtual Library. "Jewish Victims of the Holocaust: Hidden Children," www.jewishvirtuallibrary.org/hidden-children-of-the-holocaust. Accessed December 29, 2018.

Klein, Christopher. "10 Things You May Not Know About the Nuremberg Trials," 31 August 2018, www.history.com/news/10-things-you-may-not-know-about-the-nuremberg-trials. Accessed June 16, 2019.

"Kristallnacht." *Holocaust Encyclopedia*, United States Holocaust Memorial Museum, https://encyclopedia.ushmm.org/content/en/article/kristallnacht. Accessed September 2, 2019.

Levy, Esther V. *Legacies, Lies and Lullabies: The World of a Second Generation Holocaust Survivor*. Sarasota, FL: First Edition Design Publishing, 2013.

"Liberation." *Holocaust Encyclopedia*, United States Holocaust Memorial Museum, https://encyclopedia.ushmm.org/content/en/article/liberation. Accessed September 9, 2018.

"Liberation: An Overview." *Holocaust Encyclopedia*, United States Holocaust Memorial Museum, https://encyclopedia.ushmm.org/content/en/article/liberation-an-overview. Accessed September 9, 2018.

"Liberation of Nazi Camps." *Holocaust Encyclopedia*, United States Holocaust Memorial Museum, https://encyclopedia.ushmm.org/content/en/article/liberation-of-nazi-camps. Accessed September 9, 2018.

"Life in Shadows: Hidden Children and the Holocaust." August 28, 2003–September 6, 2004, United States Holocaust Memorial Museum, Washington, D.C.

"Life in Shadows: Hidden Children and the Holocaust Study Guide." United States Holocaust Memorial Museum, Washington, D.C., 2003.

Linder, Douglas O. "The Nuremberg Trials: An Account," *Famous Trials*, https://famous-trials.com/nuremberg/1901-home. Accessed June 19, 2019.

Liphshiz, Cnaan. "Yellow Star Houses Project Challenges Official Hungarian Holocaust Commemorations." *Jewish Telegraphic Agency*. April 1, 2014, www.jta.org/2014/04/01/global/yellow-star-houses-project-challenges-official- hungarian-holocaust-commemorations. Accessed May 19, 2019.

Lipstadt, Deborah. *Denying the Holocaust: The Growing Assault on Truth and Memory*. New York: Plume, 1994.

Lipstadt, Deborah. *The Eichmann Trial*. New York: Schocken Books, 2011.

"Lodz Ghetto." *Yad Vashem*, www.yadvashem.org/holocaust/about/ghettos/lodz.html. Accessed May 19, 2019.

"Martin Bormann." *Holocaust Encyclopedia*, United States Holocaust Memorial Museum, https://encyclopedia.ushmm.org/content/en/article/martin-bormann. Accessed September 2, 2018.

Miller, Yvette Alt. "Holocaust Survivors' Torment After Liberation." *Aish*, June 1, 2019, www.aish.com/ho/i/Holocaust-Survivors-Torment-After-Liberation.html. Accessed June 15, 2019.

"Nazi Camps." *Holocaust Encyclopedia*, United States Holocaust Memorial Museum, https://encyclopedia.ushmm.org/content/en/article/nazi-camps. Accessed June 27, 2019.

"Nazi Propaganda." *Holocaust Encyclopedia*, United States Holocaust Memorial Museum, https://encyclopedia.ushmm.org/content/en/article/nazi-propaganda. Accessed September 14, 2019.

"Non-Jewish Resistance: Overview." *Holocaust Encyclopedia*, United States Holocaust Memorial Museum, https://encyclopedia.ushmm.org/content/en/article/non-jewish-resistance. Accessed August 6, 2018.

"Perpetrators." *Holocaust Encyclopedia,* United States Holocaust Memorial Museum, https://encyclopedia.ushmm.org/content/en/article/perpetrators. Accessed September 2, 2018.

"Perpetrators, Collaborators and Bystanders." *The Holocaust – The Nazi Genocide against the Jewish People*, www.holocaust.com.au/The-Facts/Perpetrators-collaborators-and-bystanders/Perpetrators-collaborators-and-bystanders. Accessed September 2, 2018.

"Postwar Refugee Crisis and the Establishment of the State of Israel." *Holocaust Encyclopedia*, United States Holocaust Memorial Museum, https://encyclopedia.ushmm.org/content/en/article/postwar-refugee-crisis-and-the-establishment-of-the-state-of-israel. Accessed December 26, 2018.

"Propaganda." Online exhibit, United States Holocaust Memorial Museum, Washington, D.C.

Ray, Michael. "Nurnberg Trials." *Encyclopedia Britannica, Britannica.* www.britannica.com/event/Nurnberg-trials. Accessed June 16, 2019.

Ray, Michael. "Walther Funk." *Encyclopedia Britannica*, May 27, 2019, *Britannica.* www.britannica.com/biography/Walther-Funk. Accessed June 24, 2019.

Rees, Laurence. *The Holocaust: A New History.* New York: Public Affairs, Hachette Book Group, 2017.

"Rescue." *Holocaust Encyclopedia*, United States Holocaust Memorial Museum, https://encyclopedia.ushmm.org/content/en/article/rescue. Accessed December 28, 2018.

"Resistance." *A Teacher's Guide to the Holocaust*, Florida Center for Instructional Technology, College of Education, University of South Florida, 2005.

"Resistance during the Holocaust." *Holocaust Encyclopedia*, United States Holocaust Memorial Museum, https://encyclopedia.ushmm.org/content/en/article/resistance-during-the-Holocaust.   Accessed August 6, 2018.

"Resistance Inside Germany." *Holocaust Encyclopedia*, United States Holocaust Memorial Museum, https://encyclopedia.ushmm.org/content/en/article/resistance-inside-Germany. Accessed August 6, 2018.

"The Return to Life in the Displaced Persons Camps, 1945–1956: A Visual Retrospective." *Yad Vashem*, www.yadvashem.org/yv/en/exhibitions/dp_camps/index.asp. Accessed December 21, 2018.

Roleff, Tamara L., ed. *The Holocaust: Death Camps*. Michigan: Greenhven Press, Inc., 2002.

Rosenberg, Jennifer. "Hidden Children of the Holocaust." ThoughtCo., May 25, 2019, thoughtco.com/hidden-children-of-the-holocaust-1779661. Accessed December 29, 2018.

Ross, Steve. "Sunday Spotlight: Harry Smith interview with Steve Ross." Sunday Today with Willie Geist. NBC, July 29, 2018.

Rubin, Janet E. *Teaching about the Holocaust through Drama*. Woodstock, IL: Dramatic Publishing, 2000.

"Rudolf Hess" *Holocaust Encyclopedia*, United States Holocaust Memorial Museum, https://encyclopedia.ushmm.org/content/en/article/rudolf-hess. Accessed September 2, 2020.

Sharples, Caroline. *All You Need To Know…The Third Reich: The Rise and Fall of the Nazis*. Chippenham, UK: Connell Publishing, 2018.

Shuter, Jane. *The Holocaust: The Camp System*. Chicago: Heinemann Library, 2003.

Steinbacher, Sybille. *Auschwitz: A History*. Translated by Shaun Whiteside. New York: Ecco (Harper Collins), 2005.

"Survival in Hiding." *Facing History and Ourselves*, www.facinghistory.org/holocaust-and-human-behavior/chapter-9/survival-hiding. Accessed December 29, 2018.

"Teaching About the Holocaust: A Resource Book for Educators." *Holocaust Encyclopedia*. Washington, D.C.: United States Holocaust Memorial Museum.

Teeman, Tim. "Architect Daniel Libeskind: How to Transform Horror into Art, From Auschwitz and the Holocaust to 9/11." *Daily Beast*, May 23, 2019, www.thedailybeast.com/architect-daniel-libeskind-on-how-to-transform-horror-into-art-from-auschwitz-and-the-holocaust-to-911.

"Theresienstadt." *Yad Vashem*, www.yadvashem.org/holocaust/about/ghettos/theresienstadt.html. Accessed June 28, 2019.

"TOPF." *Holocaust Encyclopedia*, United States Holocaust Memorial Museum, https://encyclopedia.ushmm.org/content/en/article/topf-and-sons-an-ordinary-company. Accessed September 2, 2018.

"Trials of War Criminals." Yad Vashem: Shoah Resource Center, The International School for Holocaust Studies, www.yadvashem.org/odot_pdf/Microsoft%20Word%20-%205887.pdf.   Accessed June 19, 2019.

"Volkswagen." *Holocaust Encyclopedia*, United States Holocaust Memorial Museum, https://encyclopedia.ushmm.org/content/en/article/volkswagen-1. Accessed September 2, 2018.

"Warsaw Ghetto." *Yad Vashem*, www.yadvashem.org/holocaust/about/ghettos/warsaw.html. Accessed May 19, 2019.

Wolf, Diane L. "What's in a Name? The Genealogy of Holocaust Identities." *Genealogy*, October 6, 2017, pp. 1, 19.

Works cited (theater activities)

"BBC ON THIS DAY | 27 | 1945: Auschwitz Death Camp Liberated." *BBC News*, BBC, January 27, 1945, http://news.bbc.co.uk/onthisday/hi/dates/stories/january/27/newsid_3520000/3520986.stm.

Friedmann, Pavel. "The Butterfly," 1942. www.hmd.org.uk/resource/the-butterfly-by-pavel-friedmann/.

Hagen, Uta and Haskel Frankel. *Respect for Acting.* New York: Macmillan, 1973.

"Nuremberg Laws." *Holocaust Encyclopedia*, United States Holocaust Memorial Museum, https://encyclopedia.ushmm.org/content/en/article/nuremberg-laws.

Pokrass, Dmitri. "Zog Nit Keynmol." 1943, *SaveTheMusic*, https://archives.savethemusic.com/bin/archives.cgi?q=songs&search=title&id=Zog+Nit+Keynmol.

UN General Assembly, Universal Declaration of Human Rights, December 10, 1948, 217 A (III), www.refworld.org/docid/3ae6b3712c.html.

Sachs, Nelly. "Chorus of Orphans by Nelly Sachs," translated by Teresa Iverson.

"Second Day, Wednesday, 11/21/1945, Part 04," in *Trial of the Major War Criminals before the International Military Tribunal.* Volume II. Proceedings: 11/14/1945-11/30/1945. Nuremberg: IMT, 1947. pp. 98–102.

Shakespeare, William. "Act 2, Scene 2." *Hamlet.* Lit2Go Edition. 0. Web. https://etc.usf.edu/lit2go/94/hamlet/1673/act-2-scene-2/.

"Theresienstadt." *Holocaust Encyclopedia*, United States Holocaust Memorial Museum, https://encyclopedia.ushmm.org/content/en/article/theresienstadt.

Index